I0214026

MIKAMI Kayo

The Body as a Vessel
Approaching the Methodology of Hijikata Tatsumi's Ankoku Butō

Translated by Rosa van Hensbergen

Ôzaru

Books

The Body as a Vessel
by MIKAMI Kayo

Original text © MIKAMI Kayo, 1986
English translation © Rosa van Hensbergen, 2016
Front cover "Gibasan" photograph © YAMAZAKI Hiroshi, 1972
Front cover calligraphy © YAMAUCHI Seijō, 1993
Photographs by NAKATANI Tadao used by kind permission of Butoh Laboratory Japan
Photographs by FUKASE Masahisa used by kind permission of Fukase Masahisa Archives

Every reasonable effort was made to track down the copyright holders for all content used in this publication. Please contact us if you become aware of any copyrighted material used inappropriately. Material believed to be out of copyright has been edited to correct obvious errors and conform to modern typographical conventions, while retaining the original text as far as possible.

The rights of MIKAMI Kayo to be identified as the author of this work and Rosa van Hensbergen to be identified as the translator of this work have been asserted in accordance with the Copyright, Designs and Patents Act 1988.

All rights reserved. No part of this document may be reproduced, copied, distributed, transferred, modified, or transmitted, in any form or by any means, electronic or mechanical, including photocopying, recording, or by any information storage or retrieval system, without the prior written permission of the copyright owner; nor can it be circulated in any form of binding or cover other than that in which it is published and without similar conditions including this condition being imposed on a subsequent purchaser. In no event shall the author or publisher be liable for any damages caused in any way by use of this document.

Published by Ōzaru Books, an imprint of BJ Translations Ltd
Street Acre, Shuart Lane, St Nicholas-at-Wade,
BIRCHINGTON, CT7 0NG, U.K.
www.ozaru.net

First edition published 12 April 2016
Printed by Lightning Source
ISBN: 978-0-9931587-4-2

Contents

List of illustrations

A Note on the Text

A first draft of this text was translated at Mikami Kayo's house with Shimmyo Shuta, during the winter of 2013. The initial process of translation involved working through the text systematically with both Mikami and Shimmyo, addressing and discussing moments of difficulty, and finding ways to render these into English. The subsequent editing has taken place over the following years.

The text that formed the reference for this translation was an unpublished revision of the book *Utsuwa toshite no shintai: ankoku butō gihō e no apurōchi* [The Body as a Vessel: Approaching the Methodology of Hijikata Tatsumi's Ankoku Butō] (ANZ-Do, 1993) – the revised version has since been published by *Shumpusha* in 2015 (ISBN: 978-4-86110-465-7). This translation represents something closer to the revised edition, with notes added to the appendix from Hijikata workshops taken in 1978 and 1985, and an Ashikawa workshop taken in 1990, and an Afterword containing edited translations of two more recent essays by Mikami along with English reviews of her dance. There are also many additional photos, largely from Torifune Butoh Sha productions.

In addition to a Japanese bibliography, the original book gave references for secondary but not primary sources, and gave no page number references. We tracked down as many of these as possible, and these have been added to this edition. Mikami provided many of these, and we have endeavoured to format them consistently, though in places differences in referencing conventions may have resulted in some discrepancies. Japanese words have been italicized, with long vowel sounds indicated by macrons. Japanese names have been ordered last name first, and titles of texts or performances have been referred to in Japanese, in abbreviated form where full-titles were particularly lengthy, and with English glosses contained in brackets where necessary. However, where English titles or Romanized names were originally included, or are in common use (e.g. Tokyo not Tōkyō), these have been retained rather than applying the above principles.

Rosa van Hensbergen

On the English Translation

The Publication of Hijikata's Butō-fu and the Translation of Hijikata's Language into Japanese

This revised edition of *The Body as a Vessel: Approaching the Methodology of Hijikata Tatsumi's Ankoku Butō* (ANZ, 1993), brings together my MA and doctoral research into the *ankoku butō* method of Hijikata Tatsumi. The difference in subtitle between my MA thesis, 'Hijikata Tatsumi Research: Considering the *Butō* Method' (1991), and my doctoral thesis 'Hijikata Tatsumi Research: Theory of the *Ankoku Butō* Method' (submitted to Ochanomizu University in 1997), reflects a change in the academic reception of *butō*. At the time of writing my MA, *butō* had already started to become popular abroad, under the name 'butoh', whereas '*ankoku butō*' was criticised within Japanese academia as a dance associated with white paint, baldness, nudity, and the exposure of emotions. In other words, '*ankoku*' still held negative connotations.

When I started my graduate research on Hijikata back in 1988, I was told by a well-known aesthetician that my work was to translate Hijikata's language into Japanese. Hijikata was both an incomparable dancer and a genius with language, but his style was often obfuscatory. At that time, his coded notational language, *butō-fu*, had not yet been made available to the public, and nor had his collected works or the materials now available at the Hijikata Archive. I worked along with two other disciples to gather up the *butō-fu* that had been scattered as the basis for my graduate research. This became the first study to publish and decode Hijikata's notational language. The importance of this work was acknowledged in reviews of the book: "There has never been an attempt like this one to investigate the origin of *butō* through such a full use of original notational resources. The value of these materials is a landmark for *butō*, representing a text that can help *butō* dancers reach a greater precision in their training." (Nagaoka Yuri, *Jiyū jikan* [Free Time, Magazine House, July 1993]). "For audience members like me, this book will offer a totally new perspective on *butō*." (Yamaga Seiichi, *Tokyo Artsscene* [Tokyo Arts Scene, 1993]). The well-known dance critic, Ichikawa Miyabi, also thanked me for making available materials that could never otherwise have been accessed.

Although my work was the first of its kind, and in some sense established the field of Hijikata research, I still had reservations when it came to publishing. Everyone who met Hijikata had a clear idea of 'my Hijikata', and so it was intimidating to be the first one to theorize his method. Since publishing my work, I have had encouragement from young *butō* dancers and researchers, who tell me it is there '*butō* textbook', or '*butō* bible', or that it 'changed Japanese dance' altogether. I also received the kind words from Murobushi Kō that it was 'the most reliable book on Hijikata'. All the while, I still felt that maybe I had closed Hijikata up in a small room inside myself. But the words of my second teacher, Noguchi Michizō, helped bring me confidence. He told me I had 'done a good job, and taken the right approach', but he also told me: 'Hijikata was an even greater person than you think he was.' The only way I have left to meet with this greatness is to continue dancing.

In 1998, the Hijikata Archive was established and Waguri Yukio released his *Butō kaden* CD-ROM containing recordings of the *butō-fu*. In 2005, Hijikata's *Collected Works* was published. I am privately content that my book, *The Body as a Vessel*, could contribute in some small way to this growing field of Hijikata research.

The Body as a Vessel was begun with the purpose of helping me to grow as a *butō* dancer. Around the time of its publication I cofounded the company Torifune Butoh Sha, and began to perform and teach workshops both in Japan and abroad. This revised edition of *The Body as a Vessel* constitutes the continuation of my research through teaching and dancing.

Since the publication of my original book, I have had a number of requests from foreign dancers and researchers for an English translation, but I was focused on developing my own dance at that time. When I finally decided to try and get the work translated, around 2001, I sent off an English summary to the researcher Sondra Horton Fraleigh, to request her editorial support. She responded with the comment that she had just been reading a text with the 'same idea' as mine. That text was in a 2001 special edition of *The Drama Review*, edited by Kurihara Nanako. Kurihara had requested to see my MA thesis nearly a decade earlier, in 1993, claiming 'she couldn't understand Hijikata's Japanese', and I had directed her towards my forthcoming publication, *The Body as a Vessel*. A year before I attained my doctoral dissertation in 1997, Kurihara submitted her thesis to NYU. As Kurihara had never presented her work in Japan, I had no sense that she was working on the 'same idea' as me, until Fraleigh informed me of this. Nonetheless, I hope that the research that will come from the texts she translated, and the more extensive research now possible with the establishment of the Hijikata Archive, will contribute to understandings of Hijikata's work. [A further discussion of Mikami's contentions with Kurihara is contained in 'The Reception and Transformation of Hijikata's *Ankoku Butō* 2' section of the Afterword].

During the winter of 2013, I was able to work with Rosa van Hensbergen and Shimmyo Shuta to draft an English translation of this text. It was fortuitous that we were able to take the time needed to work together on this task. I can't say whether the publication of an English translation would have pleased Hijikata. In response to the rising popularity of 'butoh' abroad, Hijikata would say, from the upstairs room of Asbestos Studio: 'It's all of a muchness!' I am still trying to figure out what Hijikata's words meant, feeling him follow behind me whispering: 'Hurry, no don't hurry'. All I know is that I want to go on dancing into old age as Hijikata was unable to do.

This translation would not have been possible without a lot of help along the way. 10 years ago, Sagawa Mitsunori was kind enough to draft a preliminary translation. Following this, Joshua Gibbs expressed an interest in translating the book, and it is through him that we made contact with the publisher, Ben Jones, at Ōzaru Books. I cannot thank everyone enough for their assistance in making this possible. My only hope is that it can contribute in some modest way to the development of *butō* research.

Mikami Kayo
December 2015

Preface

Hijikata Tatsumi and I, A First Meeting

The image of 'Christ in Passion' crossing the stage and dissolving into particles of light and the image of a devil devouring its offspring. How could two such images move me to the same emotion? The devil figure comes from Francisco Goya's work *Saturn Devouring One of his Sons* (c. 1819-23), and the Christ figure comes from the last stage performance of Hijikata Tatsumi in October 1973.[1] Hijikata's sole movement was to walk slowly across the stage. It only lasted a few minutes, but in that moment I had an unexpected revelation that moved me to tears: that I was forgiven, and that I existed.

Watching the vision of Christ shine brightly and then disappear, I felt purified and saved. Tears began to fall and so did questions: 'was my world-view at that time the right one?' I was 21 years old, and I was afraid. I was afraid to face the 'truths' of the world, and so I had turned away.

The following summer, I visited the Prado Museum in Madrid and saw Goya's painting in the flesh for the first time. Standing before it, I felt Goya's agony and struggle wrought in paint, and cried for a second time. The tears fell heavily on both occasions. Like stones, they sent out ripples; ripples that would grow into waves and eventually engulf my entire life.

It wasn't until the summer of 1978 that I found myself face-to-face with Hijikata. At that time, I was trying to be a responsible citizen and had taken up work for a newspaper company. To do so, I'd also silenced a voice of 'truth' inside myself, and that still feels like the failure of my 23rd year. Hijikata was the person I most deeply wanted to avoid, but retrospectively it seems an inevitable coincidence that I met him again at that juncture.

The first words Hijikata said to me were: 'Do the crippled beggar!' I recall trying hard to 'become' one, whilst all the while he beat on his drum and shouted: 'Liar! Liar! You've been veiling your life with words and strange habits! Leave that smartly acted life behind you!' Hearing those words, I began to walk in the direction of 'truth' for the first time.

To become Hijikata's disciple meant to abandon an everyday life – he always asked for 'all or nothing' – so the question became whether I could give up everything to dance, give up everything to *butō*, whether I could relinquish work, friends, family, and even an attachment to what it means to be human. He demanded that you push yourself to the point of crisis. He seemed to believe this was the only way to approach the question: what is *butō*?

I was Hijikata's disciple from 1978 to 1981. I'm his disciple even now. But it was during those years that I was involved in weaving that vision of *butō*. Before meeting Hijikata, I had been so confined by an *idea* of freedom that it was sometimes hard to breathe. I was like the flying bird Hijikata often described: 'even the bird that appears to fly is rarely free.' I only began to breathe again once I gave up all my time and words to Hijikata. It was then that I realized only a longing for dance would bring me freedom.

On January 22, 1986, after five years away, I visited Hijikata's studio once more. I entered to find him lying on the floor, still as a stone. He spoke out: 'I don't need the future. I just want the now.' The words cut straight to my heart. And then it was as if he asked: 'Is that what *you* want?'

For five years I had been unable to face Hijikata, I had lost my path, but returning at that moment I saw the way open clearly before me: it had to begin with dancing; it had to begin with Hijikata. What were Hijikata's thoughts? What were his aims? Why was it that Hijikata had become like a Christ to me? How could an art form so dramatically transform a person's life, as it had mine?

In searching for some answers to those questions, I began researching the methodology of *butō*. And though it will always be of regret to me that I only began this search after Hijikata's death, the chance to continue discovering such 'truths,' seems the best way to repay him for his teachings. These various reasons motivated the research and writing of this book.

Mikami Kayo
April 1993

Acknowledgments

I would like to acknowledge my gratitude and indebtedness to both my teachers, Hijikata Tatsumi and Noguchi Michizō, as well as to Hijikata's late wife, Motofuji Akiko. I would also like to thank the support and guidance of Asai Kiyoshi, professor of Japanese Literature at Ochanomizu University, and Ishiguro Setsuko, professor of Dance Studies.

1. Introduction: Themes & Methodology

The Emergence of Ankoku Butō and Butō

Nikutai no hanran (Revolt of the Flesh, 1968), by Nakatani Tadao

Ankoku butō is a dance form said to have begun in the 1960s with the work of the avant-garde dancer, Hijikata Tatsumi. Hijikata had used the title '*ankoku buyō*' from as early as 1960-1, but did not officially adopt '*ankoku butō*' until 1963. Despite this, the starting point of *ankoku butō* has often been considered to be 1959, as the year of Hijikata's notorious performance, *Kinjiki* (*Forbidden Colours*). *Ankoku butō* is conventionally seen as a dance "born of an inherently Japanese physicality, with the bow legs, wide-set stance, and squatted position that comes from a low centre of gravity;"[1] a dance of "gestures buried in the darkness,"[2] brought to light in the twisted expressions and deformed movements of white-painted bodies.

As the movement expanded during the 1970s, the epithet '*ankoku*' was dropped, to leave only '*butō*'. Under this title, a whole lineage of dancers has trained: the first-generation were those involved with Hijikata's work from the outset; the second-generation studied directly under Hijikata; the third-generation trained under the second; and then further dancers trained under these, or were influenced by *butō* without direct exposure to Hijikata or his works. Today, there are also a number of international performers and contemporary dancers who consider themselves to be post-*butō*, or to perform a kind of high-tech *butō*.[3]

The expansion of *butō* from the 1980s has led to its worldwide recognition as an important representative of Japanese contemporary art, with the anglicized term 'butoh' now internationally known. It might even be said that a positive critique of *butō* has been reimported into Japan from abroad. In spite of this, negative responses to *butō* still litter the Japanese media, where it is frequently described as a "dance form lacking technique, full of shaven heads and white-painted bodies."[4] There even remains some confusion in popular media as to the distinction between *buyō* and *butō*, to such an extent that *buyō* or ballet dancers have been mistakenly called *butō* dancers. At the same time, such confusion may be taken as proof of *ankoku butō*'s influence, in that its global reach seems to have exceeded that of such forms as *buyō*.

Drawing a distinction between *buyō* (舞踊) and *butō* (舞踏) is nevertheless imperative. The dance scholar Gunji Masakatsu has written on the etymology and varied usages of both terms. In particular, he notes the superimposition of the term *butō* with *buyō* in 1904, when the dramatist, novelist, and critic, Tsubouchi Shōyō, introduced the compound *buyō* (舞踊) in his treatise, *Shingakugekiron* (On A New Music Drama, 1904). Prior to this there had been no unified concept or compound for *buyō*, and instead the single characters *mai* (舞) and *odori* (踊) had been in use. The variant compound *butō* (舞踏) had in fact been deployed within the Heian-period court (794-1192) earlier, to describe dancing with the hands (舞) and with the lower body (踏). This latter compound came to refer to dances imported from China and the West during the Meiji period (1868-1912). And so Tsubouchi's use of *buyō* stood partly against *butō*, as a term for foreign dance styles. This term *buyō* gradually became standardized in reference to a wide range of dance styles during the Taishō period (1912-26).[5]

From this point onwards, *buyō* was the term used to encompass such diverse styles as traditional Japanese performing arts and classical ballet. Indeed, when modern dance was imported from Germany and America during the late Taishō–early Shōwa period (1926-36), it also came under the heading of *buyō*, despite its clear challenge to the other more traditional Japanese dance styles denoted by the term.

Hijikata's use of *butō* in the 1960s cannot be said to concretely refute the term *buyō*, and yet it is a choice of etymological importance. The *tō* of *butō* derives from the notion of trampling the earth, which might be seen to oppose the upward directionality of Western dance forms. The cultural anthropologist Yamaguchi Masao has pointed out a comparison between *butō* and the traditional movement of *henbai*, in which a stomping motion is used to draw up energy from the earth and simultaneously settle the unrest of evil spirits. This earthbound motion, he indicates, is characteristic of Eastern movement, as opposed to the elevation and upward reach of Western dance.[6]

Hijikata's reclaiming of the term *butō* worked along the same lines of reversal as Tsubouchi Shōyō's coinage of *buyō* had done earlier. *Butō*, unlike the then widely applied term *buyō*, did not indicate any correspondence to established forms of Eastern or Western dance, but rather signalled the manifestation of an entirely new genre. His choice of *ankoku* was equally rich with implication. According to Hijikata's wife, Motofuji Akiko, the possibility of *shikkoku butō*, or 'dance of pitch blackness,' had also been floated, but *ankoku* was chosen for its associations with the genre of *ankoku eiga*, or *film noir*, which had, with its dark depiction of the French underworld, become popular in Tokyo during the 1960s.[7] Gunji describes the dance form in related terms, as "the underside of an accepted history; the darkness that lies beneath the everyday. That is, the reverse side of all things."[8]

Despite the lack of any clear definition when it comes to *ankoku butō*, it has still spread amoeba-like to the world. And while recent years have seen a more general shift towards placing the 'body' at the centre of cultural interests – with contemporary dance and performance art becoming a rich source of inspiration for architects, artists, and philosophers alike – *ankoku butō* might still be considered a forerunner. Indeed, *butō* dancers like Ōno Kazuo and groups like *Sankai Juku* have come to represent contemporary Japanese art abroad.

Hijikata himself, often referred to as a "charisma of darkness,"[9] occupies a central position in the wider history of the avant-garde. In this respect his contributions might be compared to those of Sergei Pavlovich Diaghilev, whose work with the Ballets Russes, and collaborations with Jean Cocteau, Pablo Picasso, and Igor Stravinsky, can be said to have facilitated the emergence of Vaslav Nijinsky's revolutionary movement. Writing in 1960, Mishima Yukio identified a comparatively revolutionary movement in Hijikata's genre-defying *ankoku butō*, considering it to carry an artistic "purity," which set it beyond the usual limitations of the "avant-garde." For Mishima, Hijikata was confronting the fate of the late-twentieth century artist: pursuing a solitary pathway into the contemporary "wasteland." It was this artistic "purity" that set Hijikata's *ankoku butō* aside, and established it as a forerunner to the 1960s underground theatre movement *shingeki*.[10] *Butō*'s widespread influence on other art forms, however – on music, the visual arts, literature, and theatre – is also what problematizes the attempt to define it.

Ankoku Butō and 'Butoh'

Despite being valued alongside *nō* and *kabuki* by the international community, *butō* is still considered unorthodox within Japan. It can be considered, not only as a form of expression, but as one of the first original contemporary art forms to have spread overseas since the end of the Meiji Period. From the 1980s onwards, *butō* activity has experienced a global upsurge – beginning in Europe and America, and spreading to dance and theatre festivals worldwide. This is evidenced by the subtitle of the 1989 *Mary Wigman Modern Dance Festival*, where *butō* is employed in its original kanji (舞踏), and by the general proliferation of foreign *butō* dancers abroad. The reach of its influence extends to many other art forms – opera, ballet, theatre, music, art, and philosophy – and well beyond Japan.

The state of *butō* academia has shifted in conjunction with this, with increasing numbers of conferences, papers, and PhDs themed around *butō*, as well as more and more foreign researchers visiting Japan in the name of *butō*. That *butō* receives more interest abroad, might be signalled by a comment directed to Professor Matsumoto Chiyoe, during the 22nd *CORD* (Congress on Research in Dance, Hong Kong, 1990), when a foreign researcher asked: 'why are there no Japanese researchers in the field of *butō*?' This international fascination with *butō* is not only in response to its status as an original Japanese avant-garde dance form, but also indicates its global relevance. *Butō* more broadly affords a new perspective on modern rationalist conceptions of the body as a medium, and presents a possible future for dance within the framework of post-modernism.

The poet Shibayama Mikio has suggested that the issues raised by *butō* are not for the dance or art world alone. Indeed, he took the widespread dissemination of *butō* as an indication that it had already reached a certain height, commenting: "I have seen the evidence in Salerno, Istanbul, New Orleans, and beyond… fragments of Hijikata have been scattered and are dispersing still." Hijikata worked beyond his native "island-nation insularity", "taking a great step" to cross the "borders of [national] blood, whilst at the same time retaining the essence of a 'Japanese archetype.'" In order to achieve this, he "drew on all the resources of his time, and on his own talents, all the while seeming to do so for himself alone." It is precisely here that his originality lies. Every time Shibayama perceived one of these fragments of Hijikata in a piece of theatre, dance, or music, he felt "the world was too quick to despair," for these fragments carried "Hijikata's notion of 'eternal revolution:' the last resort when all other options had been exhausted," and a way to transform the human experience in its current state.[11]

What Shibayama's words suggest is that *ankoku butō* transcends the categories of art or race to engage directly with questions of human existence itself. Although art may always strive towards such an engagement, Hijikata exceeded its normal reaches, and achieved what might be considered as one of the most significant contributions to the history of twentieth-century art. It is not too much to consider Hijikata's *ankoku butō* to have revolutionized the twentieth-century human experience.

Research Objectives and Methodology

At the time of research, there were no academic theses published inside or outside of Japan that solely addressed the work of Hijikata Tatsumi.[12] Several works had more generally addressed the state of *butō*, and these informed the eventual shape of this thesis.

Joan Elizabeth Laage, a movement analyst and *butō* dancer, wrote the thesis *Embodying the Spirit: The Significance of the Body in the Contemporary Japanese Dance Movement of Butoh*, submitted to

Texas Women's University in 1993. From 1987 to 1989, she studied *butō* in Japan under Ōno Kazuo and Ashikawa Yōko, and since then has performed as a *butō* dancer. Her thesis is informed by experiential research conducted in Japan, as well as a wide base of knowledge relating to the traditional Japanese Performing Arts, Eastern Philosophy, Religion, and Sociology. She divides the thesis into three sections: 'the body concrete – the human form and proportion;' 'the body ethereal – the concepts of "spirit" and "self," the use of imagery and energy;' and 'the body adorned – the coatings and coverings.' As both a researcher and *butō* dancer, Laage's approach resonates with my own. She similarly considers the multiple and contradictory aspects of the *butō* aesthetic as stemming from Hijikata's life and work.

Susan Blakely Klein's published MA thesis, *Ankoku Butoh: The Premodern and Postmodern Influences on the Dance of Utter Darkness*, submitted to Cornell University in 1989, is divided as follows: 'The Origin and Historical Context of Ankoku Butoh;' 'The Butoh Aesthetic and a Selection of Techniques;' and 'Analysis of *Niwa* (The Garden).' In order to assess the historical significance of *butō*, Klein interviewed a number of *butō* performers and critics, such as Ōno Kazuo, Nakajima Natsu, Gōda Nario, and Motofuji Akiko. This is framed within a comparative analysis of the *butō* and *nō* aesthetic, based on an extensive knowledge of *nō*.

Sandra Fraleigh, professor at the State University of New York, has developed her research into the *butō* aesthetic by taking workshops with Ōno Kazuo, Nakajima Natsu, and Ashikawa Yōko, among others. Beyond Fraleigh, there are further researchers whose work I have not yet been fortunate to encounter.

In the studies above, we can see *butō*, and Hijikata's work in particular, being approached from either a cultural-historical or aesthetic perspective. Despite this, it is apparent that Hijikata's work is available to far more diverse approaches than those adopted to-date – from such fields as theatre studies, anthropology, philosophy, and the fine arts. The fact that there has been no comprehensive study of Hijikata's *ankoku butō* could be accounted for by the limited video and academic resources available, and by the limited number of texts in English on the subject. In Japan, in particular, this may be put down to the persistence of outraged responses to *ankoku butō*, and to the fact that it is still perceived as insurgent within both academic and artistic fields. Its reputation as esoteric and mysterious can, at the same time, be considered to be a result of limited resources being available.[13]

Such challenges to *ankoku butō* research are exacerbated by those problems endemic to dance studies more broadly. The transient nature of each performance, its unrepeatability, means that resources are always secondary in nature – either filmic footage or critical responses. Even interviews with *butō* dancers and their rehearsal notes, cannot be analysed in direct relation to performances. This challenge is particularly acute in the case of *butō*, as a result of Hijikata's particular resistance to the easy consumption or comprehension of performance; as he would often say, 'you'd better come if you really want to see.'

At the time of researching this thesis, the footage that had survived was not made widely available by the Hijikata Tatsumi Memorial Archive (then based at Asbestos Studio), and only a few choreographic notes were made available by Hijikata's wife, Motofuji Akiko, in the publication *Hijikata Tatsumi to tomo ni* (Together with Hijikata Tatsumi, 1990). With the Hijikata Archive moving to the Keio University Arts Center, the distribution and promotion of materials has greatly improved, but there nevertheless remains a scarcity of published notes taken by the pupils of Hijikata. Even where these are available, they continue to present the challenge of conceptual obscurity and an enigmatic relation to the choreography itself. Without a systematic approach to these notes, their obscurity (as is characteristic of Hijikata's writing more generally) makes impossible any access to his creative process. Hijikata's utterances, often wilfully enigmatic in nature, are drawn from his own physical sensations, and present an impenetrability that has stalled significant advances in Hijikata studies.

Despite the challenging nature of his achievement, Hijikata received recognition early on from a handful of significant figures, such as Shibusawa Tatsuhiko, and is even considered by some to have been responsible for one of the major 'events' of the twentieth century.[14] Matsuyama Shuntarō, scholar of Indian philosophy, has even gone so far as to draw similarities between *ankoku butō* and Buddhism. The original intentions behind the fundamentals of Buddhism may not continue to be self-evident, he argues, but their rootedness in Buddha always remains apparent. And similarly,

> as time passes, the reality of Hijikata's *ankoku butō* may become gradually obscure to subsequent generations, but irrespective of how *ankoku butō* develops or comes to be understood, there can be no question of the fact that without Hijikata there could have been no *ankoku butō*.[15]

Matsuyama's words signal the importance, but also the challenge, of taking Hijikata as the starting point for *butō* research.

Research Aims

This research aims at the elucidation of Hijikata Tatsumi's *ankoku butō* technique, and hopes to initiate a systematic approach to his work. In order to launch an investigation into *butō*, as an art form that overcomes ethnic and artistic frontiers, I will first return to *ankoku butō*, as the point of origin. *Butō* dancers and *butō* groups cannot help but trace their work back to the deciphering of Hijikata's *ankoku butō*. It is Hijikata's work, above all, that has made a significant intervention in the history of twentieth-century dance, and expanded the horizons of dance on an international level.

Where dance forms such as ballet usually operate on the level of physical technique and form, Hijikata's *ankoku butō*, as noted by Gōda Nario, is opposed to such limitations. As a result of this, the *ankoku butō* technique must be approached from multiple angles, and traced methodologically from the process of creation to the final performance work. Only by contemplating Hijikata's technique directly, rather than by locating his work historically or cultural-historically, can we consider the lasting influence it may come to have. And only by adopting a direct approach may the over-abstraction of theory (which might fixate itself on isolating idiosyncrasies in Hijikata's terminology – such as *ankoku*, or 'darkness,' and *suijakutai*, or 'weakening body') be avoided. For Gōda, the abstruseness of this language, though resulting from the complexity of Hijikata's own artistic sensibility, makes it highly problematic to approach *butō* abstractly, or to frame it in comparative relation to its historical moment.[16]

This research sets about an enquiry into the nature of *ankoku butō* from a similar standpoint to that of Gōda, in that it favours direct analysis of Hijikata's *ankoku butō* technique over a predominantly historical approach. In order to elucidate Hijikata's method of creation, training, and the conception of *ankoku butō*, I examine the choreographic work, which I consider to be the embodied locus of his thinking. *Ankoku butō* is more than a theory of technique; it is an exploration of human existence, which finds its ultimate expression in "form." For, as Hijikata saw it, "life turns to form."[17]

Research Methods

The research presented in this book is a continuation of the work undertaken for my MA thesis, 'Hijikata Tatsumi Research: Considering the *Butō* Method'. As described in the preface, it was whilst watching Hijikata dance that I felt a kind of purification. This experience of purification, of dissolving into something eternal, of feeling the categories of space and time disintegrate, still arises when I dance *butō*. The question of where this purification arises from is still what drives my exploration of Hijikata's work.

It was only during the writing of my MA thesis that some clarification was brought to my understanding of the *ankoku butō* technique, as I had learned it from 1978 to 1981. Creating and performing works internationally since that time, I have also been brought closer to what I understand to be the Hijikata philosophy – that there is 'no knowledge before you have danced,' and that 'cognition *is* movement, and movement, cognition.' Hijikata would often refer to such ideas, and they should inform the research of *butō* as much as the dancing of *butō*. In revising the research of my MA,

I have brought to bear my performance experiences as a dancer, and also included a number of materials not previously used: foreign criticism on *butō*; Hijikata's book, *Yameru maihime* (Ailing Danseuse), which exposes the motivations underpinning the *ankoku butō* technique; the record of Hijikata's Last Workshop; and a personal account from Ashikawa Yōko of how she received and modified Hijikata's technique.

Drawing on these materials, my method follows a systematic approach to *ankoku butō* research, as follows:

1) As an entry point to this research, I outline the state of Hijikata criticism inside and outside Japan and sketch an overview of his reception internationally.

2) I go on to consider the early history of Hijikata's creative and intellectual development prior to the founding of *ankoku butō* – those formative years in which his world-perspective and *butō*-perspective were first seeded. In order to clarify Hijikata's life and philosophy, I take *Yameru maihime* (Ailing Danseuse) as a central text with which to examine his native landscape, or 'primal topography,' and from which to extract the motivations behind *ankoku butō*. I then examine these motivations in light of the later development of *ankoku butō* techniques.

3) Here, I focus principally on the nature of Hijikata's language, as found in the written texts and records of his talking, using this language as a tool with which to examine the 'method of bodily expression' that is developed through his *ankoku butō* technique.

4) This chapter evidences the importance of Gōda Nario's criticism to my own standpoint on *ankoku butō*. It also traces various approaches to Hijikata's principal works and to the shifting development of his *ankoku butō* technique, framed in relation to the backdrop of his life as a *butō* dancer.

5) The resources made use of in this section range from my experiences training with Hijikata; Hijikata's workshop notes on the practice of *butō*; and the notes taken by four disciples (including myself), documenting Hijikata's image-language. Using these materials, I extract a theory of Hijikata's *ankoku butō* technique, and examine it from three perspectives: that of a *butō* dancer's body, that of a *butō* dancer's mind, and that of a *butō* dancer's movement.

6) Here, I evaluate Hijikata's *ankoku butō* technique from the perspective of movement, analysing 'walking,' which forms the foundation of *butō* movement, and the 'choreographic forms,' which are defined by Hijikata as the minimal movement to still carry meaning.

7) In this chapter, I take records of Hijikata's Last Workshop, and records of Ashikawa Yōko's workshops (attended after Hijikata's death), to draw a structural overview of Hijikata's choreographic practice, and evaluate the characteristics of *ankoku butō*.

8) In the conclusion, I attempt to synthesize my personal experience of purification when watching *butō* with the methodological precision of *ankoku butō*, in order to reach some understanding of Hijikata's life and work.

Appendix Materials

There are a number of material limitations to the research conducted here. I have not been fortunate enough to watch many of Hijikata's performances, and never performed alongside him. Although I learned directly from Hijikata, it was for a fairly short period of time. Moreover, the workshop notes made use of only cover a brief span and were taken down by a limited number of his disciples, at a time when Hijikata's technique was no longer under formation. The notes were taken shortly after the period when Hijikata formalized his image-language, and as such there are inevitable interpretative challenges to their analysis.

At the time of research, the records contained in the Hijikata Memorial Archive were largely undiscovered, and certainly unpublished. These records, as well as private notes taken by Hijikata's disciples during choreographic and physical training, offer direct insight into his teachings and techniques. It is my hope that in making these notes more widely available, new approaches to Hijikata's work may be facilitated. The extensive appendix of Hijikata's image-language is included with the intention that it may provide an important resource for future researchers and practitioners in the field.

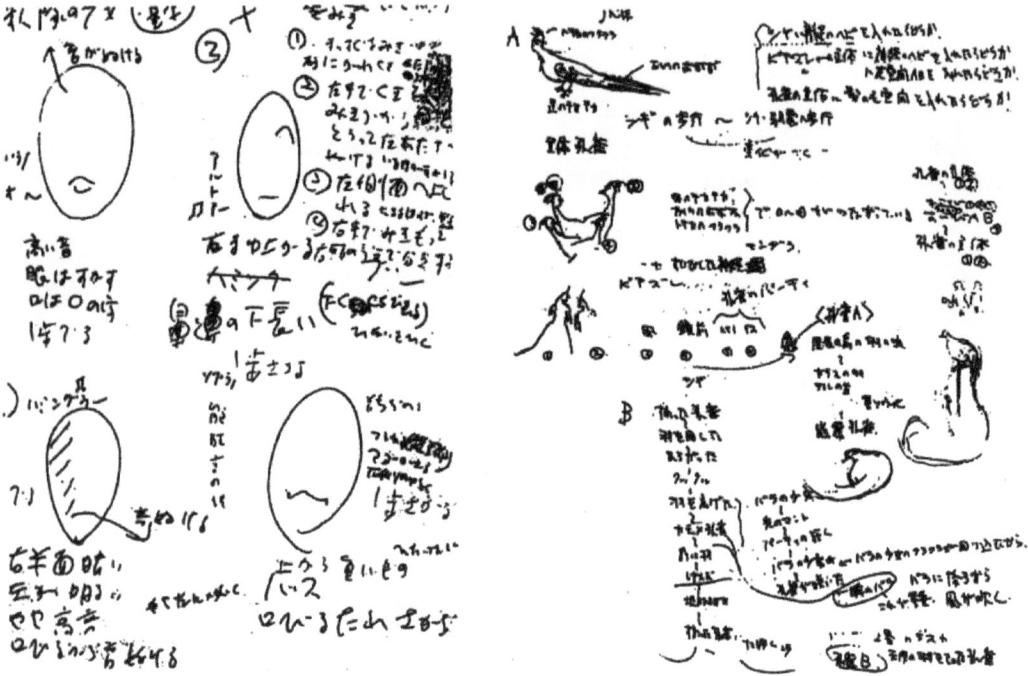

Notes taken by Mikami Kayo (1978; left) and Ichiyoshi Shunzō (1977, right)

The materials used from Chapter IV onwards consist of notes taken by four of Hijikata's disciples (including myself), and cover a four-year period, from 1977-1981. According to Gōda Nario, Hijikata had consolidated his *ankoku butō* technique earlier than this: during the middle period (1974-76), when working with *Hakutōbō*.[18] This period of consolidation can be considered as Hijikata's most productive period – despite the fact he did not perform onstage after 1973 – for it was during this time of close work with Ashikawa Yōko that he achieved enough distance on his own work to refine and detail the *ankoku butō* technique.

Shortly after this period, Hijikata retreated for a second time (from 1978-82) and began preparations for *Tōhoku kabuki keikaku 2*, a project that regrettably remained unfinished at his death. The notes taken by pupils during the period before this final project offer the closest thing to a documentation of the completed *ankoku butō* technique. Nonetheless, the notion that they offer any conclusive statement on *butō* stands in opposition to Hijikata's own philosophy – as he would claim: "In *butō* there is a process that cannot be taught – of registering the signs within your own senses. I can only teach you what can be taught."[19]

It has been said of Hijikata's *ankoku butō* training and creation that his choreography is shaped by a rich and highly evocative vocabulary. There is a sense of gravity in the way Hijikata verbalized his *ankoku butō* technique, as in the explanation he gave to Ashikawa Yōko during a *Hakutōbō* rehearsal: "One of us has to die if the other is to possess a form."[20] The language Hijikata used can be considered as the objectification of his physical training and creative method. The record of this language is collected alongside illustrations in the notebooks of his disciples. These workshop notes, in which are recorded Hijikata's instructions, might be divided as follows:

1) The shaping conditions of 'walking:' the basis of *butō*.
2) The shaping conditions of the 'choreographic forms:' *butō*'s smallest movement unit, organized into 'phrases, and 'etudes.'

3) Hijikata's musings and explanations.

For Hijikata, *butō* does not only take place under direction in a studio, life also contains the qualities of *butō*, and the *butō* disciple's life is also a training ground. For this reason, it seemed valuable to include my personal experiences of everyday life as a disciple of Hijikata.

Hijikata's weeklong open workshops were held in 1978, 1984, and 1985. The records taken at these workshops overlap in places with the general workshop notes taken from 1977-81, revealing the essence of Hijikata's maxim that he would 'only teach the truth.'

In addition to the notes employed in this book, I would like to acknowledge a debt to those whom I interviewed on the subject: Waguri Yukio, who was one of Hijikata's principle male dancers in the 1970s, and whose workshops I attended in 1990; Tamano Kōichi, who danced under Hijikata from 1960 onwards, and often performed as a principle dancer; and Yamamoto Moe, who was Hijikata's disciple from 1974-76, and had experience performing his choreography. Finally, I am also greatly indebted to Hijikata's wife, Motofuji Akiko, with whom I often spoke on the subject of Hijikata and *butō*.

Butō Criticism from Abroad

Although from the 1960s onwards Hijikata received several invitations from abroad, including from the Rockefeller Foundation and a number of international theatre festivals, he never left Japan. Despite this, the successes of the likes of *Sankai Juku* and Ōno Kazuo meant that *butō* spread worldwide from the 1980s onwards.

In this section, I address criticism from abroad, making particular use of that housed in the *Lincoln Center for the Performing Arts Library*, New York, and with a focus on texts addressing the works of *Sankai Juku*, Ōno Kazuo, Nakajima Natsu, and *Hakutōbō*.

The Style of Butō

The American dance critic Deborah Jowitt remarked that "Hijikata's original insistence (was) on cultivating the Japanese, indeed the *local* body. […] Hijikata's experiments with bowed legs and clubbed feet implicitly warred against both westernization and ideals of perfection."[21] If Jowitt's statement is taken as representative, it suggests that the American perception of Hijikata is that his "bowed legs" symbolize a pre-modern body, a body that challenges institutionalized culture and modernization, a male body lying close to the earth.

Foreign commentators on *butō* tend to cast Hijikata as a father figure and Ōno (often adopting a feminine persona) as a mother figure. This signals an important dynamic in the inception of *butō*: *butō* was partly triggered by Hijikata's admiration for Ōno, he worked with Ōno in most works of the 1960s, and most of Ōno's significant performances were directed by Hijikata. From the 1970s onwards, however, a divergence might be noted between more improvisational styles derived from Ōno, such as that of Kasai Akira, and more choreographic styles derived from Hijikata, such as the 'spectacular' performance-style of *Dairakudakan*.

Awareness of *butō* on the global stage grew from the 1980s onwards. Following in Ōno's footsteps, Nakajima Natsu (trained by both Hijikata and Ōno in the 1960s), and the group *Sankai Juku*, began to find favourable reception abroad. Anna Kisselgoff, a dance critic for the *New York Times*, and frequent commentator on *butō* from the mid-80s onwards, captures this vogue for *butō* in her article: "Dance That Startles and Challenges Is Coming From Abroad." Kisselgoff considers *butō* to come from an unexpected place and estimates it to mark a new direction for dance. The progressive and new quality Kisselgoff identifies – the originality of *butō*'s expressiveness – is offset by a comparison with the American emphasis being placed on "pure dance and formal concerns." She argues that Japanese *butō* groups "place man in a universe that must be destroyed before it can be created anew," considering the overall *butō* theme to be the suggestion of a cosmic image. *Butō* stands alongside other foreign influences, such as Pina Bausch from Germany or Jean-Claude Gallotta from France, as a threat to the "American preserve." Kisselgoff elaborates on their differences:

> [T]he sprawling free spirit of current French dance has its roots in the student upheavals of 1968 while the German and Japanese variants have emerged from the troubled legacy of World War II.[22]

The commentary offered by Kisselgoff, as well as those by other foreign *butō* critics, might indicate several distinct stylistic categories. Firstly, *butō* as a 'spectacular' dance, seen in the "flashy theatricality" of groups such as *Dairakudakan* and *Sankai Juku*.[23] Secondly, *butō* as a dance related to the individual, as in the solo work of performers such as Nakajima, who takes a "journey into her own traumas and their universalized expression," which might be said to leave a deeper impression than the 'spectacular' genre of *butō*.[24] Thirdly, *butō* as a free expressionist movement, as in the case of Ōno, who was able to remove the boundary between a "theatrical lets-pretend" and "an ecstatic imaginary universe."[25] And finally, *butō* as that style of dance brought to America in the 1990s, exemplified by Ashikawa in *Hakutōbō*, as a dance of intimate atmosphere that makes use of a varied score, free from either "extreme slowness" or "extreme distortion."[26]

These stylistic subdivisions in *butō* might be considered within a more general framework of relation to other dance styles, as Kisselgoff indicates with her description of "the Japanese Expressionist style known as butō." This description gestures towards a relationship with German Expressionism and modern dance, but may also point us in the direction of *kabuki* drama. *Kabuki* and *butō* (with the use of white body paint and grotesque expression) both generate a "sense of devastation."[27] The representation of *butō* as a dance of extreme slowness points in another direction – towards the heritage of *nō*. In *butō*, as in *nō*, the extreme slowness comes from the use of shuffling steps, which generate a particular vision of time and space. The slowness of *butō* has not always been met with favourable response, as when Jack Anderson writes, in his 1986 review of *Sankai Juku*: "it was hard to understand why so many actions had to be taken at such a ponderous pace."[28]

Butō's slowness is of course not its only mode, as Kisselgoff writes, citing the critic Hasegawa Roku, "Butō in the 1960's and 1970's used leaps and fast movements," and the "essential themes" of *butō* are not only related to slowness, but rather "[c]ycles of death and rebirth, subliminally linked to images of Hiroshima."[29]

The critical interest which *butō* generated overseas has been part of what might be termed the 'Asian-boom' in Western culture. The particular responsiveness of a Western audience to its sensibilities is documented by Suzanne Asselin when she claims: "through its oriental symbolism which sometimes tends to fall into mysticism and incomprehensibility," the audience is required "to relinquish every illusion of rationalism" and return to "the imaginary realm of the human body" in a way that transcends the "super-ego." She even goes on to claim that "[t]he audiences will be disappointed if [*butō*] fails to accomplish onstage the Japanese discourse and the philosophy Zen."[30] Andrea Rowe indicates something similar in her comment on the astonishing encounter between "the fragility of eastern culture" and the West that occurs in butō.[31] And Kisselgoff similarly discovers something particularly Japanese in the distillation found in *kabuki*, *haiku*, and Japanese dance.[32]

From these reviews we find *butō* tends to be framed in one of two ways: either in terms of the genealogy of German modern dance, or in terms of a tradition of Japanese Performing Arts, such as *kabuki* and *nō*, and in relation to Japanese perspectives of life and death, as found in *zen* philosophy and in the expressive form of *haiku*.

Butō Technique

Although within Japan *butō* is still considered an 'emotional and amateur dance form lacking in technique,' overseas it is appreciated for its 'admirable and extreme degree of muscular control.' With such diverging responses, it is hard to locate the core of *butō*.

In Western criticism, there is often the drive to discover what lies beneath the technique of muscular control that allows for *butō*'s slowness and distortion. Critics also take an interest in more abstract techniques, such as what Kisselgoff identifies as the "distillation of energy to convey a heightened emotional state – visualized through the human body."[33] This relates to a sense of the governing "concept of metamorphosis and transcendence," seen in *butō's* shifting landscape of figures – infants, old women, rocks, trees, representations of Buddha, fantastical creatures – and might be termed an "outer image of a spiritual change."[34] Deborah Jowitt has also commented on the metamorphic qualities of *butō* when watching *Hakutōbō*:

> [Who] move as if monitoring the flow of blood, as if sensing the impact of air not just on their bones and muscles, but on their pores. They are constantly metamorphosing. [...] I can't see specific mutations, only the never-ending process of becoming.[35]

The "constantly metamorphosing" movement of *butō* dancers has also been read in almost opposite terms as a "static mime-dance form."[36] The process of transformation is so perfectly crafted that the image could have been there for centuries. For Marcia B. Siegel, this is particularly true of Nakajima Natsu's work, in which she sees "no cause and effect [...] only stages and states of feeling."[37] Of Nakajima's work, it has been noted that "[t]he most fundamental relations are processed by Nakajima just by sitting onstage without a slightest motion." Such a "spiritual transformation of the performers" comes as a surprise to the American audience, in that it undoes the expectation of dance as a rhythmic form of movement expression.[38]

Butō is a dance that conveys an "unpredictable" and "potent" energy, an accumulated vehemence in its sequences of gestures.[39] Movements are internalized, and then unpredictable: a "bent-knee stance" gives way "to a stretched flailing shape in a transformation scene of astonishing intensity;" or Nakajima shifts in a state of imbalance, crosses the stage, lies on the floor, and then suddenly awakens in some vision of a lost fragment of Mary Wigman's *Witch Dance*.[40] If such scenes convey an "unimaginable strength," then this strength comes from the *butō* mind condition, which moves beyond logical understanding. It is this quality that Tobi Tobias notes when he writes that in Ōno's work there are often series of "riveting and almost inextricably moving images," as though they emanate a light that eclipses problems of "deficiencies in structure and logic."[41] We find here a strong draw towards the idea that *butō* might operate beyond logical comprehension. Tobias describes this in more detail when he writes of Ōno:

> [He] is like a mad genius who has long ago obliterated the line between theatrical let's-pretend (which remains within the pretender's control) and an ecstatic imaginary universe of which he is the sole inhabitant.[42]

This sense of another state being inhabited, is also perceived by Kisselgoff when watching a *Hakutōbō* performance:

> Like a Kabuki performer taking on a demonic shape, [Ashikawa] seems to enter another state of being before subsiding into serene calm.[43]

Or by Siegel when commenting on the "divided state of consciousness" of Nakajima, when:

> [H]alf of her throws itself into expansive gestures [...] half isn't there – eyes closed, head lolling, body cut off from the act.[44]

The *butō* mind condition being detected here is common to Ōno, Ashikawa and Nakajima despite their differences in approach: the latter two work more choreographically, while Ōno works heavily with improvisation. The detection of a division in consciousness also relates to *butō*'s frequent reversal of audience and performer roles. An example of this might be read in Jowitt's description of the terrifying effect Ashikawa had, when she raised her head on stage like one of the dead noticing the living.[45]

The techniques used to achieve such an effect in *butō* are, nonetheless, met with some confusion, as when Siegel writes: "You can stare at it till yours eyes hurt, searching for a sign of life, and suddenly you notice that the dancer has turned into a baby or an old woman, and you missed the transformation entirely."[46] Or when Bonnie Sue Stein exclaims: "*Butō* is: / shocking / provocative / physical / spiritual / erotic / grotesque / violent / cosmic / nihilistic / cathartic / mysterious."[47] The accumulation of adjectives used to describe *butō* here indicates the many directions in which it might lead us, but also the challenge it therefore poses to interpretation. Indeed the "effect" of *butō*, whilst deeply moving, often stirs a sense of perplexity, as described by *butō* critic Ichikawa Miyabi, who accompanied Ōno's 1980 European tour and 1981 New York tour. Ichikawa recalled a number of the audience wept at the deep impression it left, reflecting that a Western audience watching *butō* seemed to perceive the weight of a body submitted to endless transformations. This *butō* body brings to stage a vision of the deconstruction of "the microcosm" and a denial of the universe. It brings a sense of destruction or apocalypse which can be seen as a meeting ground between East and West, as "[t]he performers and audiences [are] tossed into the same melting pot searching the way to live at the end of modern times."[48]

A number of the themes highlighted by critics above have also been brought out in relation to my own work as a performer, which has been considered in relation to *kabuki*, *nō*, or the Hiroshima atomic bomb (though such connections were not intended in making the work). My work has also been met with a sense of perplexity, as when a ballet dancer said to me: 'It looks like you are coming and going between this world and another. How are you doing that?'

It is my own experience as a dancer, as well as my consideration of other works, that has led me to consider *butō* as some kind of meeting ground between the souls of the audience and of the dancer – as they move towards each other without heed of bodily limitations. The meeting is made possible by the partial dissolution of a bodily reality, and the emergence instead of a spiritual reality. It locates itself in the realm of some shared origin, the site of chaos to which we have returned, where selfhood is erased and life expands on a cosmological scale. This expansion can overcome national or artistic boundaries to move audiences and critics worldwide. It is precisely *butō*'s will towards the eternal that foreign criticism is so responsive to.

Critical Approaches to Hijikata

At the point of writing this book, there were three significant resources available on Hijikata: *Hijikata Tatsumi shō – nikki to in'yō ni yoru* (Homage to Hijikata Tatsumi: based on diaries and memorabilia, 1987), by the modern poet Yoshioka Minoru – a document of Hijikata's relationship with Yoshioka and other artists; *Hijikata Tatsumi to tomo ni* (Together with Hijikata Tatsumi, 1990), by Hijikata's wife Motofuji Akiko – containing memoirs of their early days, when *ankoku butō* was being formed, as well as detailed information on each of Hijikata's dance works from the 1960s; and my own unpublished thesis, *Utsuwa toshite no shintai – Hijikata Tatsumi ankoku butō gihō e no apurōchi* (The Body as a Vessel: Approaching the Methodology of Hijikata Tatsumi's Ankoku Butō), which formed the basis of this book. In addition to these, a number of novelists and artists have offered non-critical commentaries on Hijikata, expressing their respect for him as a performer and friend.

Hijikata has often been cast in relation to one of three cultural historical frameworks: that of postmodern Western art, that of the Japanese performing arts with their tradition of gestural and physical techniques, and that of anthropology with its analysis of peripheral figures or marginal groups. The three intersect where they engage with the issue of consciousness, and its potential to move beyond a form of rationalism codified in language, towards the alternative "wisdom of the body."[49]

Butō and Western Modernism

Hijikata's work, emerging in the mid-1960s, can be considered to marginally precede postmodern Western dance. Ichikawa has drawn a comparison between the two, claiming "where postmodernism surpasses modernism, *butō* does so by returning to premodernism." Ichikawa considers this retrograde movement to entail a return to "eastern monism," or the uniting of the body and mind.[50]

Ichikawa's comment resonates with that of the scholar Amagasaki Akira, who considers there to be a movement in the arts towards "the incarnation of existence."[51] This emphatic corporeality is also something indicated by Shibusawa when he argues that the substance of Hijikata's *butō* is the "expression of the crisis that lies within the body."[52] This "expression" speaks beyond the theatre of modern dance, as a "total recovery from the fractured subjectivity of modern art."[53] It is a form of expression that expands beyond the parameters of a Western conception of the ego.

Butō and the Japanese Performing Arts

Butō instead marks a return "to premodernism" through the rediscovery of an ethnic body.[54] It seems to revolt against the *kabuki* inheritance, by embracing "the taboos of a Western aesthetic," but this in fact comes from within "the inheritance of a *kabuki* aesthetic."[55] The relationship *butō* has to the Japanese performing arts has been written of by the director Suzuki Tadashi, when he claims that "[*butō*'s] achievement lies in its presentation of the dying figure," which reveals a "consciousness of time and space, similar to that of *kabuki* and *nō*, in that it arises from an acute awareness of the flesh."[56] That is, an awareness of the *Japanese* body. According to *kabuki* critic Takechi Tetsuji, this relies on "the idea of paddy farming" and "*namba*" (the traditional way of walking with synchronized leg and arm movements). Takechi argues that the essence of Hijikata's philosophy can be found in paddy farming, and that to return to such a point will contribute to "the value of a new Japanese culture that is not borrowed from the West."[57]

To consider *butō*'s relation to *kabuki*, "not in terms of folklore, but in terms of retracing its roots" from *kyōgen* to *nō*, *nō* to *bugei*, and from ancient performance rituals to paddy farming, we can place Hijikata's work in a long tradition of bodily practices. At the same time, Hijikata's work might also be seen to carry the aesthetics of Japanese folklore, as indicated by Kobayashi Masayoshi when he describes his impression of *Shiki no tame no nijūnana-ban* (Twenty-Seven Nights for Four Seasons, 1972), and of seeing "Hijikata crawling on four legs" writhing like an animal:

> [Hijikata] traced the very edge of human life, and confirmed its existence in an expression of sympathy towards all other life forms. In that moment, Hijikata went further still, passing through his personal darkness, and encountering all living things.[58]

Passing through his personal darkness, Hijikata came close to the world of Japanese folk culture; that is, a world in which there is an essential "sympathy" and "responsiveness" to all "living things" and to the surrounding universe. His work occupies a place within this Japanese surround. As Yamaguchi Takeshi has speculated: *butō* oscillates between "here and there [between life and death], as a native place for the Japanese." Yamaguchi perceives Hijikata's body to "work as an instrument" channelling universal currents, which might give expression to the Japanese philosophy of life and death, of "already seeing the end in the beginning."[59]

Limitations to Both Approaches

To consider Hijikata's work as a movement beyond modernism, an embodied return to a state of premodernism, offers too limited an approach. For any "single expression" or "single concept," as Suzuki Shiroyasu points out, will not be able to offer the way to "rescue the body of folklore, which has been rejected by a Japanese consciousness since the Meiji period." To attempt such a singular or methodological approach can only lead to the "dictation of expression."[60] Indeed, Hijikata's work can never be viewed from a single perspective, as Matsumoto Koshirō has written:

> Taken within one context, Hijikata Tatsumi's *butō* reveals the body in a state of liberation, of 'rebellion.' The body is released through the discovery of new value systems. Taken within another context, this is a body weighed down by history and oppressed by a new form of stylization.[61]

Hijikata's *butō* emerges from the unexpected, it marks "the erasure of a catalogue of bodily gestures," and the liberation from a "systemization of the body." At the same time, it can be read in inverse terms, as the "dictation of expression" and as the suppression and stylization of the body.[62] The way to find a route through these varying interpretations of Hijikata's *butō* is by adopting as direct an approach as possible, as Matsumoto indicates when he claims that Hijikata criticism ought not to "analyse in terms of historical context or circumstance, but address the history of Hijikata's body directly."[63] It is with this direct approach to the "body" in mind that I specifically orientate this thesis towards Hijikata's performance work and technique.

Butō and the Grotesque

Both a Western framework and Japanese performing arts framework share some common ground in their re-evaluation and perception of the body. As Matsumoto has pointed out, approaching Hijikata's work either in terms of its Japanese performance heritage, or in relation to contemporaneous postmodernist practices, can only result in a limited interpretation. To take another framework for considering the work, we might introduce the idea of the grotesque.

The grotesque, derived from the Italian word 'grotto,' may be considered as something "mysterious," or "strange."[64] Yamaguchi Masao relates Hijikata's work to a theory of the grotesque in relation to its engagement with questions of centre and periphery, city and village, and in terms of its reappraisal of marginalized agricultural communities. Yamaguchi argues that we see in Hijikata's movement the image of a farmer crawling on the ground, which expresses "the idea of the grotesque, the release of an animalistic quality that lies inside the human." This results in a "violent strain to push beyond the neat organization of civilized life."[65] This violent revolt against established order can be drawn from Hijikata's physicality, as Gunji describes it: "the graceful stands in contrast to the ugly", "the bow legs, the hunched back, and the contorted limbs" go beyond the aesthetics of *kabuki* and recall an earlier time.[66] In the past, "the disabled were bringers of happiness, and considered as gods of wellbeing." Likewise, the "taboo of a white-painted body transforms into something bitter, something foul, and is then elevated into something sacred."[67] This is the standpoint of the grotesque.

Tōno Yoshiaki writes that "laughter in the face of the grotesque occurs specifically at moments of historical change," when the grotto, like a mouth, opens beneath the feet and reveals "unperceived monsters shining in the dark."[68] Considering Hijikata's work in light of these descriptions of the grotesque, I have been able to reconsider my own feeling of salvation when watching Hijikata's movement for the first time. As Kobayashi describes, there is some sense of returning to an originating scene that arises in the presence of the grotesque:

> In some sense the grotesque is that which has not once appeared before our eyes, that which has not once been seen. And yet, though no memory exists, somehow a memory is preserved, so that when it presents itself, we feel that it has been seen before. This is the meaning of *Urszene*.[69]

Kobayashi considers the *Urszene* in relation to structures of psychological trauma. Its description, here, also carries a general sense of the meaning of the grotesque, as the "hidden essence of things," revealed when an aesthetic criteria or order breaks down.[70]

The feelings of salvation, purification, and nostalgia, which arose the first time I saw Hijikata dance, may have derived from this "hidden essence of things," which lies at the heart of the grotesque. Considering the darker aspects of *ankoku butō* in terms of the grotesque might allow for a new approach to the complexities of Hijikata's work.

2. A Portrait of Hijikata's Youth and his Native Landscape

Hijikata's Childhood

[Previous page:] Hijikata Tatsumi on a fence in Tōhoku, *Kamaitachi* (Weasel's Cut, 1965), by Hosoe Eikō

Hijikata Tatsumi was born as Yoneyama Kunio in Akita, Tōhoku, in 1928 (the third year of Shōwa). He was the tenth child (and sixth son) of eleven, to be raised in a house that was half farm, half soba restaurant.

The cultural environment of Tōhoku, as Hijikata himself has indicated, lies at the source of his movement technique: the images of cross-legged infants bound in *izume* (straw baskets), or the particular walk that comes from trudging the Tōhoku soil. The movements of Hijikata's *ankoku butō* were born in the rice fields of a snowy country and produced by a lifestyle that deformed the arms and legs. His movement materials were connected to literary images of Tōhoku as a place of darkness and poverty.

The connections between Tōhoku and Hijikata's *ankoku butō* movement have been discussed by Ichikawa Miyabi in terms of a folkloric body moulded by the specific climate of Tōhoku,[1] and by Yoshimoto Takaaki in terms of the specifics of Tōhoku's topology.[2] Both consider the bow legs, the character-types, and the expressive qualities of Hijikata's *ankoku butō* to derive from this Tōhoku heritage. *Ankoku butō*'s imaging of Tōhoku and of figures trudging in rice fields marked the turn away from ballet towards a new sensibility. For Hijikata, Tōhoku became a kind of mythos, a place where dance could discover its roots, a universal site. He would claim "there is even a Tōhoku in England." Tōhoku represented darkness, a primal site in which thinking was born, for "thinking itself is darkness."[3]

The aura that surrounds Tōhoku also surrounds Hijikata himself, with a number of myths springing up around his early life. The idea that his family dwelling (something between a farm and soba shop) was one of poverty is somewhat misleading given that his father was a village mayor's son. Hijikata could even afford Western clothing when attending Akita University Elementary School and, despite being one of eleven, was able to go on to Technological College. His cultural resources were also unusually varied, in that students lodging at his house from Akita Teachers College would expose him to a number of influences, such as *Tai Kwon Do* training. In other words, his upbringing was unusually rich in both economic and cultural terms.

At the same time, growing up in Tōhoku, with local trades mainly consisting of human trafficking, army work, horse breeding, and gold mining, images of poverty must have been deeply imprinted on Hijikata's imagination. Despite the nostalgia this might imply, Hijikata's treatment of Tōhoku might be considered ironic. These images were the symbolic residue of a pre-war Tōhoku – not a specific geography but, for Hijikata and those of his generation, a kind of primal Japanese topography that had since been lost. At the same time, his claim that Tōhoku can be discovered even in England, suggests a universality that extends beyond – even ridicules – specific Japanese associations with the term. Interpretations of Hijikata's *ankoku butō* in terms of geographical or cultural specificity run the risk of exoticizing Japaneseness in ways that lose sight of Hijikata's vision.

For Hijikata, Tōhoku was the familiar environment from which to launch himself: "a perfect climate from which to launch a great leap, and the right temperature to keep things frozen in their place." For Hijikata, climate and imagination were closely linked. He considered there to be an originating scene from which man must either choose to launch a great leap, or be condemned to remain frozen. The particular strain generated between leaping forward and remaining fixed afforded a contradictory sense of forward motion: "fusion occurs due to discontinuity […] life moves forward due to discontinuity."[4] Hijikata's "great leap" configures a relation between the climate and the dark place in which thoughts arise. He considered the problem of Tōhoku's darkness to be not only one of latitude, but of universal human life, and of the existential anxiety that attends it. This anxiety, termed by Hijikata a form of "pure starvation," was deeply bound up with his own sense of a homeland.[5] The relationship between a homeland and a "great leap" out of it can also be traced in Hijikata's statement: "my home was my theatre."[6]

Hijikata's notion of a home as a theatre was born in the darkness of a *kakumaki*, or large heavy cloak, which his mother would throw over him and his siblings when fleeing her violent husband along a snowy night-time road. Hijikata claims to have received his first training in the art of *makumozō* (literally, 'imitation membrane', but rather a sort of cloaked somnambulism) under this cloak, with his legs all twisted in sleep, and "clinging desperately with the thought of being torn off and thrown away."[7] This is the beginning of a *butō* consciousness: a state of half-sleep and half-wakefulness; a desperate movement in the thick of sleep.

The training of *makumozō* that took place in the *kakumaki* theatre of Hijikata's childhood was not the only training he received at that time. Watching his busy mother with "no time to dream," Hijikata discovered a "life dance" – that "all life was dance, and dance was the very soil of life". His *butō* training began with sleeping children, or in the dance of a mother with no time to dream. He perceived that all life was dance, and that a theatre could even be made of the home.[8]

Central to this perception was Hijikata's close relationship to his mother. He recalls, for example, the unexpected reassurance of being violently beaten by his mother when he lost the military decorations his father had won in the Sino-Japanese and Russo-Japanese wars – a feeling that seemed related to the *ankoku butō* method. It was as though Hijikata was preparing for some part in the drama, *Mother of Eyelids*, as though he was determined to make his mother into *the mother*. For Hijikata, this mother-son relationship was characterized by a sensation of deep blushing, which he experienced when addressing her as 'mother.' Hijikata observed this dynamic with eyes that could pierce to the inevitable in human nature, and discovered within it the beginnings of what would later become *ankoku butō*.

It was from this beginning that the necessity for an *ankoku butō* language grew. Hijikata's accounts of his homeland, his family, and his sister, who he would claim had been sold into prostitution, can assist in locating his emotional and nostalgic associations. "I have a sister living inside my body,"[9] he claimed; and just as he "kept the dead sister alive inside [him]self", he also "raised in his body" the memory of dressing up in his older sisters' *kimonos*, and of combing and setting his hair, in a custom now lost.[10] As a child, Hijikata was already observing the movements and processes of the body and the workings of consciousness in a way that would characterize the *butō* way of seeing.

Hijikata saw his father as a "serious and frank man," who had moved to Akita city from a large house overflowing with young people and female servants.[11] He had moved to Akita in order to offer his children a better education, having been told by relatives that his talents would go to waste in the countryside. Hijikata's mother was "large and bright," a 21 *kanme* (almost 84 kg) woman with high blood pressure, and a shaved patch on top of her head. For Hijikata, these were parents who showed "unprecedented independence": a "man who could accomplish anything," and a woman who could rise at three, carry her hatchet to the *doma* (a traditional room with a dirt floor), and split the ice in the water jug.[12]

Hijikata's childhood scenes became the imaginative foundation for something far more expansive. He recalls seeing his mother cooking rice by the hearth with hair that looked alight, and wondering whether "she was burning along with that fire," or whether some strange creature had just dropped into the *doma*.[13] This grew from wonder to fantasy, as he watched "that strange creature in the house cooking rice – no woman. Children are born, plop, plop. No longer the stuff of folklore, but something 'international.'"[14] The image grows into something "international," as Tōhoku represents a place not only in Japan, but existing anywhere in the world. Tōhoku is not only Hijikata's native land, it is *the* native land, or 'primal scene,' harbouring associations of the mother-son relationship and of the world as a dark theatre.

The urge to explore the secrets of Tōhoku's darkness may be what drove Hijikata to finally write the work, *Yameru maihime* (Ailing Danseuse). This work is central to an understanding of Hijikata's perception of Tōhoku, his motivations for dancing, and the origins of *butō*.

Yameru maihime (Ailing Danseuse)

Yameru maihime was serialized in the magazine *Shingeki* from 1977 to 1978. By this point, Hijikata considered the *ankoku butō* methodology to be largely completed. He had begun to be mythologized by the Japanese avant-garde community. Having earlier wavered between focusing on writing or dance, this marked the most extended example of Hijikata's literary talent, revealing him to be "not only an incomparable butoh dancer, but also a genius with language."[15] The world portrayed in *Yameru maihime* is based on the people and landscape of Hijikata's childhood in Tōhoku. He left Tōhoku for Tokyo at the age of 24 to pursue his ambition of becoming a dancer, and did not return until 1965. Hijikata returned in 1965 with Hosoe Eikō in order to shoot a series of photographs, *Kamaitachi* (Weasel's Cut, 1969), and this seemed to anticipate a realization that he must draw from the materials of his own life rather than focusing on the West.

This realization meant returning to memories stored in his own body – for "the body's flesh, as a bundle of memory," is like a landscape haunted by recollections of the dead and the living.[16] These memories would come to the stage in the work *Shiki no tame no nijūnana-ban* (Twenty-Seven Nights for Four Seasons, 1972), and inform the completion of his *ankoku butō* methodology, which occurred during his work with *Hakutōbō* (1974-6). Hijikata's *ankoku butō* methodology makes use of various figures and scenes that correlate to those described in *Yameru maihime*, which was published shortly after this period of *Hakutōbō* activity.

Reconsidering *Yameru maihime* in light of Hijikata's death ten years later, it seems he was trying to efface the preceding eighteen years as a *butō* dancer and make space to contemplate the next stage. As the poet Nakamura Fumiaki has pointed out, *Yameru maihime* seems to be a kind of settling of accounts, in which Hijikata reviews his entire personal history. Nakamura found that the motivation behind *Yameru maihime* only revealed itself in light of Hijikata's final performances, produced after the 10-year silence that followed its writing. *Yameru maihime* seemed to come out of a hunger or desire for a time when "art and society" no longer matter.[17] It can be read both as an incredible autobiographical poem that overlays the people, places, and objects of Hijikata's life, and also as a treatise on the *butō* perspective. The experience of reading this book might be compared to that of viewing a *butō* performance, in that both are open to multiple interpretations.

Yameru maihime is closely related to Hijikata's theory of corporeality, to a body in revolt, as suggested in a description by Uno Kuniichi: "[Hijikata's] use of language evades all sense of hierarchy, and even moves beyond the idea of anarchy," this work is "neither poetry nor prose, and yet both poetry and prose." This is a book that offers no explanatory context, neither straight poetry nor prose. It is not a memoir, and yet "to reverse that completely, one might also say it is a memoir of all that has happened, a record of real living" and of the "mysterious things that also exist in the world." For Uno, *Yameru maihime* catalogues "the differentiation and nuances of things, of insects, of air... their moment to moment transformations; time under observation; perpetual enumerations;" it describes a "mysterious conception of life and death, of the past, and a mysterious ordering of memory." In *Yameru maihime*, "matter joins matter, life forms join meteorology, there is the condition in which the body is always entangled... the 'I', in constant living, constant dying."[18] To try and disentangle the "I" of *Yameru maihime* and assign it a clear subject, located in time and space, is almost impossible. The depictions of childhood in this book, might call up nostalgic recollections, but they also imaginatively "generate a future," and at the same time suggest an "immediate present," in a complex model of simultaneity that is considered by Uno to bear a close relation to the temporality of *butō* dance.[19]

The originality of *Yameru maihime*'s descriptive approach has also been written of by the manuscript editor, Miyoshi Toyoichirō, in terms of a stream of consciousness: when Hijikata "starts writing, a stream of associations flows out and thickens like tendrils that cover and veil a trunk, leaving branches still growing and intertwining, until subject and object become indistinguishable and sentences grow dense in obscurity."[20] This use of language bears some relation to that of

Surrealism, but is very far from derivative, as French Literature specialist, Nishitani Osamu, has pointed out. While both "upheave the meaning of language from an everyday context," in Surrealism this involves a conscious estrangement and disruption of the flow of language, whereas in Hijikata's work it involves the creation of a "dancing text," in which conflicting "dualisms of metaphors in words and sentences are neutralized."[21]

Hijikata's treatment of people, places and things in *Yameru maihime* relates closely to the movement methodology of *butō*. Its style moves beyond the framework of a clear subject-object relationship, working to eliminate established boundaries. Its continuous shifts in perspective refuse a subject-orientated consciousness, suggesting a movement of the mind that can be taken as the functioning of a *butō* dancer's consciousness. This transforming consciousness moves through cycles of creation and disappearance, as places fade and are refound.

The text's descriptive twists and turns bring objects and figures into focus for an instant before once more disappearing them into the dark. Within the remarkable expanse and elaborate disorder of this descriptive tapestry, traces of both the light and darkness of Tōhoku can be found. The darkness of descriptive chaos and fragmentation is offset by the clarity of figures outlined in detailed accuracy. This chaos, generated by a lack of clear context, places the reader or viewer in a state of confusion. At the same time, the precise detailing of places and figures inevitably draws them into the world of the text. Something similar can be found in accounts of viewing Hijikata's performance works, when Japanese and foreign audiences describe shedding tears without being able to explain why.

Pure Starvation: the Motivation for Ankoku butō

The salient theme of *Yameru maihime* is Hijikata's childhood: memories of his early days and the people who surrounded him in infancy. Hijikata's mode of description is nonetheless far from nostalgic in any conventional sense, as the following citation makes apparent:

> That time rolling off the roof with a ceramic insulator in the mouth. That incident alone banished a man from his hometown. Considering those palms clasping a bundling cloth, [I] become suddenly scorched pitch black.[22]

This man, banished from his hometown for cutting the electricity with a "ceramic insulator," was none other than a young Hijikata. Hijikata had been painfully divided: on the one hand "unable to go too far"[23] from the "relief of feeling myself protected by something,"[24] and on the other hand driven away to "witness things reaching their end."[25] He had known that to stay or go would ultimately equate to the same thing: a "pure starvation, or a starvation that could never be satisfied."[26] He felt forced to take hold of the insulator, and stop the flow of a community; to become the boy who takes up the insulator and is utterly alone; to become the boy who is "scorched pitch black." In this we might discover some of the motivations behind Hijikata's creation of *ankoku butō*.

Indeed the source of *butō* movement can often be discovered in these descriptions of rural life, as when Hijikata wrote with slight irony in a performance pamphlet: "compared to ploughing a field, war is easy."[27] This comparison is made sense of by Hijikata's account of the severity of farm labour: "the labourer goes past the point of exhaustion… [bent over] like the character 'ブ.'"[28] For Hijikata, the adults who laboured in the fields of his childhood were locked in a cruel fate. This cruelty began in infancy, when the children, imprisoned in their *izume* (straw baskets), "cried and cried" but couldn't be heard by those adults, because their "cries came from within a system in which the voice cries out but reaches nobody." Children, like their parents, were locked in a struggle against fate, born to live and die bound within the same shackles. Hijikata wrote of past hardships: "you can't imagine how in the past there were more summers fit for hanging yourself in" – an image which conversely brings dead bodies to mind.[29] Misery and poverty may have plagued the "great landscape" of Hijikata's past, but there was always some light to see by,[30] for "whether driven to ruin or insanity, a suitable sun would always shine."[31] He felt this misery and ignorance to be associated with the cruelness of fate, recollecting: "a stupidly honest scene of repeating forms extending on, as though something was gradually accumulating."[32] This was the scene of life, better accepted than avoided, because "you can cry and regret, but people still die in their turn."[33] For Hijikata it was certainly better to accept life's fate, than to seek a life "cooking honeycomb toffee."[34] He felt a "need to pull apart the world," and to confront a sense of impending crisis.[35] Turning to this "great scene," like a landscape of ruin, Hijikata wondered "how to approach the blue sky." This experience of puzzlement in the face of the sky, of "not knowing what to do," was the discovery of "pure starvation" for Hijikata.[36]

This discovery dates back to his childhood. Hijikata remembers his red-faced and "serious brothers," stoked with *sake* and told to "fight bravely," being sent off to war, later to return as no more than rattling bone-filled urns.[37] He recalls how his sisters "suddenly disappeared," like pieces of discarded furniture.[38]

Filled with a sense of absence, Hijikata grew self-aware of his place within the universe, feeling like "*Kurama tengu* [a mythical long-nosed mountain hermit], whose weak existence nobody under the high blue sky understands."[39] Hijikata knew he must take the "ceramic insulator" and exile himself to a state of "pure starvation." The feeling of "pure starvation" discovered in the "beautiful blue sky" lends the world of *Yameru maihime* a sense of open-mindedness and transparency.

Figures in the Landscape: Butō and the Body

In the darkness of the *doma* steam rises from the hearth, and a boy is left alone in a spacious room. Out in the rice fields, adults inhumanly labour in the heat. How does Hijikata remember this boy's world so well – the figures, the objects, the phenomena of childhood, the stables, the blacksmith, and the adults around?[40] These memories are called up without moral judgment, objects are placed just as they are, viewed through the eyes of a child. The world is felt with a child's sensibility, with a child's sense of its own body, the figures of *Yameru maihime* are recalled in relation to the body: "all things, even the pumpkin's flower wilting, or the horse's face wasting, are the talk of the body."[41]

The figures and images of *Yameru maihime* pass by one by one, endlessly on. First comes the "scribble of a tiny infant," floating in a haze of "dislocated forms, like odd things or a barely distinguishable fake atmosphere."[42] Then there is the "fool who might look strong" but is reported "to go limp in a *sumo* fight," and that "kid from a poor house" with his "face of pure poverty," who wilts at the scent of red or blue sugar-water. Then there is the "woman who enters a room with her hair on end, as if electrified,"[43] and the "senile old woman, ridden with time-feeding lice."[44] There is the "infant with its bag of excrement, like a small hernia,"[45] and the "woman who looks a bit easy, but turns out to be frigid," selling chickens on windy days.[46] There is the woman in a room, who talks "like a crow opening its mouth,"[47] the "woman crying" beneath a quivering lamp,[48] and the "schoolgirl who doles out whiffs of toilet."[49]

Whatever kind of "hell these people were living in, the things that lay hidden in their bodies" remained unseen,[50] and their "screams remained sealed" in daily life.[51] Hijikata's thoughts were formed among these suffering bodies and silent screams. He recalls the times when an outburst would occur, when you enter a house and find "one or two gods who are internally broken," the kind of "people who can't suppress the violent passion of their spirit," and so release a scream "in a shrieking tone, whilst holding a poker in their hands." For Hijikata these outbursts were the moment when a person really "tasted exactitude – the moment before impotence."[52] Insanity was something related to the bodily mechanism, and not something to be observed from the perspective of psychology. Such bodily descriptions of figures in *Yameru maihime* underlie Hijikata's *ankoku butō* perspective, and deeply inform his movement technique.

The Character of the Ailing Danseuse

Yameru maihime is a title that closely relates to Hijikata's particular emphasis on the sickening or 'weakening body.' He describes how, the "person weakened by sickness, thrown between rest and wakefulness, is always mourning in the dark part of the house."[53] In the landscape of Japan's past, such figures as the sick, the insane, the disabled, and the homeless, were not exiled, but lived their extraordinary lives within ordinary society.

The lying body of a sick person was not hidden, but "released like a fish onto tatami," so that its "outline appeared as a wish," a wish for life's transience, a wish for a life beyond the everyday. This "person weakened by sickness" revealed "the darkness of the other side, the darkness of a resurrection beginning." Hijikata acknowledged the point where existence itself emerges in the process of dying, and discovered a "resurrection beginning" in this ailing figure.

The ailing figure appears as a symbol of fate, seeming to say: "before you is certain death," before you lies the surface of existence, which veils real time and space.[54] To hear these questions, and confront the question of death, perpetuates a kind of anxiety in existence, and fuels the "wish for a release, like after the excruciating pain of a brutal thwack in the shin with a stick."[55] That is to say, bodily pain releases the self from superficial anxieties, and brings a realization of the desire for existence itself.

The young Hijikata moved in the direction of pain and towards the darkness of death, as though "striding across the shadows of deformity and apathy" that fall between the glow cast by a healthy life and the deep shades of death. He "dragged his body along the root laid by the ailing danseuse," until he was completely "mixed up in [her]," recalling with an overwhelming sense of "sweetness, nostalgia, and despair," how he "decided to dance with her, that princess, to hold her temperature in an embrace, and absorb it into [his] veins."[56] As a child, Hijikata was forced to confront the sickness of the ailing danseuse, and to acknowledge that there is a "resurrection beginning" in death. This was a lesson that "cannot be learned or taught," the "deep sigh of growing up."[57]

Hijikata felt a sense of crisis at being absorbed into this "great landscape" without making a disturbance within everyday life. This was connected to his strong desire to break through the sky, as though it were a single plate, and to draw closer to the ailing danseuse as a means of escaping this "great landscape."[58] Hijikata saw that to break this sky would open a route towards the ailing danseuse and towards *butō*, and away from the rhythmic use of the "body's energy" that characterized Western dance. The result of this was what Shibusawa has described as "a proper expression found in the forms of discontinuity or weakness," as "a dance founded on a Japanese ethnicity."[59]

Ogano the Mute

Hijikata tended towards the "direction of straying,"[60] trailing figures like "that mute woman in the neighbourhood, Ogano, who was impregnated by an oilman." He recalls how as a child, "whenever [he] saw this woman, [he] hid [him]self and trailed her, always keeping her keenly insight."[61] The child always has a simple curiosity towards individuals with mental or physical disabilities, mad people, and beggars, who live in a village. These were the tricksters of a closed community, its ventilation fan, presenting the children with an intensified form of existence, a dense humanity, a sense of the weight of social deprivation.

Hijikata's childhood was a period when the house was still built on "arbitrary rules that had long become lukewarm and rotten," when the light to live by was one bleeding from the "deadened silence of day," rather than the "glassy beams" of "half-rotten light" that stream through an "old glass screen like milky water in a rice-bowl." When that light from the "deadened silence of day" streamed in, people went out to work in the fields, leaving only a "*fukusuke* doll placed in the darkness of the living room." The solitary *fukusuke* doll was placed in the alcove of a wide tatami room, its silhouette cut from the spilling darkness and the stillness of day, its small form in the wide room appearing "transformed into the outline of a figure on a distant pathway."[62]

In the stillness of day that hung around the darkened house, "lady Ogano" would go out walking. Ogano was rumoured to be "the mute one who drunk breast-milk mixed with beast-milk," which dribbled down from "ear to throat." The children had an "eerie" curiosity for Ogano, certain that there was some depth behind her "pretence of ignorance," and some sound being heard "in the world of the mute." They would watch Ogano "spread into her surround in some unknown way, as though preparing for something," and they knew they could be "no match" for her. She seemed to have a "curious elegance" and "acrobatic style, free from the strangeness of a woman with trouble in her womb," and from the strangeness of a woman's "itches, her bodily secretions, her saliva, her pus, and tears." She lived "in a body that floats on its dysfunction."[63] Ogano's muteness revealed the essential body. Hijikata was able to see this essential nature of the body and of existence, and develop out of it the movement and methodology of *butō*.

The Old Woman

Hijikata counted old women by the sheet: one sheet, two sheets. "They were not human anymore, but the single type of lightness that couldn't fly."[64] They were nostalgic "old women, always catching at cheap rainbows," and caring for the children who "wanted spoiling." The children were always trying to prolong their state of "lovely" dependency, by feigning shallow breaths and tears as though close to death, whenever someone noticed their "unusually high temperature."[65] All they really wanted was the "reassurance" of seeing themselves through others' eyes, but their parents could not offer that kind of affection,[66] driven like machines to "guzzle, guzzle, gobble angrily, work the body like a tool, grind it to the bone," and so it was the old women to whom they turned.[67]

The old women would "spread their legs as wide as they wanted and envelop a child in the fold of their crotch." They would run after the child who smelt "like peppermint" and give them a fright. The children would "hurry quickly between these old women's crotches and the sweet shop, winding their way like a smoke bomb," and growing up gradually in this constant to-and-fro. The old women would "mimic swaying soldiers who succeeded to the rank of Private, or an aeroplane (wherever *that* came from), flying on one engine," bringing life to the community and "rejuvenating the surrounding people and wind." They were the only receptacle in a community that could carry the children, and their lightness was a "kind of beacon."[68] There was something comforting in seeing the "instability of their weakened legs mimicking other legs, their legs being undone," which arose when watching "their coupling with the surrounding weather," and their movement "like one dazzled whilst swimming, like one dancing."[69] It was as if they "mimicked light like an albino," with their backs bent in the light of the fields, like "mud-men, a species of cracking," like "the dead who couldn't speak of what they knew,"[70] like "women coming from the rice paddies, full of water," with their "farm-working clothes, sticking like smoke to their smoked flesh."[71]

Hijikata observed these people as though they were things or particles, like paper, smoke, mud clods, or stuffed objects. He refused to limit the human body to a fixed state of the flesh, treating it instead as though it were a thing, constantly transforming. He sought out those figures who gave ventilation to a community and whose roles were removed from the everyday, figures whose bodies provided for them despite pain: the sick, the physically disabled, and the elderly. He found a way to show these figures – their existence as transforming things – through the body.

In a Place Near the Gods

Hijikata had always turned towards those who might reveal the clear form of human existence. Even as a child he saw things through the eyes of an adult, and had a talent for "solving any calamity, a seedling that emerged sprouting from his body, feebly and unwilled."[72] At the same time, he wanted to remain a child, to go out "drinking soda and dancing wildly"[73] in a place reserved for children: "the place closest to gods."[74]

These children were "playing a cheap game, like the pleasure of being blown by wind down a dreary path," running around, until the day, "in its totality, fused with heated nerves." With "tails growing from their behinds," these children forgot the passing of time, "playing with their tales plumping and wilting" until dusk.[75] A river would flow behind them as they played, making "the eerily life-like sound of a machine." One of the children was "the hungry boy who gave the buzz of an electric shock when touched," another was the "green-bottomed boy, like an offering, coloured by the green paddy." It was like their "thinking stopped," and the only awareness left was the "smell that comes from the water-pump game."[76]

Back inside the house, Hijikata recalls the feeling of "paradise" inside a "closet that embraces sickness or weather, like wind to the breast, and allows drifting smells to melt down the head." In that cupboard he arrived at new thoughts, feeling "ahhh… at last, I have drifted ashore," at last arrived at "that distant place where, nostalgic daytime gestures exist, like that of shielding from the sun".[77] He discovered a similar comfort in the "stable with its cosy warmth." He experienced "the smell of straw, bran, and tree-stumps mingling" with the darkness, as a kind of confirmation that he was just the same "regular boy" who always visited. Into that darkness he would wander, find the "resting place of a fence bar, polished by horse's saliva, on which to place [his] neck whilst jutting out [his] teeth," and then ask: "why was I born?"[78] He remembers afterwards, the moment of it growing dark outside, the sudden shift from "broad daylight, where vegetables covered with deadly poison threw ninja stars at one another,"[79] to the fall of dusk spreading across the landscape, which "started from the angle of a small animal's fleeing foot nearby."[80]

Those days when the adults returned home, and the "rain fell reluctantly" on, were boring for the children. They wanted their "favourite things, after hail," like "the colour of the flame made by coal," or the lost cockerel that had wandered into the blacksmith's *doma* (a traditional room with a dirt floor), or the "stout night hanging" on into day. The blacksmith's *doma* was the stage for their favourite scenes. The blacksmith was an old guy with a sturdy frame who made "free plates for spinning tops," and who would "hold his stout penis in his palm and take a rusty metal piss." Going to the *doma*, the children would take turns to perform their One Man Show from the anvil. One boy would adopt "the varying tones of pathos" and "pronounce forth: 'you're divorcing me?'" Another boy, with "one sleeve of his *kimono* off, glaring out into empty space, and dribbling saliva in his enthusiasm, would shout: 'you're betraying me!' and it was as if something half *Tange Sazen* [the samurai hero], half ghost had appeared."[81] Then there would be the final figure of that boy whose role it was to curl up stark naked on the earth floor of the blacksmith's *doma*. The *doma* had become the stage for *butō*, the "place nearest to gods," where the children could be themselves. They could escape the spell of relationships to adults, and exist in a pure expression of life, from within the darkness of life's "great landscape."

The children and other figures that appear in *Yameru maihime* seem to be cut out of the surrounding scene, at once void of any particular context and at the same time existing in a very certain place. There is a kind of nostalgia in detecting this place that cannot be located, which might be similar to the inexplicable sense of nostalgia felt by an audience watching *butō*. There is a memory, which cannot be articulated, and a time and space that opens out into the originating scene. The heart's mechanism turns with long distant memories, and it feels like "molecules in activity are falling in love."[82] The tears of the audience seem to say: 'I don't cry from sadness or laugh from gladness, I cry from friction.'

The world presented in *Yameru maihime* is also that "unbounded universe," which causes "the neutralization"[83] of "thinking on ethics, religion, or cosmology."[84] In *Yameru maihime* we see the physical disability within the healthy man, and the solemn existence within the physically disabled man. This is the perspective that forms the basis for *butō* creation, and it arises from a sense of "pure starvation." This "pure starvation" simultaneously accepts and resists man's fate, it is the act of taking hold of the ceramic insulator that sets you on a path towards *butō*.

3. Hijikata's Historical Context and the Development of his Ideology

Hijikata's Ideology in its Infancy

Hijikata Tatsumi with the riot police (1969), by Fukase Masahisa

The Period in which Hijikata Lived

Hijikata Tatsumi was born in 1928, the third year of the Shōwa period. The year held a particular significance for him: "the year I was born, Zhang Zuolin was killed by a bomb, and Hitomi Kinue was running… it was a time when the sky of Asia was about to become ominously overcast."[1] This same year, ceremonies were performed around the country to commemorate the Emperor Shōwa's inauguration (1926), and rumours began of a Shōwa Reformation. The shadow of fascism was descending.

Hijikata died in 1986, just three years before the Emperor Shōwa. With his lifespan almost exactly coinciding with the Shōwa period (1926-), it was like Hijikata was a real "child of Shōwa."[2] We might ask, then, what the Shōwa period meant to Hijikata? Politically, it was an extremely turbulent time, spanning Japan's pre-war militarism to its post-war Americanization. It was a time that oscillated from tension to relief, restraint to emancipation, from oppressive government control to democracy and individual freedom. Japan's defeat in the Second World War brought about drastic changes to its political and social infrastructures, and was followed by a time of unprecedented and rapid economic expansion that repositioned Japan as a major economic power. Artistically, however, the Shōwa period was characterized by conflicting attitudes towards modernism and postmodernism. The arts were confronted by this conflict across the board, and Hijikata was no exception.

Hijikata was born and grew up in Akita prefecture in the North of Japan. His interest in Western culture began around the age of 19, when he started practicing German *Neue Tanz* and reading widely in Western literature. Hijikata's encounter with classical ballet techniques at that time, led to his search for an individual expressive style. His transition from an affiliation with modernism, to an interest in postmodernist practices, was a common trajectory for artists at that time. A number of Japanese artists, Hijikata included, first turned to Western role models, and then returned to a sense of their individual and national identity. In this sense, his artistic journey was not unique.

The period of Hijikata's maturation as an artist, corresponded to broader social shifts in Japan at that time. The rapid modernization that began after the Second World War, and accelerated with Japan's subsequent economic growth, led to a dramatic shift in Japanese values. The 1960s were characterized by unrest over the renewal of the US-Japan Security Treaty, and this led to a number of counter-cultural movements, which were staged in solidarity with the international unrest of the times. The cries going up overseas for a "restoration of the body," were responded to in Japan with a cry for "the restoration of the Japanese body!"[3] This climate of change brought about a particular turning point in Hijikata's artistic practice, and can be seen to be the conditions that spurred the development of *butō*.

Encountering Neue Tanz

In 1947, aged 19, Hijikata graduated from Akita Institute of Technology (now Akita Industrial High School), and began working for Akita Steel Manufacturing Company. During this time, he was also taking *Neue Tanz* lessons at Masumura Katsuko's Dance Studio. Masumura was a disciple of the eminent modern dancer Eguchi Takaya, who had studied under Mary Wigman in Germany. Hijikata recalls his first experience of dance at that age:

> Coming of age, I was the person who chose to dance, I was the person who wanted something solid. And considering a solid dance, I chose German dance. What I am today is a result of this.[4]

> I was significantly influenced by Germany, especially the *Hitler Youth*... to imagine those orderly boys coming into class, and making all the girls swoon.[5]

The Hitler Youth inspired a curiosity in the pre-war high school students of Japan, and for Hijikata in particular, their aesthetic left its mark – the strapping vigour of the Hitler Youth represented the height of a controlled and purified beauty. Another Akita dancer was also influenced by this German aesthetic: the pioneer of Japanese modern dance, Ishii Baku. Attending one of the dance recitals given by Ishii when he returned home from abroad, Hijikata commented that, "the dance of Ishii Baku was just the mimicking of a foreigner, wearing eye shadow under his eyes. Despite that, I thought it was good."[6]

During his school days at Akita Institute of Technology, Hijikata played rugby, read widely in literature, and enjoyed left-wing magazines like *Kaizō* (Reformation). At the same time, he was a tough young boy who would drag his friends along to fight, painting charcoal around his nose to make it look more prominent, and donning a stylish cloak to attack his enemies in. He not only looked the part, but also had a particular way with language; friends recalled his poetic language as being hard to understand, but nonetheless adding to his charisma. Having encountered Ishii's dance, Hijikata decided to perform his own dance at the cinema *Asahikan* in Akita city. In this dance, he adopted low positions, as though preparing to fight. Shortly after this performance, Hijikata and his friends joined a troupe of farmer comedians and toured the suburbs of Akita for about a year.

The influence of Western culture and new thought on Hijikata's *ankoku butō* was apparent, but there were also traces of Japanese folk arts: *gidayū* (a form of melodic story-telling which Hijikata would hear sat on his father's knee), *bon-odori* (a 'ghost-dance,' still practised in the *Nishi-monai* area), and *kagura* (a type of Shintō dance). Indeed, the roots of *ankoku butō* can be traced to Hijikata's Japanese heritage. His wife, Motofuji Akiko, recalled to me how Hijikata would claim that: "as long as Mount Taihei exists, I can create as many dances as I choose." While Japan may lie at the foundation of *butō*, foreign cultures, philosophies, and dance forms still played an important role in its formation.

Modern dance is said to have started as a form of individual expression, in opposition to classical ballet. This was imported to Japan by Ishii Baku among others, who had studied in Europe and America during the Taishō and early Shōwa periods. In the pre-war years, the mainstream modern dance style was that of *Neue Tanz*.[7] This began to shift, however, with a revived interest in the Japanese performing arts during the eight years following the war. Although most dancers moving to Tokyo still came under the influence of Eguchi's school of *Neue Tanz*, rather than Ishii's school of modern dance (*Yōbu*), there was still an increasing awareness of new directions in the modern dance scene. 19-year-old Hijikata, with his hopes of becoming a dancer, wanted to be at the forefront of this scene.

Moving to Tokyo: Encountering Ōno Kazuo's 'Poison Dance'

In 1949, aged 21, Hijikata set off to Tokyo for the first time. Whilst there, Hijikata chanced to see Ōno Kazuo's dance recital at Kyōritsu University Auditorium in Kanda, and was deeply shocked. He recalls this first experience of Ōno's work:

> I met with a strange performance. A man wearing a chemise, overflowing with lyricism, randomly cutting the air with his chin. The impression remained for a long time afterwards.[8]

Ōno had been training with one of Japan's pioneers of German Expressionism, Eguchi Takaya, but had become dissatisfied with the established style, and begun to develop his own. The impression of a 43-year-old Ōno performing in a chemise, not long after the end of the war, was a powerful one for the young Hijikata – he dubbed the dance a 'Poison Dance.'

It was this performance that inspired the 24-year-old Hijikata to move to Tokyo three years later, in 1953. His only baggage was a "cartful of books."[9] Shortly after arriving, Hijikata began attending the Andō Mitsuko Dance Institute, which he funded through manual work as a wharf labourer and warehouse guard. He later described his existence during this period as a "miserable state of poverty."[10] At the Andō Mitsuko Dance Institute, Hijikata enthusiastically signed up to learn Western dance forms such as classical ballet, jazz, and flamenco. He also had the opportunity of performing a dance choreographed by Andō in one of the first music programs, when television broadcasting in Japan was still in its infancy.

Hijikata's stage debut was at Andō Mitsuko's 1954 recital, in a piece called *Karasu* (Crow). He took on the stage name Hijikata Kunio, an allusion to Hijikata Toshizō, a *shinsengumi* (samurai guard) from the late Edo period, who represented to Hijikata a figure of historical avant-gardism. By this point, Hijikata was already receiving critical attention from the likes of performing arts critic Andō Tsuruo, who made a point of recommending him to the critic and reformer of *kabuki* dance, Takechi Tetsuji, in 1955-6. In 1957, Hijikata would be asked to feature in Takechi's work *Musume Dōjō-ji* (Dōjō Temple Daughter), which brought together *kyōgen* and traditional Japanese dance. By 1958, he would perform with the Unique Ballet Group, coordinated by Andō Mitsuko and Horiuchi Kan. Also in 1958, he danced alongside Yoneyama Mamako and Ōno Kazuo in the ballet pantomime *Hanchi kiki*, presented by Ningen-za Group and the Contemporary Theatrical Art Association, performing the 'movement' part of 'Stillness and Movement' within the 'Dance of the Earthen Doll.' Around this time he changed his stage name. Taking the old word for his favourite direction, *tatsumi* (southeast), he recreated himself as the dancer Hijikata Tatsumi.

Hijikata Tatsumi became a student of the Tsuda Institute of Modern Dance, which presented a variety of experimental works that took their inspiration from German dance. The studio director, Tsuda Nobutoshi, was married to Motofuji Akiko, who would later become Hijikata's wife. It was with the support of Motofuji that Hijikata presented his first substantial debut in 1959, *Kinjiki* (Forbidden Colours) – often considered the starting point of *butō*.

The Background to Hijikata's Ideology

Bleeding Nature

Having moved to Tokyo, Hijikata became associated with young artists like the stage designer Kanamori Kaoru, the artist Kawara On, and the photographer Narahara Ikkō. He recalls the initiation rite to enter such circles:

> After a strict examination at Kuroki Fuguto's *atelier* in Ikenohata kuromon-chō, you said 'I love Rimbaud' once, and got in. Looking back, this mad initiation was a considerable thing.[11]

Hijikata, like his artist friends, drew inspiration from foreign literature – writers like Lautréamont and Jean Genet. They came together with the desire to connect through culture: "human and human feelings were attracted to each other like magnets."[12] Hijikata recalls how he offered a piece of cake to his roommate, Kojima, in a bunk-bed dorm in Hiroo. The boy, who "seemed to be carrying out dubious night-work," started sobbing. Hijikata had been reading Genet's *The Thief's Journal* at the time, and it dawned on him that "if you give sweets to a thief in the daytime, they'll start to cry."[13] The desire for an artist community these Rimbaud-lovers shared, didn't last long. Hijikata recounts:

> The romance was gradually collapsing. People who used pistols came among us, mixing as new members, and the group fell to Second Rank [...] The means to murder began to lose all seriousness.[14]

What Hijikata meant by this, might be read into another comment of his: "like criminals, friends were those who could be sniffed out." Hijikata had lived his "adolescence like a cur," and so friends were those with the "dimension of smell." For him, "the word *world* was only nonsense," whereas "nature bleeding could overrun the realms of sociology and history."[15] He obsessively "pored [his] eyes over these concerns," arriving at the disappointed conclusion:

> Friends that I met in Tokyo were residents of a transparent and mechanical 'world' that had no relation to bleeding nature and no smell.[16]

Those people he met in Tokyo had a notion of the 'world' that was no more than "nonsense," they bore no relation to the "bleeding nature" which Hijikata sought. For Hijikata, dance was the art of "murder." The crime of creation had to carry the "seriousness" of bleeding, and the brutality of suffering.

> In the rehearsal studio, trying to blend in, I would bring together Chopin and a jockstrap, but suffer from a relentless diarrhoea of misery.[17]

Western dance training, bringing together physical exertion and classical music, was a source of suffering, for Hijikata. This was to be endured and not avoided, for "however much [one] bleeds," through bleeding the "dance becomes flesh and blood."[18] At the same time, Hijikata realized that the suffering of "dancing in the rehearsal studio,"[19] was not enough to bring about his own "dance experience," and so he began to seek out a philosophical basis on which to construct a new form of movement.

A Challenge to Ballet: "Leap Without Leaping, Turn Without Turning"

Hijikata trained in various forms of Western dance: flamenco, jazz, ballroom dance, and classical ballet. He revered the inherent elegance of classical ballet, refined over many centuries, but also felt that to master its technique required the inherited physique of long and straight limbs.[20] With one leg shorter than the other, Hijikata had never been able to fully straighten his legs. This fuelled an envy for ballet dancers like Motofuji. His crooked limbs and uneven stance were a serious handicap to effecting the straight-lines of ballet. Ballet's strict aesthetic and training was one to which his body would never adhere. But Hijikata was able to transform this handicap to his own advantage.[21] He inverted the formula of ballet, proposing, "to leap without leaping, and turn without turning," to borrow Motofuji's words.[22] This was Hijikata's challenge to the spins and leaps of ballet, and clearly reveals his point of departure for establishing a dance that would go beyond westernization and the modernization of Japan. It was at this moment, that Hijikata turned towards a Japanese physicality as the basis for a new form of contemporary dance. This reorientation can be taken as the substantial starting point of *ankoku butō*.

"Dance Experience"

Hijikata had spoken of a theory of "dance experience" from the time of the *Kinjiki* debut in 1959, but it was not until 1961 that he founded his own dance school, and 1963 that this came under the name of *ankoku butō*. Hijikata realised that to "experience" dance, meant more than the "experience of dancing in the rehearsal studio," and required finding "outdoor theatres everywhere in Tokyo."[23] He found such theatres in unlikely places, forming "friendships with male prostitutes in Kurumazaka, Ueno," and becoming an audience to:

> The patchy head growth, the feet of 11 *mon* [approx. 26.4cm], and the *rouge*, all frozen to death in a public toilet. Gathering these tools, any lazy choreographer can make a dance.[24]

Hijikata embraced these figures, feeling the "Tokyo mind-set" to be another form of "nonsense."[25] He rejected the elevation of artists who made "imitation art," "impotent art," or "terrorism dance," as those who had never been wounded or bled, and were poisoned by the "Tokyo mind-set."[26]

Hijikata's descriptions of this period of his life are unusually straightforward in style, as when he wrote: "days and months passed by, and friendships were formed from a hatred of hunger."[27] But these were not friends to "go to the end" with, to share a hunger with.[28] They were people who entertained the "nonsense" of the "world," and loosened their "ties" with the sugary sweetness of the "Great Japan's Sugar Manufacturing boom." For Hijikata, that kind of "sweetness was awful to eat."[29] It represented the trend for a model of democracy that was no more than a "cheque that bounces,"[30] and Hijikata "refused the deception" of that bouncing cheque:

> What I call dance – the use of aimless flesh – is the hated enemy of a production-based society, and so necessarily becomes taboo. The common ground my dance shares with criminality, homosexuality, and festival or ritual practices, is found in this candid act of displaying aimlessness.[31]

Nonetheless, since "the audience pay to come and enjoy evil," Hijikata conceded, "we must give them compensation." He understood that "Tragedy had to be prioritized on the side of production," and that "rose-coloured dance, as well as *ankoku buyō*, had to splash blood in the name of evil experience." This need was apparent in "the body's habit of holding within itself a mysterious sense of crisis." For Hijikata, "sacrifice lies at the root of any work, and dancers are the illegitimate children of this idiosyncratic experience." They are the ones who experience sacrifice through their bodies. He rejected outright any "dance of show," and criticised, in particular, "humorous dance, which holds even less potential for shame than comic dance." For Hijikata, the dancer "had to become the person shamed."[32]

Hijikata's dance came from a place where "blood splashes," from "bleeding nature," it was not a "dance of show," but a dance rooted in the "sacrifice" of a "person shamed." It revealed a sense of desperation, resulting from the need to push onwards to the end. This form of "dance experience" was "not a matter of shared understanding," but "the act of continuing to experience. A dance that has become flesh and blood, absorbed into the body as a kind of penance caused by the fear of belief."[33]

For Hijikata, "dance experience" was a form of shared suffering that could speak without discrimination; it was a form of 'love', similar to that described by Jean Genet, which could "give songs to the voiceless."[34] Hijikata's "dance experience" required each dancer to work through their own process of suffering and discovery. This method formulated the creative process as one of "drawing and erasing drawing and erasing" (Appendix 1). Hijikata articulates more broadly his conception of the *ankoku butō* method in the following passage from the text '*Keimusho e*' (To Prison):

> I am savouring a depth of esotericized gesture, a scream in the face of relentless everydayness. I am working out today's mode of walking, on the surface of a dark earth that could not unite dancing and leaping. The dark earth of Japan was a dance teacher that taught me many ways to faint as a boy. [I] must take that sensation of treading directly to the theatre. Where, using it to challenge a footwork tamed by flooring, I become a naked enlisted soldier.[35]

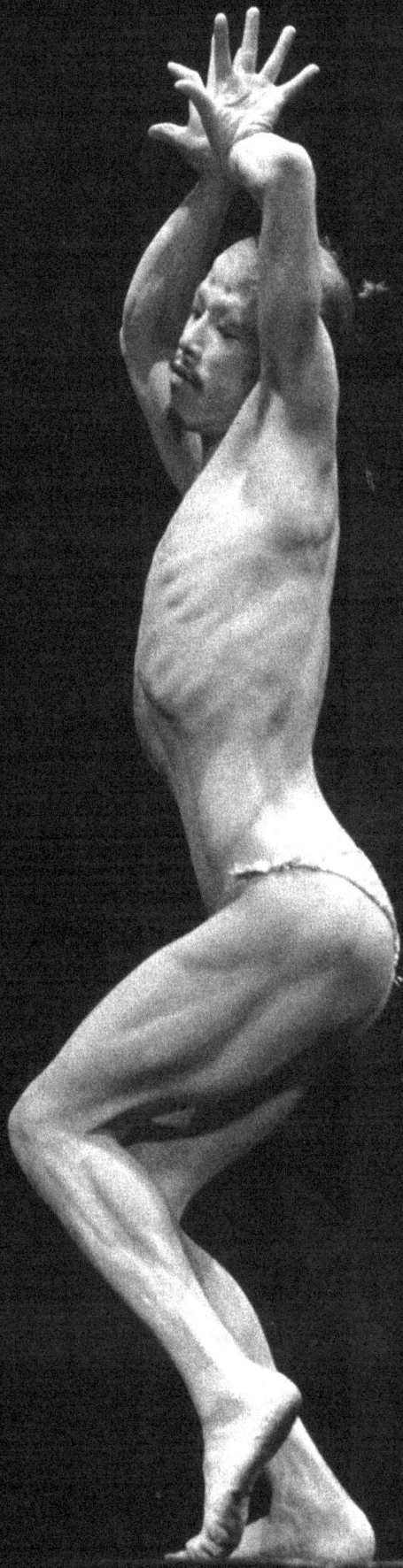

4. Hijikata's Principal Works and the Methodology of his Technique

[Previous page:] Hijikata Tatsumi (left) and Tamano Kōichi (right) during a rehearsal for *Nagasu kujira* (Fin Whale, 1972), by Hosoe Eikō

Hijikata's career as a choreographer and dancer spanned nearly 27 years, from his debut of *Kinjiki* (Forbidden Colours) in 1959, to his early death in 1986. Critics, such as Gōda Nario, have tended to divide this career into three distinct periods: the Early Period (1956-68) from *Kinjiki* to *Hijikata Tatsumi to nihonjin – Nikutai no hanran* (The Revolt of the Flesh: Hijikata Tatsumi and the Japanese, 1968); the Middle Period (1969-78), containing *Shiki no tame no nijūnana-ban* (Twenty-Seven Nights for Four Seasons, 1972) and *Hakutōbō*'s Performances; and the Late Period (1979-86), focusing on *Tōhoku kabuki keikaku 2* (Tōhoku Kabuki Project 2, 1985).[1]

The Early Period (1959-68): Kinjiki → Hijikata Tatsumi to nihonjin – Nikutai no hanran

Principal Works of the Period: *Kinjiki* (Forbidden Colours, May 1959); *Banzai onna* (Banzai Woman, December 1959); *Yome – Shi-gatsu jūkyū-nichi taian* (The Bride – Nineteenth of April, a Lucky Day, April 1960); *Hanatachi* (Flowers, July 1960); *Shushi* (Seed, July, 1960); *Kiki* (Kiki, July 1960); *Toritachi* (Birds, July 1960); *Kinjiki* (Forbidden Colours, July 1960); *Divīnu shō* (Extract from Divine, July 1960); *Antai* (Dark Body, July 1960); *DANCE EXPERIENCE 3 shō* (Dance Experience Chapter Three, July 1960); *Shorijō – Marudorōru no uta yori bassui hitomaku* (Processor – Scene of an Extract from Maldoror, July 1960); *Seikōshaku* (The Holy Marquis, October 1960); *Han'in-han'yōsha no hirusagari no higi sanshō* (The Early Afternoon Esoterica of a Hermaphrodite Chapter Three, September 1961); *Satōgashi yon-shō* (Sugar Sweets Chapter Four, September 1961); *Reda san-tai* (Three Phases of Leda, June 1962); *Anma – Aiyoku o sasaeru gekijō no hanashi* (Masseur – Story of the Theatre that Advocates Lust, November 1963); *Barairo dansu – A LA MAISON DE M. CIVEÇAWA* (Rose-coloured Dance – A la Maison de M. Civeçawa, November 1965), accompanied by the, *Watashi no musume tenjisokubaikai-jō* (The Exhibition and Sale of my Daughter, November 1965); *Seiaionchōgaku shinan-zue – Tomato* (Tomato – An Educational Illustration for Beneficial Sexual Love, July 1966); *Keijijōgaku* (Metaphilo-physics, for Takai Tomiko, July 1967); *Butō June* (Dancing Genet, for Ishii Mitsutaka, August 1967); *Onnatachi* (Women, for Nakajima Natsu, August 1967); *O-June shō* (An Extract of O-Genet, for Ishii Mitsutaka, June 1968); *D53264-ki ni noru tomodachi Bioretto Nojeiru no hō e tsuneni tōi no ite yuku fūkei PACIFIC 231-ki ni noru butō-jō yōko* (Dancing Girl Yōko on the Pacific 231, with the Ever-Receding Vista of her Friend Violet Nojail on the D53264, August 1968), *Mandala yashiki* (Mandala Premises, for Takai Tomiko, September 1968), *Hijikata Tatsumi to nihonjin – Nikutai no hanran* (Revolt of the Flesh – Hijikata Tatsumi and the Japanese, October 1968)

The Early Period can be divided into two halves: *Kinjiki* is representative of the first (1959-62), and *Hijikata Tatsumi to nihonjin* is representative of the second (1963-68).

In the first half of this period, Hijikata derived a number of works from Western literary sources, such as the work of Jean Genet (*Divīnu shō*, and less directly *Kinjiki*), Lautréamont (*Shorijō*), and the Marquis de Sade (*Seikōshaku*). These tended to be orientated towards expressions of "Western eroticism," and the "eroticism of sacrifice."[2] They reveal an intention towards the "expression of metaphysical notions through a pure body language," or a "symbolization of the human body," and are characterized by an "emphasis on form."[3]

In the second half of this period, particularly after *Anma*, an "avant-garde artistic line" began to emerge,[4] as well as a "tendency towards folk-style."[5] This was part of a general trend for Happenings and Events at that time. From around 1961 onwards, Hijikata began to associate and collaborate with artists from various fields, such as the fine arts, music, and literature. The works produced in this way have been considered as particularly representative of the avant-garde trends of the time, but they are not the only work Hijikata was engaged in. Far from avant-garde, some of his early works might be considered "rearguard" and nostalgic, such as *Banzai onna* or *Yome*, which both reflect a more delicate sensibility.[6]

To paint a clearer picture of this period, I will analyse in detail three of its most representative works: *Kinjiki*, *Anma*, and *Hijikata Tatsumi to nihonjin*.

Kinjiki (Daiichi Seimei Hōru, 1959)

Hijikata Tatsumi (left) and Ōno Yoshito (right), *Kinjiki* (Forbidden Colours, 1959), photographer unknown

Kinjiki was performed as part of the All Japan Association for Artistic Dance's *6th Competition for Newcomers*, held in May 1959. It is remembered both as Hijikata's debut work as a choreographer, and as the starting point of *butō*. The title *Kinjiki* was taken from the novel of the same name, by Mishima Yukio. Its homosexual overtones drew inspiration from the works of Jean Genet, or 'Saint-Genet,' as Jean-Paul Sartre dubbed him. Its structure and contents are outlined below, according to the record of Gōda Nario:

> 15-minute performance. Dramatis Personae: Boy (21-year-old Ōno Yoshito), Man (Hijikata Tatsumi), White Leghorn Chicken. The whole scene is performed on a

gloomy-stage with only suspension lighting, and no musical accompaniment except the blues harmonica in the final scene.

The sound of footsteps of a boy running and a man in pursuit. The effective use of the sound of sexual breath from a tape recorder, and the sound of groaning. Both of them with naked torsos and bare feet. Boy wears lemon-coloured shorts and a neck-scarf. Man wears loose pantaloons, with a shaved head and blackened body.

Boy enters downstage right. Man enters upstage left, approaching from behind with the leghorn in his arms, his straightened legs and heels pounding the floor, "running in a deformed manner." He gives the leghorn to the boy. The boy strangles it between his thighs.

Second half, the boy stands with the dead leghorn by his feet. The man violates the boy, the stage blacks out. Both fall stage left, clinging together. The sound of breathing and groaning from a tape player. The man cries several times, "Je t'aime." The sound of fleeing footsteps. The sound of pursuing footsteps. The sound of a blues harmonica from stage right. Scene gradually becomes light. Boy appears from the darkness, picks up the leghorn from the floor and brings it to his chest. He shuffles slowly in the direction of stage right.[7]

The audience was in uproar at the boy's strangling of the leghorn. They shouted again at the chicken's corpse by his feet, and at the scene of violation people left one after the other. Many audience members rejected the work as an "abrasion of the peace of everyday life."[8] Hijikata was so disappointed by the response, and by the narrow-mindedness of the dance world in general, which he felt only valued prissy entertainment, that he withdrew from the All Japan Association for Artistic Dance.

Despite this, several important cultural figures, Mishima himself among them, offered their vehement support, and Gōda was so excited that he exclaimed: "this dance emerged in direct contact with human existence itself,"[9] acclaiming it as perhaps the first revolutionary work in the history of Western style modern dance since the Taishō Period. Hijikata was able to convey the essence of a man's character through atmosphere alone, without taking a single step from the darkness. He was able to convey the subject matter through sound alone, with the patter of fleeing and pursuing feet. Hijikata challenged the dance world by "materializing a dance which, unlike establishment dance, did not rely on a system or method, music, explanatory notes in the program, or even dance technique." *Kinjiki* was significant in the way it "combined movement and darkness as an expression of existence itself, which would later come to characterize *ankoku butō*." With the "brutal act of strangling the chicken and the taboo of homosexuality, this confrontation of society" stirred fears in the audience, which could only find release "through the [audience's] process of accepting their inner darkness."[10]

For Gōda, *ankoku butō* overcame the divisions between audience and performer, viewer and viewed. It was the achievement of a "dance experience," or a shared experience, that brought together the darkness suffered by the audience and the sacrifice suffered by the dancer. *Kinjiki* flooded the stage with this darkness, allowing it to spill out and purify the audience, until they could see into the depths of their own existence. In this way, it laid the philosophical foundation for *ankoku butō*. It also established what would become *butō*'s identifiable aesthetic: shaved heads and nudity, expansive movements that revealed muscles, and awkward movements that appeared segmented.

Meditation in the Womb

Having seen Hijikata roll around foetus-like on the floor with protracted limbs, Haniya Yutaka described his dance as a "meditation in the womb." The perceived quality was one of stillness, because "staying still and staying motionless form the basis of dancing, and the prototype for all future human movements."[11] Hijikata had used these movements in *Hannatachi* and *Shushi*, performed on a small dark box at the July 1960 presentation of *Hijikata Tatsumi DANCE EXPERIENCE no kai.*

Around the time of *Kinjiki*, Shibusawa Tatsuhiko characterized Hijikata's dance in terms of a progression through life, starting out from the "posture of a foetus." This could "suggest the direction of life and death simultaneously." Hijikata would bend and stretch his body, "revealing his ribcage," or expand and contract his chest and abdomen "like bellows," he would move with the "convulsions and impulsions of a polio victim on unbalanced limbs," and then "suddenly stop and stiffen his legs like sticks, with an accompanying scream." This was a "dance that surprised," as Shibusawa recalled, and one that suggested the possibility of a mysterious use of the body, in a way that "absolutely betrayed the movement expectations set by the rhythms and stylized motions of classical ballet."[12]

The methodology that lay behind these movements can be better understood by reading Motofuji's notes on the creation of *Reda san-tai* (1962). Just before the audience entered, Hijikata instructed Motofuji to dance completely naked, her body painted in half-pink half-white plaster. Made to dance a *pas* within a metre of the audience, she had tried to hide herself out of embarrassment, twisting like the character 九 then 八, and finally fleeing to a nearby closet. In pursuit, Hijikata proceeded to force a marble into her anus. Motofuji later recalled how she had needed an extreme degree of technical control to raise her leg without dropping the marble – a degree of control to rival that of ballet, for which she had been awarded fourth place at the International Dance Contest in Vienna four years earlier.[13]

Hijikata was looking to generate a sense of tension. Motofuji was *trying* to dance, and so he placed her in a condition of shame, by demanding she dance naked or by inserting a marble into her anus. He was seeking a movement that came from the body alone, a bodily truth that emerged from a state of crisis. This return to the original body was another figuring of the condition of a "meditation in the womb."

Anma – Aiyoku o sasaeru gekijō no hanashi (Sōgetsukaikan, Tokyo 1963)

The first years of Hijikata's Early Period are marked by a shift from a "purely form-orientated" approach towards a collaborative approach, as in his work with various avant-garde artists for *Anma*.[14] Motofuji recalls the performance of *Anma*:

> Upon entry, the audience stepped across a variety of abstract objects and passed through Kosugi Takehisa's sonic arch. They were then seated on the stage. Before them, the first row of seats had been cleared and replaced by 100 tatami mats to form the dancing stage. The dancers were exclusively men. They were wrapped-up and carried onstage by the artists Nakanishi Natsuyuki, Akasegawa Gempei, and Kazekura Takumi. Hijikata came onstage shouting freely and riding a bicycle, which parted the tatami mats.

> Hijikata's instructions for "a gonorrhoea costume" made Motofuji think of scraps of bloodied cotton floating on the light-green waters of the Kusatsu Onsen. This image led to the preparation of under-*kimonos* made of wax-cloth on which floated shades of pink and green. Nakanishi placed a number of pegs in the hair of those dancers who wore under-*kimonos*, and asked them to hang ice bags full of purple liquid below their crotches. They appeared strange and comical. They ran around eating cake, playing baseball, and frequently tripping over. Each time one tripped, the lower part of their pink and green under-*kimono* parted to reveal the ice bag hanging from their crotch, and the audience burst out laughing. Old women from the Funabashi Health Center played the accompaniment on their *samisen*, singing *"Makkuroke bushi"* and a number of other short ballads from the Taishō, Meiji and early Shōwa Periods. They didn't have any idea what was going on around them onstage. At several points, they tried to make a run for it in fear, but Hijikata

grabbed their sleeves and held them back. He had really become the son of a Yakuza boss.

In this performance, Hijikata had painted his entire body with white chalk solution, but this frequently rubbed off, to leave him looking like a strange sculpture dancing.[15]

Anma (Masseur, 1963) by Tanno Akira (L) / Yoshioka Yasuhiro (R)

Watching this scene, graphic designer Tanaka Ikkō was astonished by the "confused sound effect" of Hijikata's booming voice shouting at the lost looking old women playing on and on as hard as they could. This "anti-moral" treatment of the old generated a confused energy, drawing together the "avant-garde" and the "anti-moral," and dissolving any clear sense of "who the audience were." The effect of this drove Tanaka into an "extraordinary state of mind."[16]

In *Kinjiki*, eroticism and violence were associated with homosexuality and the act of strangling a chicken, whereas in *Anma*, the *ero-guro*, or erotic-grotesque, quality was characterized by cruelty and absurdity. Hijikata's provocation of the audience in *Anma*, brought them into a shared sense of "crisis" with the performers, and disintegrated any distinction between "those seeing" and "those seen." It overturned the audience's expectations "one by one, onstage," not in the way a Happening might, but as a result of Hijikata's "meticulous calculations."[17] These calculations took into account the performers' expectations as much as the audience's, as with the example of a marble inserted in Motofuji's anus. Hijikata pushed for a degree of confusion and unease, that was characterized by a sense of crisis. His work was not a dance of show, but a form of creation as perplexity.

Painted White

Motofuji traces the use of white paint in *butō* back to *Anma* (1963), but it can actually be traced back further to the performance *Han'in-han'yōsha no hirusagari no higi sanshō* (1961), where the artist Yoshimura Masunobu made an "obverse intervention in dance" by covering the body of a shave-headed Hijikata until he looked like a "mummy covered with gauze and plaster." During this process, the plaster began to set from the heat of Hijikata's body. He shivered as it cooled, starting to hit himself, until bits of the plaster and gauze peeled off and hung like "keloid skin."[18] These spasmodic movements became as much associated with *butō* as the shaved head and white painted body. It was not only an aesthetic decision, but related closely to this physical technique, as Ōno Kazuo pointed out when he claimed that the "reliance on white paint" was a response to "technical immaturity." The flesh, as though receiving a cut, was forced into a state of discomfort that produced its own movement.[19]

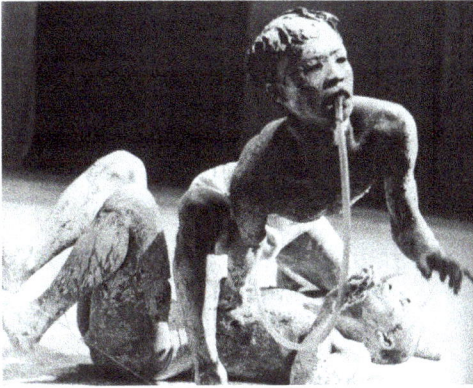

Barairo dansu (Rose-coloured Dance, 1965), by Hosoe Eikō

Yoshimura's solution of glue and plaster made an "obverse intervention in dance," that would gradually lose some of its force when replaced by the brush-on solution of face powder and water used in *kabuki*. Gunji related the white paint of *butō* to the image of an "albino" described in *Wakansansai-zue* (Illustrated Japanese Encyclopaedia). Like a fallen god, "the albino of *butō* is a taboo figure that represents the dark world, and should therefore be killed."[20] Whiteness marks "the border of darkness and light... a colour that overlaps death and life and precedes the birth of things." As this whiteness peels or sprinkles from the body, it seems that something bodily is also shed. It falls to the ground, and the traces of individuality fall away, as an "assertion of the existence of being" beyond the physical.[21]

Aesthetic Characteristics

This period in Hijikata's performance history made use of a variety of everyday objects, such as the pegs and ice bags of *Anma*. Objects were frequently part of the Happenings and performances of the 1960s, but Hijikata was particularly consistent in his use of them. Kanō Mitsuo's "edible pamphlet" made in the shape of a penis, lips, or hands, was the beginning of Hijikata's "anti-art set design."[22]

The pamphlet was made for *Barairo dansu* (*Sen-nichiyakaidō*, Tokyo, November 1965), which is best known for Yokoo Tadanori's iconic publicity poster. The performance itself had a "bright set" of artists dressed in white and pink, who were shaved onstage by a barber wearing an "apron made from naval flags." There were two statues of "Victor's Dog," stolen from a record shop, and the "richly coloured vagina" painted on Tamano Kōichi's back. Kasai Akira, Ishii Mitsutaka, and Ōno Yoshito wore "tube costumes," made by Tanaka Fujio, and danced sweetly to the music of "bunnies dancing" and "seagulls and sailors." Ōno and Hijikata danced in white dresses to a soundtrack of guitar solos and nonsense-songs from the Taishō period.[23]

In *Seiaionchōgaku shinan-zue – Tomato* (*Kinokuniya hōru*, Tokyo July 1966), Hijikata continued to use artists as performers. He also continued to make use of everyday objects, using sheets, bras, corsets, and chemises hardened with plaster and chalk as men's costumes, or having male dancers run about the stage in Motofuji's tights. Hijikata himself wore a net plate cover belonging to his children as a hat. There were window frames taken from the studio and painted like picture frames in pink and green by Nakanishi, and a rattling toy mobile painted in white fluttering before a backdrop of Michelangelo's *Adam and Eve*, reproduced in a garish style by billboard painters from Asakusa's *Rokku-za* and *Fransu-za* strip theatres.[24]

[Following page:] Poster for *Barairo dansu* (Rose-coloured Dance, 1965), by Yokoo Tadanori.

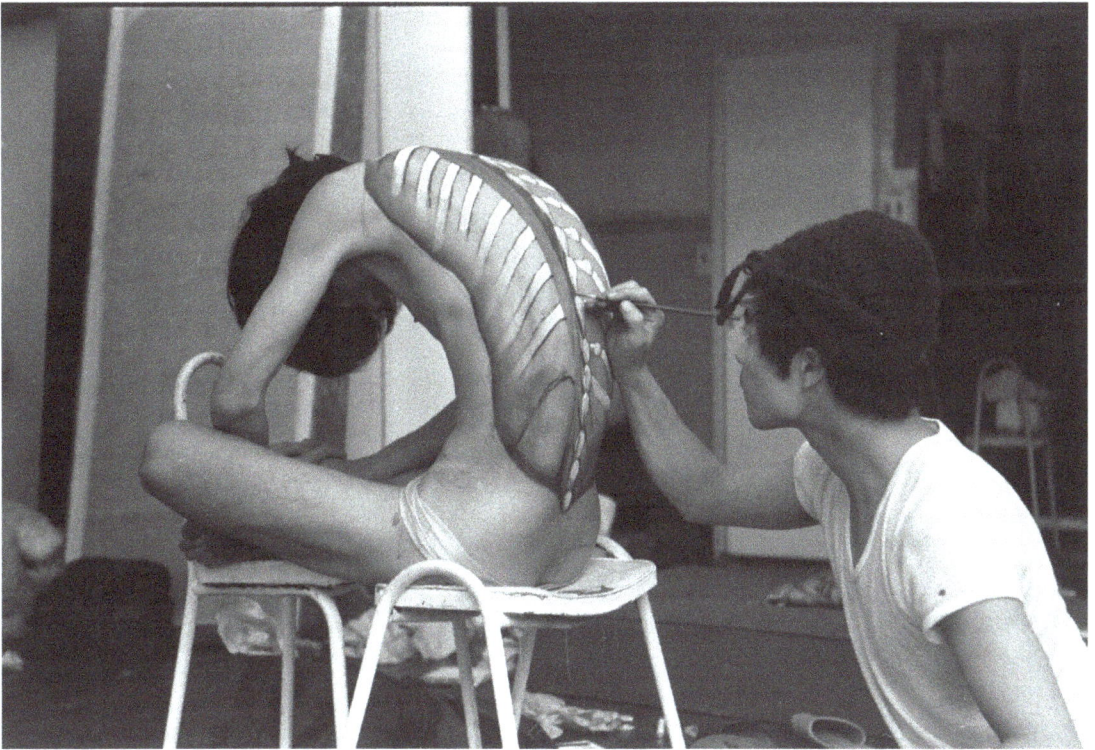

Nakanishi Natsuyuki painting a dancer's back (1967), by Nakatani Tadao

The aesthetic that emerged during this period was characterized by pale colours – pink, white, and green, as in the title, *Barairo dansu* – and by the use of materials from Hijikata's immediate environment. It made its visual mark upon a number of artists, such as Yokoo, whose meeting with the ghostly "otherworld of Hijikata" led to the realization that "within [him] too, there was the existence of another world." Yokoo recorded at the time:

> My style was completely changed by that day. I could see the world had changed from that day to the next. This work awakened me to myself.[25]

Watching Hijikata, Yokoo experienced a self-awakening, which went beyond their personal relationship as artists. This experience was shared by a number of other artists at that time, who all felt themselves to be transformed by their meeting with Hijikata.

Costumes

The gonorrhoea under-*kimonos*, the *kimonos* worn back-to-front, and the "really cheap-looking pink and blue *obi*" tied around the legs in *Anma*, rejected traditional ways of wearing kimono, and transformed them into strange "dresses." The garments seemed to hang heavy with their wearers' nostalgic sentiments, generating an "archaic feeling," and causing the illustrator Uno Akira to describe their appearance as an "experiential history" that only the Japanese could understand.[26]

Hijikata did not approach this costuming with an intention of "denying modernity to [become] conversely modern," or with the hope of staging some "scandalous idea," but with the sense of a "child's privilege of following their any caprice." The idea of a "*kimono* worn any which way" came from Hijikata's childhood, when a *kimono* had meant more than the movement of dressing and removing. It had represented a world of childhood desires, not yet "tamed by the ambiguous ways" of adulthood.[27] Hijikata maintained this child's perspective in his approach to art.

Hijikata's attitude in the works preceding *Hijikata Tatsumi to nihonjin* (1968), was one of interrogating the body's essential truths through the denial of accepted views on the body or movement. He was seeking a performance practice that was not purely decorative, but confrontational: an expression of 'NON' that broke open the reality of an existence shared by audience and performer. *Hijikata Tatsumi to nihonjin* would be the most extreme expression of this confrontation.

Nikutai no hanran (Revolt of the Flesh, 1968), by Nakatani Tadao

Hijikata Tatsumi to nihonjin – Nikutai no hanran (Nihonseinenkan, Tokyo October 1968)

Following *Anma* (1963), Hijikata began to leave behind Western influences and turn towards folklore and his own cultural history. He returned to Akita in 1965, following an 11-year absence, to create a series of photographs with Hosoe Eikō. For Gōda, this marked a turning point, after which "Hijikata attempted to bring *butō* back to the clear expression of his own time and place, as no other could."[28] Hijikata knew that to return to this heritage required an act of destruction – the destruction of his own Western concepts, the breaking down of an established relationship between performer and audience, and even the rejection of a body that desired dance. Gōda saw *Hijikata Tatsumi to nihonjin* as an act of destruction that allowed Hijikata to in some way relive his life over again.

During the performance of *Hijikata Tatsumi to nihonjin*, demonstrations against the renewal of the U.S.–Japan Security Treaty were reaching boiling point. The intensity of Hijikata's performance at this time was certainly part of a general accumulation of unrest and frustration, but it was not a by-product of this, as Hijikata clearly stated: "the 60s did not make *ankoku butō*. The times themselves sidled up to the flesh."[29] The extraordinary performance of *Hijikata Tatsumi to nihonjin*, at the age of forty, was the culmination of Hijikata's work as a performer.

> At the entrance to *Nihonseinenkan*, there was a white horse borrowed from the zoo neighing, with white chrysanthemums decorating either side of it. Paper aeroplanes were tossed at the lowered curtain as Hijikata, wearing a white costume, was carried in by many students, from behind the audience, on a sacred palanquin covered by a mosquito net. Following this, a white pig in a white baby cot and a white hare sitting quietly on a pole entered in succession. From the wings, stage pianists clad in white tuxedoes responded to Hijikata's solo with dramatically played pieces by Chopin, Liszt, Brahms, and Strauss. In the final ascension scene, Hijikata was suspended by pulleys and drawn across from the stage to the ceiling over the audience's heads. Sheets of brass, which could injure the performers, were shining on the stage, placed there by the stage designer, Nakanishi Natsuyuki.[30]

[Following page:] Hijikata Tatsumi with a golden phallus, *Nikutai no hanran* (Revolt of the Flesh, 1968), by Hanaga Mitsutoshi

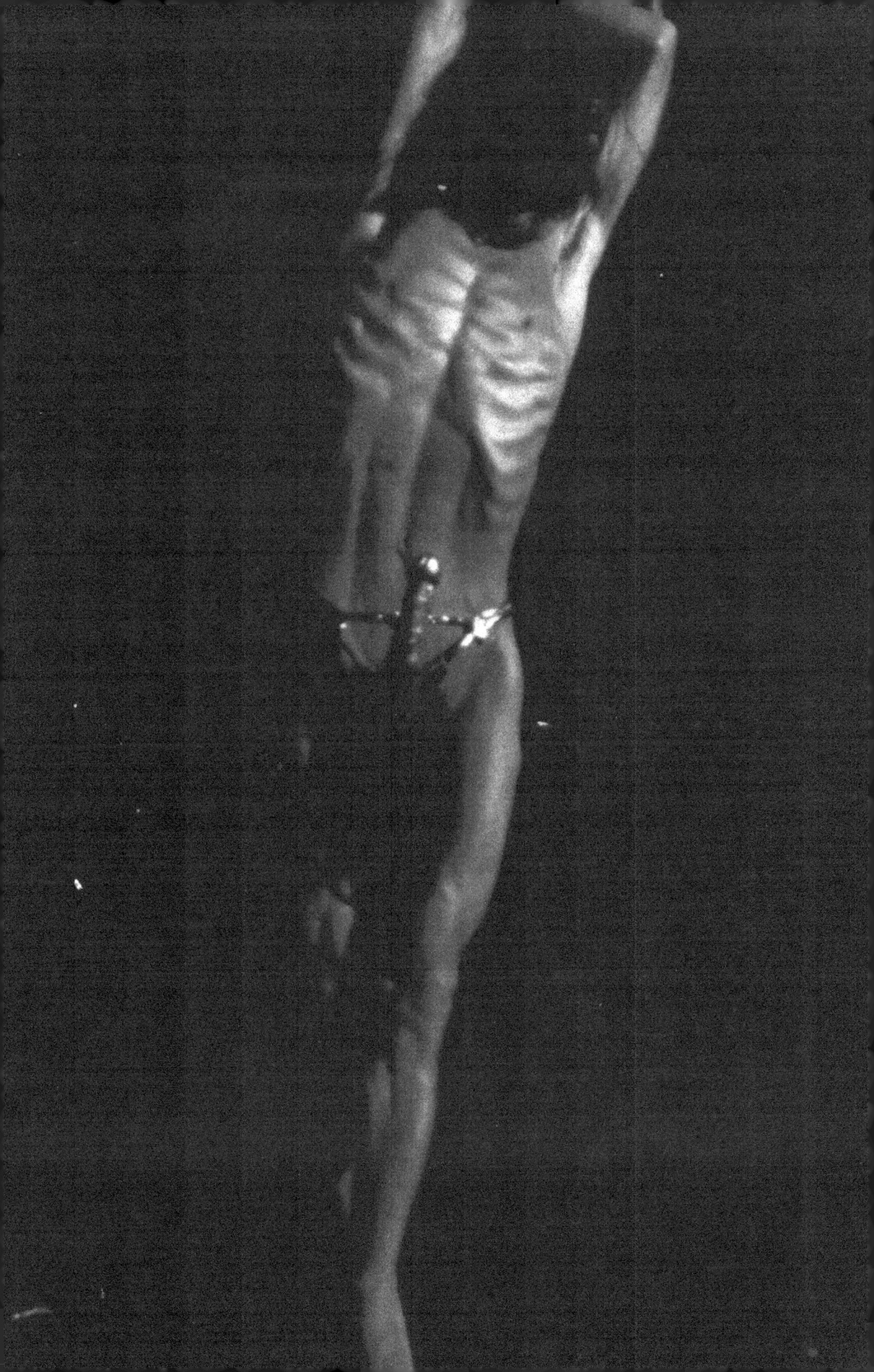

The composition of this scene was based on a method intended to alienate and insult the audience. The audience's attention was concentrated on the small rectangular space of a raised palanquin within the expanse of *Nihonseinenkan*, from which Hijikata glared back at them. This keen gaze, and the general brutality and noisiness of the piece, seemed to "challenge and threaten the audience." Hijikata hung off the neck of a strung-up rooster, killing it. An ear piercing engine-sound played, and filled the space with a strange atmosphere. There were dances of various origins – Spanish ballets, and waltzes. The performance was held by the tension of contradictory elements:

> Vulgarity (the golden strap-on) and sacredness (the ascension of Christ, pulled up from the stage in the final scene); noise and silence. Antitheses crushed each other, and collapsed in confusion, until a strange whirlwind of energy was stirred. [...] This was the careful formalization onstage of a highly personal denial of self, in which Hijikata Tatsumi used the audience's testimony of hatred, or their sense of alienation, as a source of leverage.[31]

In this work, Hijikata "exposed himself entirely, his disdainfulness, his obscenity, his brutality." He made use of various Western dance forms (Waltz, Polka, and Spanish dance), moving "continuously and blatantly out of time with their steps or music," to effect "a fast disillusionment and bring about a sense of ennui." This "ennui devastated the stage" in a way that couldn't be redeemed. It was a striking confrontation to the West, in that Hijikata seemed to dance out those Western dances that had been his training-base since the age of 19. In this piece, Hijikata "dared to intentionally sell himself to the audience," in a way he had never done before.[32]

> Directly, rather than narratively, [Hijikata] revealed his obscenity and cruelty to the audience. There was not a single personal sentiment in all of this, but rather an attempt to exist *as* the hatred, offense, and anger of the audience.[33]

As Gōda perceived it, Hijikata's performance was an act of revealing and exposing himself to the audience. This sense of exposure and shame lay at the heart of the "dance experience" of *butō*, and was key to the performances from *Kinjiki* onwards. It was not only this sense of exposure that marked out *Hijikata Tatsumi to nihonjin*, but also the lack of synchronicity between movement and sound – which Hijikata liked to describe as the use of laxatives on rhythm – that came to characterise later works.

From *Kinjiki* to *Hijikata Tatsumi to nihonjin*, Hijikata turned away from Western forms of modern dance and towards his own deepening sense of "dance experience." His methodology during this transitional period was still partially generated by an antithetical relationship to modern dance, and it was not until *Hijikata Tatsumi to nihonjin* that it was released from this structure of conflict. This can be seen as the point at which *ankoku butō* was established as an independent school.

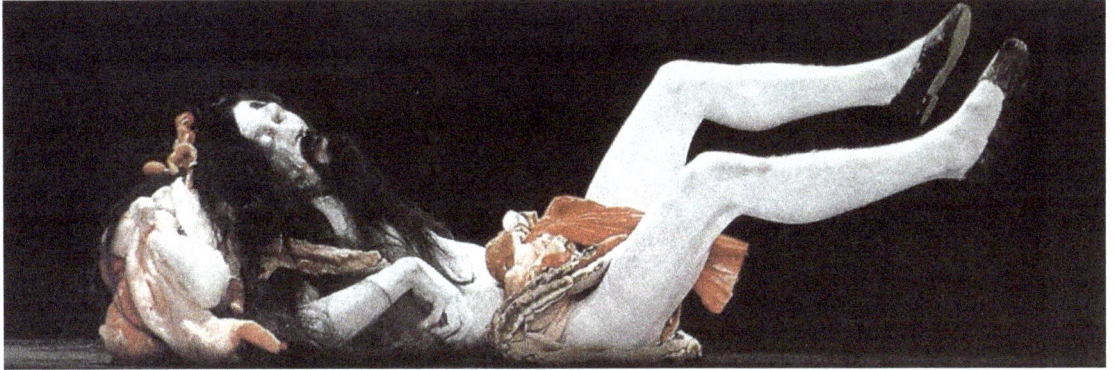

Hijikata Tatsumi in 'Gibasan,' *Shiki no tame no nijūnana-ban* **(Twenty-Seven Nights for Four Seasons, 1972), by Yamazaki Hiroshi**

Principal Works of the Period: *Supēsu kapuseru de no ichi-ren no shō* (A Series of performances at Space Capsule Theater, March-November 1969); *Oshi no shushi* (Seed of Muteness, August-December 1970); *Gibasa* (Gibasa *, August-December 1970, January 1972); *Honegamitōge shininkazura* (Vines of Death at Emaciated-Bone Pass, October 1970); *Bai-rabu* (Love on Sale, January-December 1971, January 1972); *Susamedama* (Fondling Bead, January-December 1971, January 1972); *Zannenki* (Note of Remorse, January 1972); *Yōkan* (Red Bean Jelly, April 1972); *Susamedama zenkōhen* (Fondling Bead First Half & Second Half, June 1972), *Nagasu kujira* (Fin Whale for Harpin-ha, September 1972); *Shiki no tame no nijūnana-ban*, divided into *Hōsōtan*, *Susamedama*, *Gaishikō*, *Nadare ame*, *Gibasan* (Twenty-Seven Nights for Four Seasons, divided into Story of Smallpox, Fondling Bead, Ceramic Insulator, Avalanche Candy, Gibasan, October-November 1972); *Shizukana ie zenpen, kōhen* (Quiet House First Half and Second Half, September 1973); *Tenputenshiki: Yōmotsu shintan* (Tenputenshiki: Story of the Phallus God by *Dairakudakan*, October 1973); *Hakutō-zu* (Picture of a White Peach, for *Hakutōbō*, June-August 1974); *Bijin to byōki* (Beauty and Sickness, for *Hakutōbō*, June-August 1974); *Nichi-getsu bōru* (Sun-Moon Ball, for *Hakutōbō*, June-August 1974); *Ankoku butō ebisuya ochō* (Butterfly of the *ankoku butō* Ebisuya, for *Hakutōbō*, October 1974); *Sairen-sake* (Siren Salmon, for *Hakutōbō*, November 1974); *Rapusodī in 'futashinaya'* (Rhapsody in Futashinaya, for *Hakutōbō*, January 1975); *Bakke Sensei no koibito* (The Sweetheart of Master Bakke, for *Hakutōbō*, March 1975); *Kanojora o okosu nakare* (You Shall Not Wake the Ladies, for *Hakutōbō*, May 1975); *Kohigasa* (A Little Parasol, for *Hakutōbō*, July 1975); *Usotsuku mōmoku no shōjo* (A Blind Girl Who Tells a Lie, for *Hakutōbō*, September 1975); *Ankoku butō ban kaguya hime* (Princess Kaguya: Ankoku Butō Version, for *Hakutōbō*, October 1975); *Nashi atama* (Pear Head, for *Harupin-ha*, February 1976); *Sore wa kono yōna yoru datta* (It was a Night Like This, for *Muteki-Sha*, April 1976); *Hito gata* (Human Shape, for *Hakutōbō*, June 1976); *Shōmen no ishō – Shōnen to shōjo no tame no yami no tehon* (Costume En Face – a Dark Model for Boys and Girls, for *Kanazawa Butōkan*, October 1976); *Geisenjō no okugata* (Lady on a Whale String, for *Hakutōbō*, December 1976); *Nigai hikari* (Bitter Light, for Kobayashi Saga, July 1977); *Yōji no me no naka no kusa* (A Blade of Grass in the Eye of an Infant, for *Harupin-ha*, September 1977); *Ra Aruhenchīna shō* (Homage to la Argentina, for Ōno Kazuo, November 1977); *Yami no maihime jūni-tai – rūburu-kyū no tame no jūyon-ban* (Twelve Poses of the Dancing Girl in Darkness – Fourteen Nights for the Louvre Palace, for Ashikawa Yōko, October 1978); *Saisho no hana* (The First Flower, for Nimura Momoko, October 1978); *Rōkaku no tsubasa* (Wings of the Pavilion, for *Kozensha-ha*, November 1978)

---

* Gibasa/Gibasan are both Tōhoku dialect terms for a traditional seaweed-based food.

The "mysterious term" of silence that lasted for four years following the performance *Hijikata Tatsumi to nihonjin* (1968), marked the beginning of the Middle Period.[34] It was Hijikata's most intense period of activity, and included the major work, *Shiki no tame no nijūnana-ban* (1972) as well as a string of choreographies for *Hakutōbō*. The "mysterious term" of silence that preceded it, gave birth to the myth of Hijikata.[35] Hijikata's return was marked by a series of practical training sessions for his dancers in places like *Shinjuku āto birejji* and *Supēsu kapuseru*. Gōda considers the performances that emerged out of these sessions to signal a new direction in Hijikata's work, building towards the performance of *Shiki no tame no nijūnana-ban*.[36]

Shiki no tame no nijūnana-ban marked a return to the female body, with Hijikata appearing strikingly transformed to resemble an old woman whose chest was "hollow and shrinking." His appearance was dramatic after the "masculinity" of the 1960s, with its "emphasis on muscle" and "ribs," and the black-painted and masked male dancers. It was in marked contrast to the performance of *Nikutai no hanran*, in which "the *butō* body reached completion, as an enhancement of the flesh through extreme starvation and a fine-tuning of muscle."[37]

Hangidaitōkan: Shiki no tame no nijūnana-ban (Āto shiatā Shinjuku bunka, Tokyo, 1972)

In 1970, the poet Takahashi Mutsuo came up with the name "*Hangidaitōkan*," and Mishima designed calligraphy for it. "*Hangi*" can be described as "the dead" who have been "burned for sacrifice," as "corpse[s] desperately trying to stand upright."[38] These bodies have been transformed into "things that exist plainly," as the "mirror" of Hijikata's *butō* methodology at that time. It lent a conceptual framework to the subsequent phase of Hijikata's work.[39]

Hijikata Tatsumi, Tamano Kōichi, Waguri Yukio, and others, *Hōsōtan* (Story of Smallpox, 1972), by Onozuka Makoto

Gaishikō (Ceramic Insulator) from *Shiki no tame no nijūnana-ban* (Twenty-Seven Nights for Four Seasons, 1972), by Onozuka Makoto

Shiki no tame no nijūnana-ban, as its title suggests, was performed for twenty-seven nights. It was divided into five parts (*Hōsōtan*, *Susamedama*, *Gaishikō*, *Nadare ame*, and *Gibasan*), which were not only choreographed by Hijikata, but also featured him as principle in all besides *Nadare ame*. The dances were performed late at night, after the regular film slot at *Āto shiatā Shinjuku bunka*. All in all, around 8,000 came to watch, Gōda being one of them. He recalled the work as "the wildest and most popular work of [Hijikata's] lifetime, like the dormant volcano that has suddenly erupted." For Gōda, the piece signalled Hijikata's remarkable return to Japan:

> The Tōhoku figured there, was clearly the Tōhoku of his childhood, that densely colourful pre-war Tōhoku. The wind, the sound of cicadas, the horses trotting, the whistles echoing, the local *samisen* music, and the sound of flat drums. Hijikata still carried the burden of that harsh Tōhoku: he was at once the leper, the noble lady, the great dog decorated with boils, the (Tōhoku) Christ on a wooden door. In his stillness, there was a reflection on a long lost time, the heavy illnesses and the deaths. I felt this to also be Hijikata's requiem for Tōhoku.[40]

This "requiem for Tōhoku" was divided into five sections, as noted down by the poet Suzuki Shiroyasu.[41] In *Hōsōtan* (Story of Smallpox), the men's movements were unthinkably distorted by comparison to familiar gestures – something like watching the country prostitute tending to her sick child. In *Susamedama*, there was the erotic atmosphere given by a mosquito net in summer slashed by a Japanese sword. *Gaishikō* (Ceramic Insulator) was like watching the life of an old woman in a farmhouse garden, seen from the train running along a nearby causeway. In *Nadare ame* (Avalanche Candy), there was the child's glittering dream of the stalls at a country festival or the sweetshop front. And, finally, *Gibasan* was the mock-heroic tale of one who came to save abandoned rubbish and people from the farmhouse *doma*.

Susamedama (Fondling Bead, 1972), by Onozuka Makoto

[Following page:] 'Gibasan,' *Shiki no tame no nijūnana-ban* (Twenty-Seven Nights for Four Seasons, 1972), by Nakatani Tadao

61

Shiki no tame no nijūnana-ban gave a striking impression. Hijikata's "dishevelled hair was decorated with a coquettish hairpin of coral beads," and Ashikawa moved with her "neck retracted like a bore" and the keen gaze of an Eisen *ukiyo-e*. The stage was filled with a bunch of "*geta*-clad country prostitutes, clattering like mares, and carrying their back-to-front *obis*."[42] Many other figures appeared in the performance, such as Hijikata in a padded *kimono*, Hijikata almost naked with only white silk fibre and peeling plaster hanging off him like scabs, a boy in a school cap and uniform, and a number of men with tattooed backs wearing red cloths around their waists.

In the *Hōsōtan* section, Nakamura Fumiaki describes how Hijikata performed a "dance that tries to stand but falls," a dance carrying the determination of standing just once in a lifetime, which could generate a "moment far more beautiful than a prima ballerina standing on pointe."[43] Hijikata's movement was not in opposition to gravity, but worked with it, something that would characterize the *ankoku butō* technique and the descriptions in *Yameru maihime*. The weight and stillness of this movement was described by Gōda as a condition of near-stasis,[44] in which nerves tensed and movement slowed, like the "carriage of *nō* in extreme slow-motion."[45] There was the sense of "an extended time being absorbed into the body's being," which may "look like the dancers are not moving, but is actually a technique full of the sort of energy that can transform space itself." The bodies absorbed an "extended time," closing themselves off within the distant landscape of the stage's space-time. In order to do so, Hijikata demanded a strict philosophy of 'becoming,' ordering Ashikawa and other dancers, for example, to become "chickens *becoming* chickens."[46]

Around the time of *Shiki no tame no nijūnana-ban*, the characteristic movements of *ankoku butō* were formalized. Hijikata began to integrate "bow legs" following his return from Tōhoku, considering them to be the "absolute shape – the shape of a human body raised in the Tōhoku climate," that carry memories of the weight of flesh. The "lowered centre of gravity of bow legs and the unstable balance of deformed legs are the necessary requirements of *ankoku butō*," and indicate its originality as a dance form.[47] These requirements, as well as the walking in near-stasis, the technique of 'becoming,' and the exposure of muscle through expansive or interiorized movements, can be taken as the basis of *ankoku butō*'s methodology.

Shiki no tame no nijūnana-ban was awarded the 1972 Association of Dance Critics Award. This recognition of a work that did not operate within the framework of classical, modern, or even avant-garde dance, was a milestone in the history of Japanese dance and indicated a "global dimension" to the recognition of *butō*.[48] Despite this, *butō* continued to be widely rejected, heavily criticized, and generally considered as a source of dispute and controversy.

Musical Accompaniment

Kinjiki proposed the possibility of a performance without music to Hijikata, and when he did use music in performances after this, it was as something closer to set-design or costume. In the same way he overturned everyday movement patterns, or the expected uses of objects, Hijikata's integration of music and sound was always surprising, whether classical, contemporary, *gidayū*, pop, or the sounds of everyday life.

Hijikata's unexpected use of music was noted by Furusawa Toshima, when he saw Hosoe Eikō's slides of Hijikata in Tōhoku set to Dvořák's *New World Symphony*, and felt the space "transformed into a drama of unexpected and strange atmosphere."[49] The familiar sound of this classical masterpiece (inspired by Dvořák's move from Europe to America) became an "unexpected and strange" commentary on relations to homeland, offsetting Hijikata's return to a familiar landscape with the sounds of arriving in an unfamiliar one. A similar juxtaposition of sound and movement was observed by Nakamura Fumiaki in *Hōsōtan*: when a soprano aria was sung during a solo in which Hijikata dropped his knees open, and another was sung in an angelic voice whilst three girls wearing short reversed *kimonos* and high *geta* (looking like Tōhoku women or chickens) opened their mouths heavenward like chicks. Both presented an image of "authentic folklore combined with a voice of purity, in a way that opened up a new scene," and left "a deep impression, unintended by the composer."[50]

'Gibasan,' *Shiki no tame no nijūnana-ban* (Twenty-Seven Nights for Four Seasons, 1972), by Yamazaki Hiroshi

Set Design, Costumes, and Props

In the works of this time, Hijikata flooded the stage with objects – a Buddhist altar, a lacquer tray, a *kotatsu* (heated low table), a rickshaw, a charcoal brazier, and a washbasin – to the extent that bodies seemed almost overwhelmed by them. Ichikawa Miyabi describes the importance of objects in terms of a "theory of the flesh in which the flesh is forced to change, rather than given any freedom in its relationships with other objects." This marked a shift from the earlier works, characterized by a "violent conflict between the body and the object," as in the use of possibly injurious brass plates in *Nikutai no hanran*. In *Shiki no tame no nijūnana-ban*, there was a relationship characterized by the object's "closeness to the body," which focused on finding resonances between inherited "gestures" and the landscape or environments they lived in.[51]

The inherited "gestures" of a specifically Japanese body-object relationship were already apparent in *Anma*, with the use of tatami mats, in *Nikutai no hanran*, with the use of a mosquito net, and in *Shizukana ie* (1973), with wooden doors seeming to enclose the bodies of female dancers. Ichikawa found these elements suggestive of a "nostalgic return to the mother's body."[52] The objects in use gradually became smaller in size, enclosing the body with increasing restrictions – from the mosquito net or wooden doors to restrictive costumes and headdresses – which brought the focus in to the "smallness of a shrunken body." Ichikawa recalls Ashikawa's body in these terms, as she sat hugging her knees and grinning, in an unforgettable image. This was facilitated by Hijikata's attention to the costumes, which he began to "devote himself" to, designing "costumes which entirely covered the flesh."[53] These costumes might seem little more than rags at a glance, but were actually constructed through a careful process of layering material that had been treated through dying, bleaching, washing, and drying.

Nikutai no hanran rewrote Hijikata's past relationship to the West, paving a return route to Japan for *Shiki no tame no nijūnana-ban*, and retrieving the use of Japanese "gestures" for *Shizukana ie*. During this period, Hijikata's *butō* began to discover the aesthetic it often adopts today, moving towards the "bow legs and dirtiness" of *Hakutōbō*'s performances.[54]

Hakutōbō (1974-76)

In two and a half years, starting with *Hakutō-zu* (1974), Hijikata worked with *Hakutōbō*, and in particular Ashikawa, to create a series of sixteen works. The first three of these (*Hakutō-zu, Bijin to byōki*, and *Nichi-getsu bōru*) were performed at *Shinjuku āto birejji*, and all the works after these were performed at Asbestos Studio. Each work was performed for about a week, during which time Hijikata would make continual changes, so that every night became a kind of premiere. This relentless performance schedule led to a refinement of the 'choreographic forms,' which had been built by Hijikata through an overlay of photographic, painted, and poetic imagery. The process of extracting and combining these 'choreographic forms' over a long period resulted in the incredible work *Geisenjō no okugata* (1976). The piece marked an increasing intensity of collaboration between Hijikata and Ashikawa, and can be seen as the crystallization of the *ankoku butō* methodology. Ashikawa realised the physical forms of Hijikata's *ankoku butō* theory and image-language. This was a work of sacrifice. As Hijikata would say: 'without dying oneself, form cannot possess the opponent.'

The style of the *Hakutōbō* period, as Gōda saw it, became increasingly rigid, "figuring a prominent intentionality towards a centre, and a strong exclusion of unnecessary or confused elements." In the later works of this period (*Hito gata, Shōmen no ishō*, and *Geisenjō no okugata*) there is the sense of "time and space as something like eternity, or infinity."[55] This eternal time and space is generated by a constant refreshing of the current moment, made necessary by the instability of crouched and retracted legs, or the "physical process where the fulcrum of the sole is relocated in every instant." Gōda describes the effect of this process in more depth:

> From this process of relocation, the upper half of the body is gently loosened and subtly swayed. There is no upright for the human body. This process returns the body to the human form as it really is, and reveals the existence of eternal space-time.[56]

For Gōda, "this form of sinking furnishes *ankoku butō* with an anti-realism equivalent to the anti-realism of ballet's elevation."[57] *Ankoku butō* discovered its own comprehensive movement technique during this period.

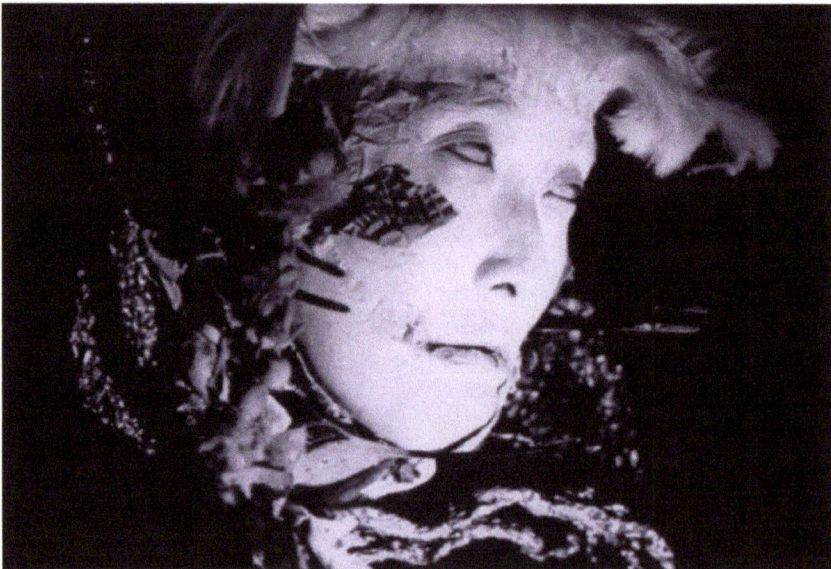

Geisenjō no okugata **(Lady on a Whale String, 1976), photographer unknown**

川羊子
. Ashikawa

[Previous three pages:] Asbestos Studio shots (1972), by Fukase Masahisa; *Geisenjō no okugata* (Lady on a Whale String, 1976), by Hanaga Mitsutoshi; *Hito gata* (Human Shape, 1976), by Hanaga Mitsutoshi

The Late Period (1978-86): Tōhoku kabuki keikaku 2

Watashi no okāsan (My Mother, for Ōno Kazuo, January 1981); *Hukku ofu 88 – keshiki e ichi ton no kamigata* (Hook off 88 – Toward Scenery One-Pile Hairstyle, for Ashikawa Yōko, April 1983); *Nihon no chiobusa* (Breasts of Japan, for Ashikawa Yōko (June-July 1983); *Taka zashiki* (Eagle Parlor, for the Northern Butō School, May 1984); *Renai butō-ha teiso kōen* (Cornerstone Performance of the Amorous Butō School, for Min Tanaka, September 1984); *Tōhoku kabuki keikaku* 1 (The First *Tōhoku Kabuki* Project, March 1985); *Shitashimi e no oku no te* (Last Hand to Friendship, May 1985); *Tōhoku kabuki keikaku* 2 (The Second *Tōhoku Kabuki* Project, June 1985); *Nihon no chibusa* (Breasts of Japan, August-September 1985); *Aburamen no daria* (Dahlia of Aburamen, September 1985); *Tōhoku kabuki keikaku* 3 (The Third *Tōhoku Kabuki* Project, September 1985); *Kyōbunkan no mae nite* (In Front of Kyōbunkan, October 1985); *Tōhoku kabuki keikaku* 4 (The Fourth *Tōhoku Kabuki* Project, December 1985)

During his period choreographing for *Hakutōbō*, Hijikata completed the systemization of his technique. Following his choreography for Ashikawa, *Yami no maihime jūni-tai*, performed at the 1978 Paris Exhibition *Ma: Space-Time in Japan*, however, he fell silent for a period of four years.

Hijikata had made his last appearance onstage as a guest performer for *Dairakudakan*'s *Tenputenshiki: Yōmotsu shintan* in 1973. In the years that followed, Ōno began to receive international attention for his performances, *La Aruhenchina shō* (1977) and *Watashi no okāsan* (1981). While Hijikata was not in the spotlight, he had in fact choreographed both Ōno's performances. It was during this period that Hijikata began to prepare for a new phase of *ankoku butō*. This final phase would be dominated by the series of performances entitled *Tōhoku kabuki keikaku*, which were left incomplete at Hijikata's death only a month or so after the performance of the fourth.

Nakamura Fumiaki recalls Hijikata's "rigid approach" in the last phase of his life in terms of a sincere desire to communicate and realise his vision. The result was of a "discontinuous continuum, as layers of meaningless fragments were repeated passionately," which resulted in a "denial from the outset, of an easy handshake between stage and audience – an etiquette of rupture."[58] The audience was denied the right to interpretation, they experienced rejection, and yet from within that darkness Hijikata extended a "last hand to friendship," offering a very bodily warmth. This "last hand to friendship," seemed to promise a new route to the shared "dance experience" of "purification" and darkness that had characterized *ankoku butō* throughout. In earlier works, Hijikata had made use of violence and eroticism to provoke the audience into an engagement with the work. This gave way to the popularisation of *ankoku butō* during the Middle Period, and to the systemisation of *ankoku butō* formally in the late period.[59]

To claim that Hijikata's *ankoku butō* technique reached completion is a paradox given the anti-technique that it was originally based on. The account of Hijikata's disciple, Majima Daiei, from the preparations for *Tōhoku kabuki keikaku 4*, is a testament to this. According to Majima, Ashikawa had danced a perfect example of the Hijikata method, only to receive the reprimand: 'Ashikawa, are you *still* dancing like that?' Hijikata would never be satisfied with a fixed methodology. He was driven by an avant-garde desire to create and destroy in continuum. The question posed to Ashikawa was an indication of the wish to destroy and rebuild the *ankoku butō* technique over again. He was moving once more into the unknown. Like Furusawa Toshimi, Gōda Nario also detected this new turn when watching *Tōhoku kabuki keikaku*:

> *Tōhoku kabuki Keikaku 4* was performed at *Studio 200*, with a black coloured cross as the stage. In the finale, Ashikawa and the other dancers broke open the

kusudama [celebratory paper ball] to shower themselves with confetti. This ultimate homage to his dancers and to himself was *the* final scene.[60]

The graceful dormant volcano... *Tōhoku kabuki keikaku*... the 'tender touch' of the fourth part presented last December... it was beautiful to all who saw it, wherever they were watching from. It was a mountain of tenderness.[61]

Hijikata's *ankoku butō* was opening out into something "beautiful" and "tender" in this final phase. Hijikata even hoped to dance onstage again after 13 years away from it, at the opening of the *Ginza sezon gekijō* from August 25-30 1986. The performance was never realized, however, for Hijikata died on January 21 of that same year. On August 21, the *Ginza sezon gekijō* held a Hijikata Memorial Performance instead, and Motofuji recounted the scene Hijikata might have performed had he lived:

Cherry blossom petals fall over the audience, the drop-curtain opens without a sound, on the surrounding wall is a cheery Mount Fuji, there's a backdrop of glossy night cherry blossoms. Suddenly hundreds of *taiko* drums descend like a flash of lightning, continuously and violently drummed, falling along with cherry blossom plectrums. The audience's breath stops, and Hijikata Tatsumi appears onstage, dancing crazily, as *Fūjin Raijin* [God of Wind and Thunder], after 13 years. Along with his crowd of *butō* dancers...[62]

Under the watchful eye of cheery Mount Fuji and dancing in the swell of a storm of cherry blossoms, Hijikata becomes *Fūjin Raijin*, slashing space as a *kamaitachi* (weasel's cut), and sending out a deep rumble with his hoard of *butō* dancers. It is as though the imagined scene extends some blessing to those *butō* dancers left living, and to the future existence of *ankoku butō*.

Tōhoku Kabuki Keikaku 4 (Fourth Tōhoku Kabuki Project, 1985), by Kamiyama Teijirō

Geisenjō no okugata (Lady on a Whale String, 1976), by Hanaga Mitsutoshi (T) / Yoshie Shōzō (B)

5. The Fundamentals of Hijikata's Ankoku Butō Technique

The Butō Dancer's Body

The Basic Concept

> My dance is not at all anti classical dance. It is about an expansion of the concept of a human being. The basic concept of my dance is rooted in the discovery of the possibility that the human body may metamorphose into anything from animals and plants, to inanimate objects.[1]

Hijikata's basic philosophy was centred on the "expansion" of what it means to be human, through the training of a body that could metamorphose into anything.

The Body's Fetters

Dance is an expressive act, mediated through the body alone. This body, always under the governance of gravity, is restrained by its structures and functions. The physical restraint of the body is the fundamental obstacle to the freedom of the expressive act, and this means the body becomes both restriction and medium. The methodology of any given dance form is only its chosen method of overcoming this restriction. Ballet attempts to overcome the limitations of gravity through leaping and turning, reconditioning the structure of the human body by opening it out using training methods such as *en dehors*. *Ankoku butō*, on the other hand, not only attempted to overcome the human being's bodily structure, but the concept of the human being itself. In order to do so, Hijikata sought a technique of metamorphosis, or 'becoming.' This meant actually "becoming an animal, becoming a tree, becoming a stone."[2]

Hijikata's methodology of "becoming" was classified by Ichikawa Miyabi as belonging to the genealogy of Shamanic possession, which is "the performance of 'becoming,' and not the performance of expression." He considers it is possible to become a given thing through the imaginative "effort of becoming the details of that chosen thing."[3] It is not always clear what precisely this "effort" entails, but what it gives rise to is a manipulation of the body that is the method of 'becoming.' As with ballet or *nō*, the *ankoku butō* body still works as a mediator of expression and reaches for a bodily existence beyond that of the everyday. The way it does so, is through this method of 'becoming.'

The Spirit of the Butō Dancer

Hijikata did not demand physical or technical ability of his disciples. He never rejected anyone who applied. He did, however, require a commitment that was total, the 'all or nothing' ultimatum. *Butō* could only be faced through complete devotion. It was a state of mind more than anything, and this state of mind formed the 'invisible technique' behind the physical techniques of *ankoku butō*. This 'invisible technique' was the reason Hijikata often chose to place a dancer with only a few months of physical training onstage, in place of someone far more experienced.[4] The basis of his creative training was mental rather than physical, it was "not the creation of dance out of experience or expertise."[5] *Butō* takes place in the space between these visible and invisible techniques, it emerges in their meeting ground.

[Preceding page:] Hijikata Tatsumi with a chicken, *Nikutai no hanran* (Revolt of the Flesh, 1968), by Hanaga Mitsutoshi

Event at Kyoto University's Western Auditorium (1968), by Hanaga Mitsutoshi

Hijikata demanded giving up everything in order to qualify as a *butō* dancer. The *butō* dancer was not the one with a particular innate talent or skill, but the one who had made a choice. This was not a one-time decision, but a continually posed challenge. Hijikata did not preschedule his classes, meaning that in order to attend, any regular commitments had to be sacrificed. Before they knew it, most dancers ended up living near the studio in order to attend impromptu night-time classes and lectures. This fostered a communal life among the dancers. Their uniform was training clothing, their food was radish leaves taken free from the local greengrocer, and their shelter was the studio or local dancers' houses. Everyday life transformed into the space-time of *butō*, as acts like cleaning the studio or taking care of the cats and dogs were shared. *Butō* was necessarily entangled with the everyday, as Hijikata described:

> The performance that is separated from life is no more than ornament. That is why a sense of crisis must be faced and cultivated.[6]

The *butō* lifestyle was in itself a training ground for Hijikata's philosophy. He used to say that: "once caught, made to die, and revived, the dancer is able to talk with winds and grasses" (Appendix 1). In order to join the "*butō koseki*," where communication with "winds and grasses" was possible, the *butō* dancer had to 'fall,' give themselves over to a certain kind of 'incompetence.' *Butō* began wherever you found yourself, the *butō* space-time unfurled out of the everyday. Throwing away everything in order to commit to this space-time was the prerequisite for joining the *butō koseki* (family register). Hijikata never rejected anyone from this *koseki*, but closely interrogated those who thought themselves cut out for its demands. In this way, disciples were taken in or weeded out.

Self-Renunciation

When I first visited Hijikata in his studio, he said to me: 'here, I'm keeping a chicken,' and pointed to Ashikawa. In a man's baggy t-shirt and long johns, Ashikawa suddenly 'became' a chicken, crawling around with a 'cluck, cluck, cluck.' That act of becoming required a renunciation of the self as a human being.

To reject the "stamp" of societal acceptance, and on some level abandon life as a citizen, was the only way to sign up to the "*butō koseki*."[7] The dancer had to abandon the condition of being a human and live as a thing inferior to a dog or a cat. This idea was present in Hijikata's title "*Hangidaitōkan*," which presented the human body as a burned and sacrificed thing.[8] *Butō* demanded a sacrifice: the relinquishment of certain freedoms and rights, and even the giving up of language. It demanded the ability to take a risk and fall instantaneously into the dangerous place that is dance. Dancing was unquestionably a dangerous game for Hijikata, a form of derangement that could lead to a burned and sacrificed body. To live divided and deranged allowed for release through self-renunciation. Living "on the edge" made a degree of spontaneity possible (Appendix 1). If Hijikata "said learn, they had to learn now." He pushed dancers and dance to a limit place, requiring an "honest" 'self-renunciation' that was more than a matter of the dancer's spirit, and rather constituted the 'invisible technique' of *butō*.[9]

The Movement of Butō

Standing and Walking

> Most dances in the world start from standing upright, but there are folded legs as well as standing ones. I have been told of this many times. When I came to Tokyo, my starting point was the walk of a condemned criminal – not walking but collapsing. Something bad will happen if *butō* doesn't take the walk of these ash columns as its starting point...[10]

The basic "upright" stance of the world's dance forms differs according to where the centre of gravity is located. In ballet, a distance is created between the dancer and the ground, as they will themselves taller using the technique of being *sur la pointe*. In *nō* the "arms draw a low close arc, hiding the waist, the knees are gently bent, and the centre of gravity is located in the hips in a natural posture that feels stable." As with ballet, the "natural posture" or "carriage" of *nō* and *kabuki* is a "standing figure" that carries the mental posture of the art form.[11] The "carriage" in *butō* is equally important, but as something constantly transforming.[12]

In *butō*, 'standing' and 'walking' constitute the basic movements. All dance practices take walking as the basic means to traverse space – not in the everyday sense, but using the non-everyday body of dance. The movement of this non-everyday body does not rely on the everyday functioning of legs.

For Hijikata, standing was a form of "collapsing," and walking was the "walk of an ash column." These descriptions of "collapsing" and "ash column[s]" feature in Hijikata's specific image-language. To access what Hijikata might have intended by these images it is necessary to consider his writing on "folded legs" and the "walk of a condemned criminal." Through this, the 'standing' and 'walking' of *butō* might be sketched.

"Walk of an ash column"

Hashira (column) is used as the counter for Japanese gods. Its use might also be intended to connote *hitobashira* (human sacrifice). *Haibashira* (ash column) is a Hijikata coinage. It calls up the image of a human burned in sacrifice, reduced to ash, and yet still retaining their shape as a column, standing. This human being has lost almost all of its human functions, and yet it maintains the sole function of being human. That is, even though this human has become "ash" they maintain their "form" as a human being. That shape – the only human function left – appears as what Hijikata has termed the "materialization of the inevitable" (Appendix 1).

The "ash column" standing upright balances precariously on the minutest point. It stands desperately working to maintain itself as an "ash column." It risks collapse at any moment from the slightest gust of wind, and this produces the effect of floating rather than standing. It is 'hung up' at the same time as standing. The only movement possible for this hanging column is that of collapse. The hanging "ash column" as it stands on the brink of collapse is the "materialization of the inevitable" that *butō* works towards. A wind blows and the "ash column" collapses, dispersing as ash to unforeseen places and unknown reaches. This directionless traversal of space is the "walk of an ash column" and so the 'walking' of *butō*.

Hijikata reconsidered the basic human acts of standing and walking. In *butō*, 'standing' is the desperate attempt of a body unable to stand, and 'walking' is the unpredictable and directionless movement of a body continually thrown off balance.

"Folded" Legs

Hijikata's frequent reference to "folded" legs recalls a familiar scene from his Tōhoku childhood. The children would be placed in *izume* (straw baskets) and tied up so they wouldn't fall out, whilst their parents worked in the rice paddies. These abandoned children's "folded" legs, tied up in the *izume* as they screamed and cried, were described by Hijikata in the following scene:

> Taken out as evening falls, it is impossible to stand. Legs completely folded and crippled... the folded joints locked in place. It is absurd and solemn – because it is desperate. Realising the legs have gently escaped the body. Where have they gone, the legs that won't return? It seems only the child's body knows, bullied by the *izume*.[13]

In *butō*, the desire to stand is met by an inability to stand. The body refuses the will to stand, but it cannot quieten that will. This body, attempting but failing to stand, and at the same time unable to control the operations of the will, constitutes the basic body philosophy of *butō*. *Butō* discovers beauty in a form of standing founded on the "desperate" attempt and failure to stand upright, on the "absurd and solemn" state of being unable to realise the will.

芦川羊子
Y. Ashikawa

Probably an expression of an ash column (*Hito gata*, 1976) by Hanaga Mitsutoshi

Absolute Passivity: the "walk of a condemned criminal"

The condemned criminal walks to the guillotine, his life persisting to the end, a human being already dead. In this one miserable man, placed in an unjust situation in the name of the law, the intense antagonism between life and death is conclusively expressed and highly condensed. A human being not walking, but made to walk, not living, but made to live. A human being not dying, but made to die... despite this total passivity, the fundamental vitality of human nature is paradoxically revealed. Sartre wrote of how 'the criminal with bound hands who stands at the guillotine is not yet dead. Short of one moment to death. That one moment of life in which death is intensely desired...' He captured the condition that is the original form of dance. Creating this condition onstage has to be my work.[14]

Hijikata described the "walk of a condemned criminal" around the time of *Kinjiki*, and it became one of the fundamentals of *ankoku butō*. The "condemned criminal walks to the guillotine," pushed by the antagonism between life and death – the will that desires life, and the body that is driven to death. The infant bound in an *izume* experiences a similar conflict, its legs refusing movement despite the will's desire to escape. The "walk of the condemned criminal" is the walk of every human being, from infancy to old age, drawn simultaneously towards life and death. A being "made to walk" that exists beyond any matter of the will. This walk of "absolute passivity" is the basis of movement in *butō*.

The "absolute passivity" of the "walk of a criminal" is similar to that of the "ash column" blown by a gust of wind, or the unpredictable movement of "folded" legs. The "ash column," holding desperately onto "form," materializes the inevitable state of the human being. The "walk of an ash column" is a movement born out of the tension of always being on the brink of collapse.

Being of the Body

The "walk of a criminal" is the desperate "form" of standing. The "walk of an ash column" is the crumbling and drifting of ash in unknown directions. They share in a desperate struggle of the body against the will, which can be traced back to the condition of infants folded into *izume*. The body that is not controlled by the will is one of "absolute passivity." This "absolute passivity" might seem at odds with another aspect of Hijikata's *butō*, that of "boundless and limitless" "freedom," but is actually closely related. The two concepts are merged in the following passage:

> Talking now of walking and eating. In my case, I almost remove the experience of walking on foot from *butō*. Why is the ghost without legs able to keep such a form? It is supported by something. Without support, it would fall like a *yukata* [traditional cotton dressing-gown]. It is supported by air. There are things like dandelions without legs, floating in a state where death repeats endlessly. Or there is the feeling a rabbit has when its fur is rubbed backwards; it detects a human body from that touch alone. In these cases, you don't walk with direction, not up, down, left, or right, but rather float. A jellyfish or a dandelion – without legs you can still go in any direction, disperse anywhere! Legs are the basic foundation of European dance, as Valéry put it, yet since childhood I have carried the single experience of avoiding legs as a tool for walking. Legs have gone never to return, where did they go? Chasing them, shadowing them. The blurred shape of those legs is still there, even when you borrow the form of a jellyfish or dandelion. The detonator of a power to be continually deceived is growing inside me – this is my method for erasing my legs.[15]

Hijikata did not want to rely on the ease of walking on feet. He wanted to "remove" this experience from *butō*. The "ash column" is like the ghost whose form is supported by air, and the "ash" is like the dandelion or jellyfish that can drift anywhere. These images share the freedom that comes from moving without legs. When legs are relied on, their usual functions constitute the limitations of movement. With the erasure of these functions they find new freedom. The child unable to move from the *izume* discovers new freedom with the departure of its legs – "gone never to return" – but is still haunted by the "blurred shape of those legs." The only way to attain this freedom in its totality is with the complete "erasing" of the legs.

"[E]rasing" the legs is facilitated by a heightened awareness: the alertness of "countless gazes." This relies on the ability to be "deceived," on the ability to believe in images, as a child might do. For Hijikata, the freedom of movement discovered in the "walk of an ash column" is achieved through the extinction of the flesh, which requires a total belief in the image. This metamorphosis is an act of the 'becoming' body, as the basis of the *butō* movement methodology.

[Following page:] 'Gibasan,' *Shiki no tame no nijūnana-ban* (Twenty-Seven Nights for Four Seasons, 1972), by Yamazaki Hiroshi

6. Modes of Walking and Choreographic Forms

Standing

> 'You have been living with domesticated movement, inflicted by extreme violence, so your concept of the body must be astray.' Saying this, I take the approach of fixing an intense gaze on his body. In other forms of dance, such as classical ballet or Spanish dance, exercises based on external form result in a uniform methodology of domestication, whereas my dance is the opposite – it fixes a gaze on the self that strays.[1]

Hijikata's *butō* training starts out from standing. It draws awareness to the body and the space around that body. It poses questions like: 'Why start from standing?' 'Where does my body end?' Hijikata urged a new interrogation of the act of standing and of the body. He forced it into a place of exposure and shame, where the desire to self-extinguish allowed for the body to really meet itself face to face.

As when the body becomes aware of itself when the back is in pain, or when the fingers are inhibited in their use, the awareness fostered by shame drew attention to the body's mechanism. At this point, the body attains self-perspective. It can be drawn close or distanced through oscillations in the degree of concentration. It can be expanded to fill the space, and then expanded further to blow through the limitations of space.

Addressing this body, Hijikata seemed to ask: 'Can you take that one step?' He posed the question to draw attention to the 'where' and 'how' of 'standing' and 'walking,' urging a moment of 'hesitation and division' before movement. This meant movement could only occur through renouncing the self and entering the 'hesitation and division' fully. This was the single step of *butō*.

Taking this single step, opened up the "secret hidden inside the body, that my arm is not my arm."[2] It revealed the "sister living inside my body, who sits when I stand."[3] This heightened awareness and interrogation of the body lies at the heart of the *ankoku butō* methodology.

Walking

Requirements of Walking

Walking and standing are the foundation of *butō* training. Walking is like the blank canvas of the *butō* body. Through returning to the base of walking, the movement and body of *butō* can be moderated and refined. In *nō*, the *kamae* (posture) forms the mental and physical training for the *hakobi* (walk), whereas *butō* starts out from the basis of the walk.

Hijikata's verbally dictated requirements for walking differ in the notes I make reference to here (those of Ichiyoshi, Akane, Harada, and myself). The differences are not only a reflection of the students' differing interpretations, but also the result of Hijikata's methodological revisions at different stages in his career; his constant process of "drawing and erasing" (Appendix 1). The most accurate record of Hijikata's final intentions for the requirements for walking must be those from the period working closely with Ashikawa before his death. I will therefore refer to those notes I made on walking whilst attending Ashikawa's workshop in 1989. These notes include the "Walk of a Measure" and "Walk by Insects," among others (Appendix 2).

Requirements for the "Walk of a Measure"

a)   become a measure and walk
b)   move without walking between heaven and earth

c) with eyes of glass, place an eye on the forehead
d) the speed of reflection is faster than that of vision
e) razor blades on the soles of the feet
f) a basin on top of the head
g) joints suspended from spider threads
h) the desire to walk goes on ahead, and form pursues after
i) traces of walking hanging in the space before and behind
j) forest in the molar teeth, threads in the hollows of the body
k) suddenly eyes stop seeing and legs stop walking; at that point, things become walking eyes and walking legs
l) walking requires moments of discontinuity, and urges the expansion of space

These requirements work as an image-language intended to generate a form of awareness that results in real changes and movements within the body. This particular set of requirements might be considered the basis of *butō* movement. Through analysing this language, the movement methodology of *butō* can be approached and interpreted.

This set of requirements does not ask for the concentration of nerves, so much as the stirring of countless sentiments. In order to accept these countless sentiments, there can be no insistence on individuality. The dancer must exist in a state of receptivity, which cannot arise through either tension or relaxation. They must stand only as a receptive "measure."

Adopting an Axis

a) become a measure and walk
b) move without walking between heaven and earth
c) a basin on top of the head

These three directions establish the body's axis. As in any other dance form, from traditional Japanese dance to ballet, establishing the body's axis precedes movement. Imagining "a basin on top of the head," the head does not shake, the chin remains tucked in, and the height stays level. To "move without walking between heaven and earth," the body becomes like a measure and the feet slide in order to avoid modulations in height. This creates the impression of gliding or floating.

Erasing the Vision

d) with eyes of glass, place an eye on the forehead
e) the speed of reflection is faster than that of vision

By imagining a single third eye, the nerves are concentrated in the forehead, the eyes are left alone to become glass eyes, and sightlines can emerge through the back of the head instead. The glass eyeballs, without willing or intending sight, instead reflect an accurate landscape, through a faster physical procedure than that of seeing. Being pulled by threads from the "forest in the molar teeth," the facial expression is erased. Eyes are the facilitators of individual expression. Whereas *kabuki* adopts an expressive use of the eyes, *nō* masks or vanishes the eyes, along with the facial expression, to allow for a deeper form of expression to emerge.[4] *Butō* neither reveals a person's character nor their individual personality or will, but attempts to return the flesh to its status as an object. By vanishing the functioning eye, which clearly expresses the human will, the body can become something like a blank slate.

Erasing the Legs

f) razor blades on the soles of the feet

g)   joints suspended from spider threads

h)   forest in the molar teeth, threads in the hollows of the body

If there are blades of razors beneath the soles of the feet, then it is impossible to stand upright. Avoiding the placement of weight on the blades of razors, a feeling of floating arises, and the knees are loosened. With this slack in the knees, the hips also loosen and various directions and qualities of movement, such as hardness and softness, can be accessed. For Hijikata, dancing was the creation of space, and this could be created through a slackening of the knees. The soles of the feet had always been considered important in Japanese traditional dance or in working the rice paddies, and this slackening of the knees was an instruction coming from the soles of the feet. The guiding of these slackened knees is therefore essential in establishing a method for steering the dancing body.

When I entered the studio, Hijikata told me: 'your joints are protruding.' This was an instruction to erase the protrusion of the joints through being suspended on "spider threads." It was an instruction to erase the visible functioning of the joints, and to transcend the oppression of gravity. The "hollows of the body," create a lightness that is internalized, so that even the functions of the internal organs are erased. The body suspended on threads without organs, flesh, or the functioning of joints, can move freely, like a puppet or piece of thin light paper. This freedom of the non-everyday body, achieved through the erasure of particular functions or needs, is created through the feeling of suspension and floating, and allows for the creation and expansion of space.

Using extremely delicate images, such as spider threads and razor blades, the nerves are concentrated locally. The concentration is not focussed on a single point, but diffused through multiple points, to open up the feeling of awareness. This counterpoise of concentration and dispersion is figured through a carefully constructed image-language, which forms the basis of the *butō* training.

Life Yearns after Form

i)   the desire to walk goes on ahead, and form pursues after

j)   suddenly eyes stop seeing and legs stop walking; at that point, things become walking eyes and walking legs

k)   walking requires moments of discontinuity, and urges the expansion of space

Movement arises from the "desire" for "form," rather than the will to walk. This spontaneous movement gives rise to a "form" that expresses the spirit of "desire," as a materialization of 'life' itself.

Hijikata proposed this paradox in his theory that the desire for life precedes form. Which is to say, form can accommodate possible movements beyond the established potential of the body or set patterns of behaviour. Through a concentration on the image, acts like walking and seeing can be paused at the same time as being created. This breaking down of the limitations of the everyday extends to the experience of time, with the disruption in temporal continuity dissolving any sense of beginning or ending, and allowing for the creation of space. The microscopic awareness of time and space implied by the "moments of discontinuity," allows for a macroscopic sense of space.

Manipulating the Body

Butō training guides the body's movement through imaginative engagement with an image-language. The way the imagination functions, for Hijikata, is related to the "being of nerves," which is the *butō* "dancer's *pointe*" (Appendix 1).

All of the instructions analysed above are ways of manipulating the body through the imagination, and suggest that an image-language is what guides sensation. The interrelation between language and movement is facilitated by the imagination, as a kind of "circuit of nerves." This circuit facilitates the progression from language-to-image and image-to-bodily transformation, which forms the basic structure of the *butō* body. In order to achieve command of the relations of this circuit, it must be observed from a bird's eye perspective, which is only accessible when the eyes are not strained in concentration on a fixed point.

The "being of nerves" of the *butō* body is not reliant on the everyday functions of eyes or legs – indeed it triggers the disappearance of an existing body – and rather draws on unlimited possibilities through the use of the imagination. The body of a *butō* dancer is like that of a puppet with slackened knees. These knees permit any movement, without jeopardizing the stability of the body's axis. The importance of these slackened joints corresponds to the "bow legs" described by Gōda in the previous chapter.

Possible Body

The modes of walking outlined above constitute the "carriage" of the *butō* dancer. In widening the range of possible movements they condition a 'possible body'. Softening the body from the feet up through the knees, to the hips and back, the body is emptied out, like a shell of skin. This is the basic form of "bow legs," or the child's "folded" legs in an *izume*, which are familiar from descriptions of Hijikata's Tōhoku.

Form: A Perspective of Negativity

"My method entirely adopts the Realist method," claimed Hijikata.[5] His movements and forms were drawn from real animals, plants, human beings, and natural phenomena, and then converted into choreography using language. The requirements of the forms are the method Hijikata used to verbally organize his choreography, amounting to over 200 image-language units. They give a sense of the wide range of diction made use of in *butō*, and provide a guideline to how Hijikata conceived of his body of 'becoming.' Each of these sets of requirements corresponds to a self-contained movement or movement sequence. They are inscribed into the imagination of the dancer to be materialized physically, as a result of necessity rather than will.

The Necessary Requirements of the Choreographic Forms

Hijikata's notion that when subjected to intense observation, or the "observing [of] observation," things exist out of necessity, relates to the importance he placed on the "materialization of the inevitable" (Appendix 1). The forms must emerge from necessity, and exist within themselves. This is facilitated by the detailing of necessary requirements, such as those written for the variation of the "cow":

* the weight is carried
* hoofs on the feet (up, *stomp stomp*, bending the knees)
* hoofs on the hands (fingers, bending)
* horns (from the nape)
* tail
* suppleness of the back – add hips
* close the armpits
* forward leaning   lengthening the nape

This is the basic form of the cow – a code for the basic materials of cow. Hijikata did not fix it rigidly, but deconstructed and reconstructed the form using his image-language. This led to variations on the form, such as the following:

Variation on Cow

- the back as a letter S
- a dahlia on the head – the head sinks down
- feathers on the hips
- a dwarf running on the back
- the left side steaming upwards *BoBoBo*
- a grasshopper on the left foot

The requirements for "cow" might be said to adopt a kind of realism. The image is conjured like a spark of intuition (the simplicity of a "letter S") or a single hair sprouting, and then grows and thickens into the image of a whole creature. The naming of the form alone assigns it a particular reality, which is then detailed and elaborated. The "letter S" generates the quality and direction of a curve, while the onomatopoeia "*BoBoBo*" suggests something bubbling under the arms, creating the unexpected motions of a cow. The precisions of language dictate the particular speed, direction, and quality of an original movement. The movement itself is not described, but the dancer is urged to consider how movement can emerge from a particular relation to the image. When the dancer's interpretation resonates with that of Hijikata, the requirements of the choreographic form become a shared language or code. The outward conditions of the form may not be dictated, but the fine detailing of inner conditions through the necessary requirements allows them to emerge with more sense of realism than would be possible with a more descriptive approach.

Naming the Forms: A Perspective of Negativity

Gōda noted how in Hijikata's performances, dancers transformed into ghosts, devils, lepers, mad people, Buddha figurines, figures of folklore, and animals such as chickens, dogs, cats, horses, and snakes. These creatures give their names to a number of the choreographic forms. Figures such as the sick and the mad occupy a position on the periphery of accepted society, and suggest that Hijikata's *butō* perspective can be considered to give preference to this place of negativity – negative, not ethically, but in the sense of outside societal norms.[6] Gunji indicated this standpoint when he described "*ankoku*" as "the underside of an accepted history."[7] Hijikata manifested this "underside," or negativity, through images of death, such as skeletons and ghosts. He established an inverse perspective on the brightness of life, drawing awareness to this underside of life, in a way not dissimilar to Buddhism.

The choreographic forms that most clearly illustrate this perspective of negativity are often those drawing inspiration from painters and paintings. *Ukiyo-e* and Buddhist art frequently feature, as do Western paintings, by artists such as Goya, Moreau, Munch, Redon, Bosch, Bacon, Turner, Bresdin, Beardsley, Michaux, Vermeer, Delvaux, Wols, and Fautrier. An attempt to classify these works would come up with the broad categories of Romanticism, fantastical art (including Surrealism), and fin-de-siècle art. The inclination to pass over ethical judgments and consider art in terms of aesthetic truth is an approach Hijikata shared with Romanticism, whilst the release of the spirit through the imagination was a quality that brought his work close to fantastical art.[8] A sense of inner searching and the possibility of spiritual release, share the same deep mysticism about the "hidden essence of things" with the theory of the grotesque, or grotto, previously discussed.

Many of the artists Hijikata drew on can be classed in terms of a negative perspective. Artists like Goya, Bresdin, and Munch, form a heritage of negativity for Hijikata's work. Using these painters' works to develop choreographic forms, Hijikata was able to articulate new movements with a precision that allowed dancers to 'become' the forms. By observing the ways in which Hijikata made use of these artists, it is possible to investigate the characteristics of the choreographic forms, and their necessary requirements.

Cow or horse shapes in *Shizukana ie* (Quiet House, 1973), by Onozuka Makoto

Goya: the Pope of Pus

In his later life, Francisco Goya (1746-1828) lost both his hearing and the security of a court life. In the *Black Paintings* and a number of etchings from this period, we can see his work had moved into the realm of the fantastical.[9] Goya was using the imagination "to gaze through nothingness," as Takashina Shūji put it, which placed him at the forefront of modernity.[10] Hijikata identified "darkness" as a necessary requirement for "Goya: the Pope of Pus," as outlined below:

- pus, saliva, discharge of ears, flesh oozing, darkness
- brain dangling down to the mouth
- elbow brushing the robe of pus
- flesh *zure* [oozing] – here *zure* [ooze] there *zure* [ooze]
- the Pope of Pus sinking into darkness
- controlling the slippage of *zure* [lags] in time = dispersion

"[P]us," "saliva," "discharge of ear," and "brain" are bodily fluids with a certain liquidity. The body's boundaries run with these bodily fluids, and the fleshly outline collapses, dissolves. Controlling the relations of the "slippage of *zure* [lags] in time" as "flesh *zure* [ooz(es)]" from collapsing flesh "here *zure* [ooze] there *zure* [ooze]," requires simultaneous awareness of different physiological areas, leading to the "dispersion" of nerves. With the "elbow brushing the robe of pus," the image arises of flesh melting and collapsing.

Bodily fluids such as "pus" are usually seen as inferior in the hierarchy of the human body, yet this very baseness gives them a particular force in the evocation of imagery. The crude and evocative imagery of such things as bodily fluids leaking or "collapsing," leads the *butō* dancer to experience a sense of transgressing the body's boundaries, as in the dissolving of skin. For Hijikata, Goya brought to mind "pus," and the body's dissolution into "pus."

The poet and painter Henri Michaux (1899-1984) is recorded to have said: "there's a spirit that exists and makes drawing necessary."[11] The aim of Michaux's painting was to depict the energy that flows between humans. He would create both "miniscule and expansive" imagery in a way that dissolved all sense of time – perhaps also a result of often drawing under the influence of mescaline.[12]

Hijikata used Michaux's work when creating the choreographic forms "Michaux: the Figure of Light," "Michaux: Droplet of Ink," and "Michaux: Three Faces." The necessary requirements for "the Figure of Light" are outlined below:

- feelers of light extending – below the nose, elbows, crotch, knees
- a mantle of light – transparent, infinitely transparent
- walk on mesh
- feelers of light extending, refracting 4 metres away – melting as a plane
- soles of the feet on razor blades – walk
- a strong smell under the nose – the nape extends
- pulled towards the back-right
- left foot lifts
- a fan in the hand
- gazed at from above
- billowing from beneath
- dispersion of directions

By imagining "feelers of light extending," the body's boundaries are expanded and the body becomes diaphanous. With "feelers of light extending" from beneath the nose, the facial expression disappears. With them extending from the elbows, crotch, and knees, the function of joints disappears. With "a mantle of light," the function of the existing body disappears, and becomes "infinitely transparent." This diaphanous body expands by "4 metres" and dissolves "as a plane" into space. As with other choreographic forms and their necessary requirements, a continuous "relation" to "feelers of light" allows for a bodily transfiguration to occur. By walking "on mesh," or sensing "the razor blades," a feeling of floating is generated, and with the gaze "from above," there is the sensation of being pushed downward. The gaze "from above" and the "billowing from beneath" create a counter-tension that urges the horizontal expansion of space. The body dissolves "as a plane," and movement in any direction becomes possible.

Through establishing a simultaneous relation to multiple images, as a "dispersion of direction," the supple body of *butō* is realised. This movement outwards is achieved in the necessary requirements for the "Figure of Light." The translucent figure, dissolving and dispersing with feelers of light, becomes like the energy of drawing on mescaline.

Beardsley: No. 1-4

Among the artists Hijikata directly referred to in his choreographic forms, Aubrey Beardsley (1872-98) was the most frequent. As one of the most celebrated figures of fin-de-siècle decadence, Beardsley is best known for his illustrations of Oscar Wilde's *Salomé*.[13] Looking at these illustrations, we might wonder what Hijikata took from their bold arabesque patterns, their decadence and sensuality, and their sophisticated world of monochrome. In the necessary requirements for "Beardsley: No. 1-4," we find an image-language that captures the essence of Beardsley's work:

No. 1
- figure made only of nerves
- fine gentlewoman wearing a long trained skirt and thin silk dress

- gaze following the nerve extending from the left fingertip
- a nerve extending from the back of the head to heaven

No. 2
- fine gentlewoman groping along a wall in darkness
- instability underfoot
- eyes attached to the right fingertips feeling along the wall
- nerves extending to the ceiling

No. 3
- a nerve extending from the chin to heaven as if appealing for help
- resting hands

No. 4
- gazing over the shoulder at an opponent
- the left hand seeking a handshake
- nerves extending to the ceiling so as not to flee backwards

Probably *Hakutōbō*, 'Beardsley – Gentlewoman Peacock', by Hanaga Mitsutoshi

Hijikata takes from Beardsley's work, a "fine gentlewoman" who is "made only of nerves;" a lady with all her "nerves extending to heaven." When the "gaze" is drawn along the nerve that extends from a fingertip, the eyes' focal point dissolves into distance. When eyes are attached to the fingertips, the body's periphery transforms into eyes or nerves. When the gaze is turned backwards "over the shoulder" and the nerve strains at the "back of the head," an awareness and visibility emerges through the back body, which weakens the focus on the front body. The "instability underfoot" in the "darkness" forces the nerves to compensate by extending upwards, becoming thinner, and more alert.

The image of "nerves extending to the ceiling," brings to mind Beardsley's elaborate line drawings. Through establishing a "relation" to them, the entire body achieves a heightened sensitivity and lengthened form.

The Flower Garden of Bresdin

The print-maker Bresdin (1822-85) detailed the depths of the human spirit. His works are "impossible to read without a magnifier," they reveal "a design harmonized by the minutiae of light and shade," and their characteristic style "when viewed at distance, displays unexpected expansion" with "elaborate details in luxurious chaos."[14] The necessary requirements of "the Flower Garden of Bresdin," are guided by Hijikata as follows:

- a picture of wild flowers, a flower folding-screen, a limited space
- thinness, diffusion and concentration
- white flower, rustle of leaves… / increasing the requirements
- minutiae – more than the finest eyesight can see, the minutiae of the blind
- relating backwards
- an outline of the upper body – something like a razor blade
- thinness of the lips
- the means of relation through the limit of wild flowers – the form of petals, the colour, the number
- the scent

Within the "limited space" of the "flower folding-screen," the requirements for sensing "thinness" and "minutiae" accumulate. By relating in turn to each detail of the flower – the "rustle of leaves," the "form of petals, colour, the number," "the scent" – a sense of "minutiae" and "concentration" emerges. By "increasing the requirements" and "relating backwards," the nerves are drawn outwards, and the states of "diffusion" and "thinness" are created. In this way, the state of "concentration" is intensified. In order to avoid the dazing effect of bringing to mind and sensing the soft "form of petals," a clear silhouette is cut thin like a "razor blade." The figure appears sharp against the atmospheric scene.

Hijikata limited the conditions of "petals" to those qualities that encourage "diffusion and concentration," in order to encourage the dancer to relate to a sense of "minutiae […] the minutiae of the blind." He identified a particular oscillation between diffusion and concentration that could occur within the "limited space" of a "flower garden," and discovered the harmony of "minutiae" within the natural "chaos."

Code for Transforming the Body

The necessary requirements outlined above, subject the body to a constant metamorphosis: dissolution into pus, diffusion into light and shade, or expansion into a network of nerves. The various bodily transformations that occur are characterized by a simultaneous sense of expansion and concentration. The body that was presumed solid dissolves by turns into liquid, gas, and particles. This is made possible through the effacement of an existing body and the freedom that comes with constant transformation.

The inspiration for "pus," "light," or "nerves extending," that Hijikata drew from the works of painters, established the vocabulary for using the imagination to relate to imagery. This worked as a tool, or code, to enable dancers to transform their bodies into various forms.

Collecting the Forms

Prescribing the necessary requirements for the choreographic forms was Hijikata's means of "materializ[ing] the inevitable" (Appendix 1). In other words, it was a means of establishing the real existence of 'things.' For Hijikata, this materialization could be discovered in Goya's pus, Bresdin's chaos of the flower garden, Michaux's light, or Beardsley's extending nerves. His selection of these artists' works was based on a perspective of negativity, but it is hard to discern exactly what this perspective meant to Hijikata.

According to Motofuji, when Hijikata was young, he would walk along the road with eyes closed, asking where the blind located their eyes, or he would decide to be 'crippled' for a month and go around in a plaster cast. I can remember walking along the road with Hijikata and hearing him proclaim before a homeless person, 'that's it!' By which he presumably meant something related to the following statement:

> The satisfied and complete body at the same time wishes to have a disability. I should have been born with a disability. This wish finally arises, as the intimation of *butō*'s first step.[15]

Hijikata's *butō* dancer might be considered as the inverse of a normal dancer. We see this in the tale of children chasing and trying to beat the 'crippled dog' with sticks and stones:

> I am in some way jealous of the dog. This is because the dog is gaining some profit. It is because the dog tempts the human child to any old place, and exposes every posture. The dog does this with his red bowls hanging from his stomach.[16]

Hijikata is suggesting that the 'crippled dog' makes use of its defect by exposing it. This trick to seduce the human is the same as that adopted by the *butō* dancer of 'taking an inverse advantage of un-freedom.' Such an approach stands in opposition to the ballet methodology, seeking to "leap without leaping, and turn without turning."[17] This was not a matter of expressing disability and ugliness, but of analysing it in order to discover an aesthetic of disability and ugliness.

The 'crippled dog' that runs presents life in all urgency. For Hijikata, this urgency brought to light the brilliance of life and a consciousness of beauty. The urgency of life emerges from a negative perspective, through relating to imagery such as pus, sores, insects' itchiness, and death. With the possibility of escape eliminated, the inevitable truths of the body are revealed. The function of negative imagery becomes this facing up to a bodily truth, established through a relation to urgency and un-freedom. This offers a way to condition the movement of the *butō* dancer.

Hijikata's use of negative imagery allowed for a new perspective on the human body, which destroyed established hierarchies, value judgments, and structures of aesthetics or truth. The negative imagery in Hijikata's method was more than a formal technique. It was a comprehensive perspective on movement.

Forced Out Movement

Hijikata's choreographic forms and modes of walking were generated through establishing a relation to imagery using the power of the imagination. This imagery conditioned the "being of nerves" (Appendix 1), while establishing a relation helped condition the concentration of the dancer. In other words, the necessary requirements both direct the concentration and also supply the momentum for the transformation of the body in space. We might also say that, for Hijikata, concentration is located continuously in the moment of awakening, which is facilitated by those necessary requirements that dictate the dispersion of nerves. Hijikata's method of creation using the negative image is clearly shown in the "Walk by Insects," below.

Requirements for "Walk by Insects" (from Ashikawa Workshop, 1989)

a) an insect on the back of the right hand
b) a second insect crawling down the left side of the nape to the back
c) a third insect crawling up from the right inner thigh
d) a fourth insect crawling down from the left shoulder to the chest
e) a fifth insect wherever you feel it
f) itching here and there   can't stand it   pushed by itchiness
g) 500 insects   beneath the chin   behind the ears   behind the elbows   behind the knees around the belt
h) 5000 insects around the eyes   around the mouth   inside the ears   between the fingers   in all the mucous membranes
i) insects in the hair
j) insects in the pores of the skin pores
k) 30,000 insects   eating from the pores   to the internal organs
l) then continuing to eat   out through the pores   surrounding the body   eating the space
m) then insects eating the insects in space
n) insects eating that situation
o) (500,000,000 insects eating the tree – insides are eaten up)
p) it is the final moment (the will i.e. insects/the texture of things)

Considering "Walk by Insects"

"Walk by Insects" starts out from the imagined reality of a single insect on the back of the hand. By sensing a single insect, the hand recoils, 'itchy… itchy.' From the neck another insect crawls, the neck evades, 'itchy… itchy.' The insect crawls up the inner thigh, and the legs float. Itching here and there, unable to stand the itchiness, movement is pushed out. The awareness is localized to the 3cm space occupied by each insect as it eats. This spreads as the insects accumulate: one, two, three. The process of walking is unrelated to the will, and begins as a result of attempting to evade the extreme itchiness. The impossibility of escaping itchiness leaves the individual no choice but to relinquish themselves to the sensation, and become danced by itchiness.

Becoming aware of the insects beneath the chin and behind the ear, becoming aware of those soft and sensitive areas neglected in everyday life, does not mean becoming numb physically through mental concentration, but dispersing into new sensations. Accumulating the places of sensation, without mixing them (mucous membranes, the pores), it is possible to draw closer to the "final moment" with precision. The images move from what can be sensed using the everyday imagination (the pores), towards an entirely new imaginative sensibility (the internal organs, the surrounding space, the insects eating the space). As even time is eaten by insects, the body erodes to become an object standing upright. "[I]t is the final moment" of a dead object, standing upright like a stick. There is "continuity within stasis" at this moment. It is a "great movement" (Appendix 1).

The "Walk by Insects" transforms the body into a form that corresponds to Ashikawa's image of the "stuffed thing" left in a storehouse for 50 years:

> When the storehouse was opened after 50 years, there was the stuffed bird bought by grandfather – full of dust and eaten all over by insects. Opening the storehouse forcefully, light flooded smoothly in, and the insect devoured stuffed thing floated gently. This stuffed thing, emptied out by insects, was blown by a gust of wind, and its loose shape collapsed.[18]

The description progresses towards an image of absolute passivity, a boundless existence, like the "Walk of an Ash Column" discussed earlier.

In terms of the movement this generates: there is a surface appearance of slowness, but an interior movement of continuous and great speed. It is the same appearance of stasis as that of the spinning top that spins at high speed. This seeming surface calm that harbours a high-energy motion was the final goal towards which the "Walk by Insects" aimed. This state became Hijikata's model for standing in near-stasis.

Forced Out Movement

> In the case of "eating," there is being eaten by insects. At first, it is the realm of the sensation of itching or tickling. Gathering up these sensations, the body, eaten out by vipers from the pores to the inner organs, transforms into a stuffed thing. A single insect cannot achieve this. When (as an object) it is eaten by insects, the thoughts that arise when moving or walking fall away… it's that strange condition.

> Leaving that place through itchiness, instead of through walking, because walking is not particularly the means to get ahead. Walking is not a signpost placed for a single purpose. Normally it starts out from walking: 'Walk', or 'Let's walk'…

> There is a fundamental difference. Not walking from the will, but being pushed out. This principle of walking does not exist anywhere else in the world. *Butō* has been reconfigured in this way.[19]

In this description of the "Walk by Insects," we can see that Hijikata's position fundamentally differs from an approach to dance that attempts to walk or move from the will, or even believes such an attempt to be possible. Hijikata did not create movement from the will, but from a principle of movement that emerges when "pushed out." Movement "pushed out" by the itchiness of being eaten by insects, might more simply be termed "leaving that place through itchiness." This movement is directionless. It is not an expression of itchiness. It is rather a question of how far one can relate to itchiness.

The acts of moving and walking are reconceived as that movement which emerges when "pushed out" of a body without will: a body as an "object." In this rejection of the will, Hijikata seemed to ask the question: "isn't it that those things which can be expressed only appear in not expressing?"[20] For Hijikata, expression resulted from establishing a relation to the image, and not from the will to express. Likewise, movement would "only appear" when it was "pushed out." This movement was "pushed out" through the desperate need to form relations. When this emerged, it was as a "materialization of the inevitable" (Appendix 1).

7. The Dissolution of Form

Nikutai no hanran **(Revolt of the Flesh, 1968), by Hasegawa Roku**

Hijikata's *ankoku butō* methodology makes use of a highly specific image-language to refine the dancer's senses and develop a dancing body that can transform itself. This is facilitated by the development of a perceptive neural network, through the careful management of the 'relations' between the body and the image. The 'walk' and 'choreographic forms' are designed as a training for this. The neural network might be considered the key to Hijikata's philosophy of mind, body, and universe. It is accessible through an analysis of the 'walks,' 'choreographic forms,' 'phrases' and 'etudes,' which are notated in the records of his dancers. This notation, and the training required to embody it, conditions the 'becoming' body of *butō*.

This final chapter focuses on the particular image-language of Hijikata's last workshop, conducted around a month before his death. This workshop reveals Hijikata's techniques for training a neural network, it reveals his construction of time, space, and physicality as they were developing in the final phase of his life. This lends new meaning to the earlier 'walks' and 'choreographic forms'. In considering this late phase, I also make use of notes taken in Ashikawa's workshops after Hijikata's death, which offer an insight into the reception and adaptation of the *ankoku butō* methodology in the years that followed.

Hijikata's Last Workshop

The theme of Hijikata's last workshop could be considered: "self-erasure that relates to mechanism" (Appendix 7). The 'choreographic forms' and 'phrases' he used were intended to transform the body of daily life into the *butō* body. This weeklong open workshop was conducted from 24 to 30 November 1985, taking place just months before Hijikata's death on 21 January 1986.

Towards Butō: The Walk

Butō training starts out with the release of a body confined by daily life, as suggested in the words cited earlier:

> 'You have been living with domesticated movement, inflicted by extreme violence, so your concept of the body must be astray.' Saying this, I fix an intense gaze on the body.[1]

Freedom was the starting point for Hijikata's *butō*. The dancer would erase themselves through fixating on an image: "a single thread," for example. Committing to a belief in the "single thread," a dancer could encounter the freedom of being moved.

A "single thread from the solar plexus" suspends the body, and "a single thread from the forehead two threads in the molar teeth threads of both ears [...] countless threads" allure the body into movement. The *butō* body moves freely as a result of these "countless threads," not moving in any particular direction. This freedom is founded on an erasure of the self as the originator of movement: "everything begins from the choice for self-destruction," "the obscurity of the origin is crucial" (Appendix 7). Through conditioning this consciousness, Hijikata guided his pupils on a journey from daily-life to non-daily life, "a mysterious journey to the interior," a journey towards *butō* space-time (Appendix 7).

Butō Movements from the Last Workshop: "<labyrinth of fingers> = dismantling the family," "the theatre of faces," "<hanganbishō>," "four eyes," "face of smell," "gaze into the skull," "face of porcelain," "Redon's single eye" (Appendix 7)

Hijikata brought attention to sites of ready awareness like the fingers or face. He then encouraged movement through establishing a relation to the *butō* image-language, rather than a reliance on the will. The necessary requirements for the image-language of "<labyrinth of fingers>," include "the movement of both elbows guided by thin threads from 10 metres ahead," "the separation of fingers on both hands," and "(dismantling the family)." The dancer's fingers become a family and begin to move by themselves. The dancer establishes a relation to the image of "dismantling," and to the "thin threads" from both elbows moving "10 metres ahead," until movement emerges without conscious design.

The faces instructed by the 'choreographic forms' of "the theatre of faces" (such as "<hanganbishō>"), involve a relation to "light, background darkness, sound, the smell of winter daphnes, awareness of the inside of the skull, temperature, and pain." The faces must shift in "an instant," "changing one after another," through an instantaneous and complete relation to Hijikata's image-language. A physiological analogy to this instantaneous relation can be found in Hijikata's observation that when a burn is received, the individual instantaneously 'becomes.' That is, they are brought into the immediacy of their body. His strict interrogation of this complete relation can be heard in the question: 'is facial expression what you are learning?' *Butō* expression is not the facial expression of emotion, but the paradoxical expression of non-expression.

Towards a Butō Body: "<transparent child of Africa>," "<rotten corpse>," "<huge ancient Lion>," "<rain on the body's illustrated record>" (Appendix 7)

These four 'choreographic forms' are intended to dissolve the borders of the body. In "<transparent child of Africa>," the body walks "together with countless maggots," and is dissolved to become "objectified," like the bones of a "<rotten corpse>."

In "<huge ancient lion>," the simultaneous imagining of whiskers on the outside of the face and "feelers" on the inside of the face, creates a "blurring" of the skin's boundaries. The "blurring" of the body's boundaries corresponds to the objectified (vessel-like) body that has been devoured by the "parasitism" of maggots and flies. The image of the lion further fades with "(the shadow of disappearing flesh)" that may be figured as the "<ghost of the lion>." Following this fading, an imaginative leap from the "<ghost of the lion>" to the "<ghost of a fly>" that buzzes around it brings an accompanying sense of dissolution between inside and outside.

In "<rain on the body's illustrated record>," the body is also imagined in a pictorial way – expanded like a stretched canvas. It is "glued dried and split walking with its condition," to suggest a sensation of dissolution and dryness.

These 'choreographic forms' are connected to the "ash column" or the "walk by insects," in that they represent a state of existence "on the edge" (Appendix 1). In the transformation from a "shadow" to a "ghost," the *butō* body is imagined not as an existing body, but as an "objectified" body – a "shadow."

Butō Space-Time: "<hydrangea>," "<brushing calligraphy>," "<the walk of a desolate cornfield>," "<the walk of the forest's interior>," "<stone in the forest's interior>" (Appendix 7)

To become the "hydrangea" spread and diluted in space, the body enters a state similar to "the fading countless brushes of countless cells," or to the image of "mould." The "mould" floats as hairs in space, like the downy strands of a "dandelion," "dividing in every direction." The similar texture of strands of "corn" develops into "countless" pieces of withered corn, which drift in any direction. The body discovers a directionless sensibility, a feeling of space, which is then closed in on "the construction of a forest using minute feelers." The sense of scale, from "minute feelers" to the expansive "forest," relates to the construction of space in *butō*. The construction of time is managed through the image of duration in the "interior condensation" of a "stone in the forest's interior." The dancer's sense of time is interiorized. Their awareness is brought to "the density of interior condensation = eyes towards the interior."

Direction and Speed in Butō: "<the stone of Maya>," "<the stone of a crocodile>," "<horse>," "<dinosaur>," "<condor (bird)>," "<the dance of birds calling>," "<dragon>," "<dead branch>," "<lightning>," "<forest>" (Appendix 7)

The "stone of Maya" and "stone of the crocodile," represent eternality – like "the speed of the centre of Mandala / that standstill." Layering this illustration of Mandala with the image of the distant time of a stone, *butō* speed becomes visible. *Butō* speed is the physical rendering of "lightning" flashing in an instant, or of "monomania towards the speed of insect's whiskers." It is an internalized speed that appears from the outside as near-stasis.

The waving form of the "letter S" seen in "horse," "dinosaur," "condor (bird)," multiplies into "a sky of a hundred forms of waves – Turner," as though to show the multiple possibilities of waves. The "sky of a hundred forms of waves" swallows the "boy," to conjure an image of an ocean-tossed body that is moved without will. The dancer's self must be "swallowed" and disappear, like the little "boy" moved by the waves. The shifting of a body moved by waves has the same sense of speed and direction as the "organic transformation of airflow," caused by "the dance of birds calling." The image-language requirements of the 'choreographic forms' shape the texture of space, time, and directionality in *butō*. These requirements offer guidance rather than dictate movement, allowing each workshop participant to encounter their own "principle of existence."

The Butō Dancer's Relation to Consciousness and Space

Hijikata's last training practice of "inner feelers" and "outer feelers" aimed to bring together the interior sensation of "peeling the skin of the face" with the exterior sensation of "peeling the skin of a cabbage." By "peeling the skin of the face" a sense of darkness surrounds the body, which is then amplified to the "darkness of a 2-metre diameter." This relates to the "outer feelers," which soften the border of skin, and create a "light of the outline," textured by small "horns, and minute branches." The "extreme minuteness" of these "outer feelers," reaching "infinitely high," is counterbalanced by the "extreme dilution of inner feelers," reaching "infinitely far." These "inner feelers and outer feelers" create an extreme sensitivity to the shifting textures of the border of skin. The *butō* dancer's consciousness is heightened by the emphasis placed on minuteness and "dilution." The "dilution" that transforms into mist develops into the final image: "when he realized he…/<pulling the steep mountain>." In order to pull the "steep mountain" at the end, the body must disappear. Its boundary of skin must become diluted with the use of inner and outer feelers (Appendix 7).

This manipulation of the body consciousness through the use of imagery was the methodology adopted in the 1978 workshop. The 'choreographic form' of the "willow tree space," uses an accumulative image-language to diffuse the body: "the eyelids, the temples, the back of ears, the armpits, the shoulder joints, the hip joints, the back, the ankles; ten, one hundred, one thousand, ten thousand, one hundred thousand, one million, ten million nerves extending out." The body becomes textured, scored by thousands of "grains of wood," eventually disappearing. Then it enters the "dandelion space," where threads extend from the body (Appendix 7):

- a single thread from the forehead
- a second thread from the back of the head
- a third thread from the molar teeth
- leaving these three in place, a fourth to the left
- leaving these four in place, a fifth to the right
- a sixth and seventh thread to the eardrums
  leaving these seven in place, the downy hairs of the dandelion, filling the space
- hairs stem from the soles of the feet, the backs of the ears, the waist
- the weak electric current of space
  a counter-current from each strand of hair towards the joints

In this particular image-language we find a way to connect the internal body and space. This is a tool to condition the *butō* dancer's movement: the speed of movement is dictated by the "electric current of space," and the sensation of floating is encouraged with the diffusion of the senses through smell, sound, and light. The *butō* body always requires "support" of some kind, as Gōda indicated with the statement: the "floating body" of *butō* "cannot be materialized without the support of air," it is an "intermediary measure – a mist, a trail of smoke, a smell," unlike other forms of dance, which "proceed from a physical methodology, rather than the physical feeling of the air." In other forms of dance, air becomes the opponent, the dancer is praised for "holding or pushing air," as a "necessary means of completing or supporting their expression." In *butō* there is "an extreme interchange with the air that surrounds the body," as all five senses are engaged in generating the sensation of mist, smoke, or smell.[2] The language used to engage these senses, makes varied use of qualities such as temperature, humidity, sound, light and smell. It persistently stimulates localized sensitivity in the body, targeting those areas that are hard to sense in daily life, such as the back of the ears, the armpits, or the anus. Even things such as internal organs or brain-capillaries become the subject of the image, so that skin is not experienced as a boundary, but is dissolved and diluted. The skin becomes sensitive to light, so that it is weakened and diffused in space. With weakened skin, the body appears to have returned to the strange original form of a corpse. This detailing of the sensations is unique to the *butō* technique.

The Rugged Mountain Being Pulled

The final day of Hijikata's last workshop (30 November), moved towards an image of death: "<towards the dying forest   towards the dying dance> / <towards light   towards death> <towards non-existence>." He seemed to be voicing a morbid anticipation of his own death, seeking out images of life in death, and of death in life. He was searching for a bodily expression that could find life in the moment of disappearing into light. This disappearance can be seen in the 'choreographic form' of "Bresden's forest" (Appendix 7):

then the branch of a tree is derived and walks in the enormous face of the forest
scent of the forest, corpses of animals, a swarm of flies
when the mists get thicker and thicker
(the extreme dilution of inner feelers and the extreme minuteness of outer feelers)
– infinitely far – infinitely high –

◎ when he realized he –
<the rugged mountain being pulled>
the space full of   a field of hydrangea
an ocean of pus
a desolate cornfield
a thick-grown field of dandelions

The disappearance of an existing body allows for the movement of a "rugged mountain being pulled" to emerge. In Hijikata's method, image-language alone can generate such a process of transformation. This does not require the assertion of muscular force, as in the rhythmical exercise of "flesh-burning" that occurs in Western dance.[3] Rather, as Shibusawa Tatsuhiko has pointed out, it is "a form of dance rooted in the Japanese climate and culture."[4] To "sufficiently express weakening or fragmentation," the body had to become like smoke, like the broken particles of an ash column.

In these final words of the last workshop, various textures allow the existing body to disappear – "diffusing, hazing, and becoming sooty." The space itself is negated and becomes hazy in the "field of hydrangea [...] ocean of pus [...] thick-grown field of dandelions." The *butō* body and its surrounding space transform under the guidance of Hijikata's image-language, to achieve disappearance, negation, and haziness.[5] This process of transformation worked from language to image to sensation to movement, beginning with the alteration of a bodily consciousness, and from a minute awareness of bodily sensations. While it may be possible to transform the everyday body using physical techniques, Hijikata used this image-language instead as his method for transforming the body. The materialization of this image-language in physical form was made possible through training the "circuit of nerves" (the circuit of image → sensation → movement). This "circuit" was the means of cultivating a consciousness of the 'possible' body.

The cultivation of a *butō* consciousness involves moving beyond 'negation' to reach for an eternal or 'infinite world.' It asks for a constant renovation of the body, and a continual effacement of the everyday body. This is equivalent to adopting a "position of hesitation." That is, movement arising in the moment of hesitation itself, as movement that is "pushed out." Sustaining a relation to the continually evolving *butō* image-language, produces a state of "hesitation" and urgency. As a result, "existence is exposed," and both the body and consciousness are transformed. This transformation is motivated by establishing relations to other living things, and these relations place the individual in a "position of hesitation."

The *butō* dancer's individuality is erased in the moment of "hesitation," and they look towards the 'infinite world.' The space of *butō* becomes visible. Dissolving the distinction between inside and outside, space becomes an extension of the feeling, breathing body.

Hijikata's Reception and Influence: The Eyes of the Butō Dancer

Following Hijikata's death, his disciples interpreted and established various methods for creating and teaching *butō*. This included dancers like Tamano Kōichi (dubbed the 'bow-legged Nijinsky' by Hijikata), who established his own group, *Harupin-Ha*. These various methods document the reception and adaptation of Hijikata's *ankoku butō* methodology. In particular, I will consider the work of Ashikawa Yōko, according to notes taken in her workshops following Hijikata's death. Ashikawa studied under Hijikata from 1967 until his death in 1986, and continued to create *butō* long afterwards. It was during the period of her performances with *Hakutōbō* (1974-1976), that the *ankoku butō* methodology is considered to have reached completion. From 1974 onwards, Hijikata had worked intensively with Ashikawa to perfect and classify the 'choreographic forms.' Ashikawa took extensive notes during her 20 years of learning under Hijikata, from which it is possible to deduce her own understanding of the Hijikata method. Ashikawa emphasized the placement of "the *butō* dancer's eyes" in achieving the negation of the self within an infinite world (Appendix 9). She stipulated the conditions of the eyes as part of the 'necessary requirements' for the 'choreographic forms.' These reveal her own vision of Hijikata's *butō*.

The Awakening Body

Butō aims towards the body of 'becoming.' Ashikawa considered this state of 'becoming' as "the continuation of a divided condition" (Appendix 9). In Hijikata's method, the *butō* dancer was forced into a desperate and urgent state as a result of having to continuously relate to the 'necessary requirements' of the 'walks' and 'choreographic forms.' This relational condition is comparable to that of Ashikawa's continual division.

Ashikawa took Hijikata's 'necessary requirements,' and continued to develop them. In the "Walk of a Measure," for example, the "basin on top of the head" and "the soles of the feet on razor blades," became the "air of sulfuric acid" and the "razor blades on the ceiling, walls, and floor", where "nothing lukewarm remains." She would go on: "I am harbouring the obstinate wish of living nowhere but here" (Appendix 9). Ashikawa pushed the body to its limit, creating a state of being divided through an expanding awareness of the ceiling, floor, and walls. When this state became continuous, the *butō* body experienced an "awakening." This "awakening body" was a concept Ashikawa developed following Hijikata's death (Appendix 9).

The "awakening body" develops a "network of nerves" that is sensitized through an extreme awareness of the network's 'mesh' and a sensitivity to the air of sulphuric acid. It is a body 'detached' from the body of everyday life. This "detachment" – the process of transforming an everyday body into a *butō* body – occurs with the shift in consciousness of the dancer, as they become aware of the placement of their eyes (Appendix 9).

Eyes of the Butō Dancer

The 'Eyes' of Eternity and the 'Deviated' Body

Ashikawa's 'walk' included instructions to "watch yourself from afar," or "corr[ect] the *zure* [slippage] of an adult walking on two legs," and "ret[urn] to the origin" (Appendix 9). For Ashikawa, the "origin" existed prior to the "domesticat[ion]" of the body (as Hijikata had described it), prior to the deviation of the everyday body. It was a place from which unwilled movement could emerge, unconstrained by the limitations of everyday space and time. Ashikawa would ask: "now or eternity?"

(Appendix 9). This was not a matter of everyday time, but the particular temporality of *butō*. It could not be accounted for by everyday physics. Ashikawa would describe it as "the descent of a waterfall that could be rising or falling" (Appendix 9). And Hijikata had spoken of it in similar terms, as the time that exists on the reverse side of another time.

This other time is like the difference between time rippling in surface waves, and the eternity of a deep ocean. To reverse the deviation from this eternity was not a return to "the time of preaching" – Hijikata felt "estranged from the world of religion or preaching" – but was conversely a way to "remain close to *this* reality."[6] At the base of Ashikawa's training was the idea that eyes should never stop watching the 'deviation' of the body. Ashikawa's method for teaching the 'choreographic forms' trained the eyes to focus on the deviation that had occurred between the body existing in eternity and the everyday body.

The 'Eyes' of Detached Eyes

The dancer stands alone in space and time, acknowledging the necessary conditions of space. Hijikata speculated on how the conditions of space might be marked by concrete obstacles, asking "why feel that concrete obstacles such as walls are an ending" (Appendix 8). He felt that the work of speaking about the body could only begin at the point of crisis. The ultimate limitation of a "wall" shares this sense of crisis with Ashikawa's "air of sulfuric acid." The question became how to enter this air of walls. For Hijikata, it related to "peeling and becoming a stain" (Appendix 8).

Taking Hijikata's "countless walls" (Appendix 8), Ashikawa developed the 'choreographic form' of a "stain on the wall," in which she specified constantly shifting eyes (Appendix 9). The externalized viewpoint of these eyes, moving from the inner leg to the back, replaced the everyday functions of sight, and caused a division within the dancer's consciousness. The dancers were told to face the concrete obstacle and imagine water coursing through and slackening the wall until the image became associated with their own bodily fluids and intestines. At this point, an imaginative body would begin to enter the wall, stirring a shift in consciousness within the remaining self. Ashikawa would continue to interrogate: 'Are the spine and ribs remaining?' The result of this was a "detachment" from the wall, and a "confront[ation]" between the remaining eyes and the eyes that had entered (Appendix 9). This imaginative encounter with eyes, resulting from "peeling" from the wall, could only arise through sustaining the double image of two bodies simultaneously (Appendix 9).

Hijikata spoke of this duality in his methodology when he described: "the 'double' (the doubled shadow) in the single point of *I*" (Appendix 7). For Ashikawa, this "doubled shadow" became the dual body that united and detached from the wall. That is, the divided consciousness of the *butō* body, into which the everyday body has transformed. For Ashikawa, "no-one is watching the dancing body they are watching the space there is no need for flesh" (Appendix 9).

The actions of this "doubled shadow" were not caused by the will of the subject, but by being made to dance. The self was "being laughed at by a shadow", and "erasing things done by" itself (Appendix 9). Indeed, the *butō* body resulted from the erasure of an actual body, and the basic technique of *butō* resulted from movement that "emerges when pushed out." Ashikawa preserved these essentials of Hijikata's *butō*, when she trained the eyes of the *butō* dancer through the imagining of a dual body.

The Second Eyes

Ashikawa talked of: an "eye on the forehead," "eyeballs on the root-tips of the arbour," "back," "eyeballs beneath the crotch," "eyeballs on the knees," and so on. The eyes on the "arbour," the face, the "hydrangea," and the strands of hair were placed along the body's extension lines, and the eyes from behind small gods, or the ceiling, came from an externalized gaze that made the dancers aware of how far their everyday eyes had deviated (Appendix 9).

The necessary requirements of a tree are found in the deviation that exists between the dancer's own eyes, watching themselves dance, and the "eyeballs on the root-tips of the arbour" (Appendix 9). The eyes of a *butō* dancer are discovered in this deviation, as when they are called to watch both the "stain on the wall" and the body that remains outside the wall. By paying minute attention to the deviation of real and imagined eyes, the existence of eyes accumulate within the "network of nerves," like the mesh of a net. The condition of the eyes generated through an acute attention to the deviation between real and imaginary bodies, led to Ashikawa's desired state of an "awakening body." This methodological approach to the *butō* dancer's eyes, can be further clarified by a description of Hijikata's:

> Sitting on the *engawa* [back porch], watching rain shower down onto the cabbage patch, and wondering when it begins or ends. As the surrounding space intermixes with this beginning-less and endless time of rain, all time and space becomes indiscriminate... aren't I rotting from the core just like the rotting cabbage... but you can't tell from the outside... If you break through the foil of seeing, you dissolve... if you dissolve, you rot, and if you rot, then the second eyes appear...[7]

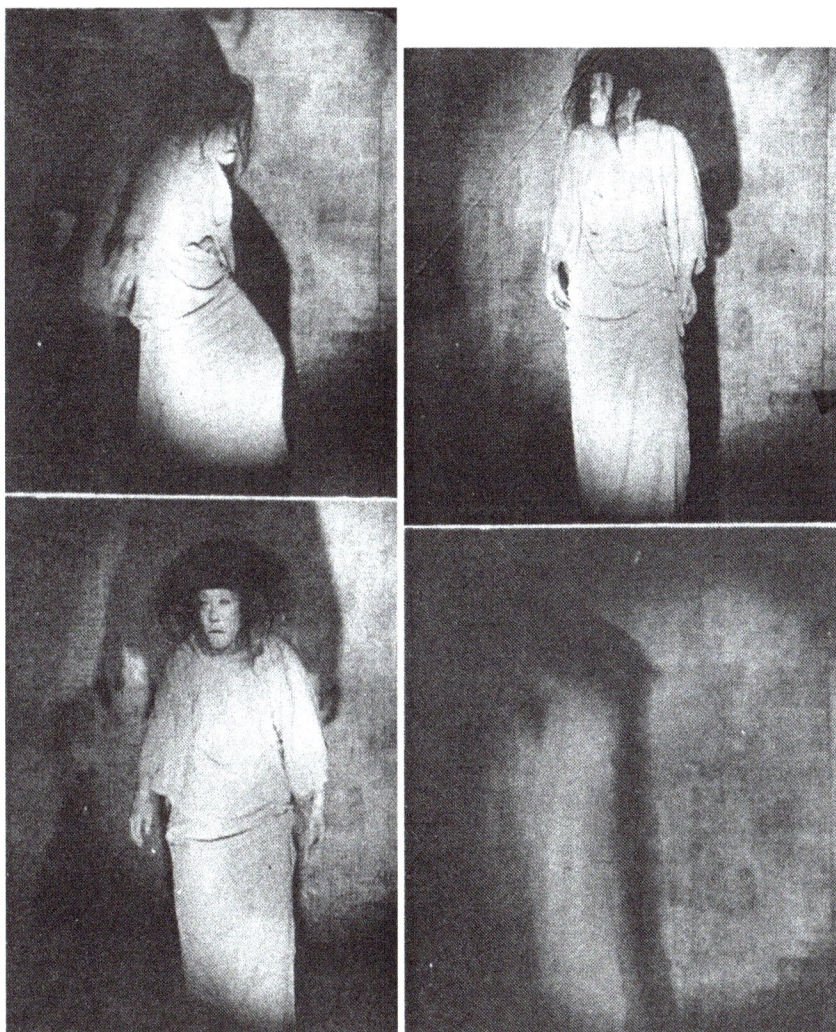

Ashikawa Yōko in Asbestos Studio (1984), by Tatsuruhama Yōichirō

Gazing through this "rain shower," any sense of space and time dissolves like the rotting cabbage. The "foil" of seeing also rots, and the distinction between seeing and being seen dissolves. This dissolution of the "foil" of seeing challenges the *butō* dancer's existing consciousness. They begin to consciously acknowledge the 'deviation' between their real and imaginary body, in a way that awakens an awareness of the *butō* eyes. These *butō* eyes, or "second eyes," as Hijikata described them, surface through the dissolution and rotting of the "foil" of seeing, making eternal space-time visible. By detaching the eyes, Ashikawa brought a consciousness to the 'deviation' between the real and imaginary body, and by placing eyes everywhere – making Hijikata's "second eyes" into third and fourth eyes – she made this deviation feel limitless.

When Ashikawa spoke of the "*butō* dancer's eyes," she was indicating the division within the consciousness of simultaneously seeing and being seen. To reach this ultimate state of consciousness, the dancer's body transformed into the highly sensitized "awakening body," with its neural network like the fine subdivisions of the mesh of a net. Ashikawa spoke of these internal subdivisions in terms of "the ability to be deceived [that] develops inside you once the body can become detached" (Appendix 9). Hijikata's *ankoku butō* used the 'walks' and 'choreographic forms' to condition the dancer's everyday body into an 'awakening body,' with a neural network as minutely detailed as the mesh of a net. In this state of being, the 'imaginary' transforms, at some point, into a 'reality'. The extension of this state of being is the promise that occurs onstage, when the dancer must truly 'become' or 'be,' in a condition of continual transformation. Ashikawa facilitated this transformation by training the *butō* dancer's eyes in a way that sensitized their neural network and allowed for their everyday body to become the "awakening body" of *butō*.

In order to achieve the subtlety of consciousness Hijikata had sought, Ashikawa indefinitely multiplied the *butō* dancer's eyes, and discovered the "awakening body" as an even more 'transparent' *butō* body. A body so 'transparent' that even its many eyes would eventually dissolve into a heightened state of consciousness.

8. Conclusion

Hijikata's *ankoku butō* theory sought to expand the notion of human existence by establishing a body that might metamorphose into any given thing. The basic movement training for this 'possible body' was centred on the 'walks' and the 'choreographic forms.' The concluding commentary of this book will be an attempt to work towards a more refined understanding of this 'becoming' body.

Shizukana ie **(Quiet House, 1973), by Onozuka Makoto**

'Becoming' Authentically

Hijikata appropriated the idea of being '*sur les pointes*' – ballet's attempt to seek height through standing on the toes – to articulate the "being of nerves" as the *butō* dancer's *pointe* (Appendix 1). The "being of nerves" was conditioned through establishing relations to the necessary requirements of the 'walks' and the 'choreographic forms.' The continuation of this relation to the image-language of the 'walks' and 'choreographic forms' led to the transformation of the body which might be considered the movement of *butō*. The space that emerges through this transforming body is the space of *butō*. It is achieved through an image-language that conditions the "being of nerves," or the *"pointe,"* of the *butō* dancer. Relating to this image-language, the *butō* dancer, like a child, becomes "easily deceivable" – they sincerely believe themselves to have become a cow, at the slighted instruction to do so.[1] The *butō* dancer's technique involves learning how to control this image-language and the "being of nerves." The "control of relations" is a way to control the neural network or the "circuit of nerves" that permits the body and sensations to transform. It might be considered a "control" of the consciousness, which hones the concentration in order to awaken the gaze. Ultimately, however, Hijikata aimed towards a technique that could dissolve even this "control of relations" (Appendix 1). This was the ultimate state of the *butō* dancer: an extreme awareness that oscillates between the intoxication of belief and a sense of "awakening." Hijikata described this as 'awakening in the comfortable state of slight drunkenness.' A body in this state can receive unlimited direction, and transform to an unlimited degree. It is, in other words, the 'becoming' body.

Hijikata carefully detailed the necessary requirements of the 'walks' and 'choreographic forms' as the training ground for this 'becoming' body. As the relations to these requirements accumulate, it becomes impossible for the will or reason to keep up. In order to receive these accumulating requirements, the dancer has to relinquish their attachment to the will or reason. This state of receptivity is the work of truly 'becoming'. It is a desperate state that results from the attempt to authentically relate to each individual requirement. Hijikata described this process as the "technique [of] methodological confusion" (Appendix 7). Attempting to relate to multiple requirements simultaneously beyond the capacities of the will, the dancer reaches a limit state. Their selfhood is discarded and they authentically 'become'.

The 'becoming' body may be otherwise termed the 'weakening body.' This is a concept Hijikata developed towards the end of his life, though he left no clear exegesis of its meaning. Nonetheless, this 'weakening body' seems to articulate the ultimate state of the *butō* dancer's body. This is not only a matter of the sick or weak body, but a highly sensitized supple body. It evokes the image of thinning out and disappearing, and the 'choreographic forms' that articulate this erasure. In this place of sickness and weakness, there is a freedom that overcomes space and time, a 'life' into which all consciousness dissolves. This is the state of the 'weakening body' Hijikata worked towards.

A State of Continual Emptiness

The 'becoming' body is the receptive body that can authentically relate to unlimited requirements. This state of receptivity is described by Hijikata as follows:

> A dancing vessel, or a vessel that invites dance in. Either way, this vessel must maintain a state of continual emptiness. When filled to excess, naturally there's a sudden intrusion, and a spirit passes through. The vessel overflows, becomes empty, and the small explosions left by the intruder as its steals out remain. The body continues to move. This state of encouraging emptiness is the rhythm of *butō*. *Butō* is the constant shifting through emptiness. The self and other are held in a state of trance. At the moment of overflowing or stealing out, you are intruded and filled up. This movement of emptiness is itself the vessel. The state of reassurance that comes from overflowing and stealing out, gives rise to the recurrent gestures of *butō*. The self that has stolen away is naturally transformed into the current self.[2]

The 'walk' and 'choreographic forms,' as specified by Hijikata, afford the concrete imagery from which movement may arise. Once established, these images are further detailed until controlling the 'relations' to these details also becomes impossible. At this point, the body must receive the requirements without any attempt to express through the will. Hijikata saw this vessel-like receptivity of the body as necessary to the *butō* body. The basic training for this body was to sensitize the nervous circuit through relating to the 'necessary requirements' of the 'walk' and 'choreographic forms.' This generated a nervous system that could receive thousands of conditions instantaneously; a "vessel" in "a state of continual emptiness." The body as a "vessel" requires the erasure of the flesh and the 'negation' of consciousness. This permits a constant metamorphosis that expands the concept of the human being, and makes visible the 'infinite world.' This was the state of unlimited receptivity Hijikata required of the *butō* dancer.

Hijikata's 'negative perspective' was born out of a desperate state similar to that of the "vessel." Through the desperate attempt to authentically 'become', the dancer revealed the "essence of that which is hidden," "the rich darkness of the human interior."[3] This might also be considered in terms of the grotesque, as a "materialization of the inevitable" (Appendix 1).

Butō is a "state of continual emptiness" in which transformation is limitless, and it is 'possible' to become any other thing. From another perspective, this is the continual process of self-erasure. For Hijikata, 'form is that which appears in the disappearing,' like the moment when "[t]he self that has stolen away is naturally transformed into the current self." This appearance within disappearance relied on the audience's gaze. Transforming what we conceive of as performance was as much the work of the audience as it was of Hijikata. The one watching and the one being watched were interdependent, and to watch necessitated the desire to be watched. At the same time, the realm of the viewer was one into which the dancer could never enter. A great wall stood between them. This eternal barrier between dancer and audience was nonetheless one that had to be broken through, and Hijikata's *ankoku butō* was not afraid to do so.

Hijikata's *butō* asked: 'isn't it that those things which can be expressed only appear in not expressing?' The attempt to express was always clearly visible to the audience. For, as Hijikata would say, the 'audience's gaze is a thousand times faster' than the dancer's. Hijikata's *ankoku butō* sought to express through anti-expression. This related to his theory of the body as something like a single droplet of water, or a dewdrop on the surface of a lotus leaf. In other words, a white sphere. A white sphere at once retains its form and at the same time takes on the colour of the autumn leaf or lotus leaf it rests upon. Even when scattered by a gust of wind, it returns to that original spherical form, and continues to reflect its surrounding landscape. This responsive droplet can receive hundreds or thousands of necessary requirements in an instant – like the *butō* body with its "circuit of nerves," or the "continual emptiness" of a "vessel." The constant transformations that shift through this droplet or "vessel" are physicalized in *butō*.

The *butō* dancer aimed to express 'without expressing'. Hijikata gave over this non-expressive figure to the subjective gaze of the audience, presenting them with 'what could be seen as a bird or a woman.' How to perceive a non-expressive performance was down to each individual audience member. It afforded them the opportunity to 'peek' inside themselves. It was an opportunity to open a door to memory, and discover a past 'life' shared by both dancer and audience. This universal 'life' was only made possible by Hijikata's willingness to acknowledge the equal importance of the audience. It allowed for a purification of both performer and audience.

Hijikata's *ankoku butō* aimed "to leap without leaping, and turn without turning;"[4] that is, to materialize without expressing. To do so, the dancer revealed their inner 'life' and the 'form' of their soul in each instant upon the stage.

9. Afterword: Mikami Kayo's Work since the Publication of The Body as a Vessel

The two additional essays featured here are part of a series of essays written at Kyoto Seika University under the heading, "*Hijikata Tatsumi – ankoku butō no juyō to henyō*" [Hijikata Tatsumi – The Reception and Transformation of Ankoku Butō]. These are followed by a selection of English reviews of Mikami's performance work, *Kenka* [Consecration of Flowers]. As with the body of the text, the citational practice does not reference individual primary works, or page numbers, but does feature a list of works cited. The late addition of these texts meant it was not possible to track down the additional references as it was for the body of the text. The principle texts cited in 'The Reception and Transformation of Hijikata's *Ankoku butō 1*' are as follows: Noguchi Michizō, *Genshoseimeitai toshite no ningen* [Human Beings as Original Life Bodies] (Tokyo: Mikasashobō, 1972); Noguchi, *Noguchi taisō karada ni kiku* [Noguchi Taisō: Listening to the Body] (Tokyo: Hakujusha, 1977); Noguchi, *Noguchi taisō omosa ni kiku* [Noguchi Taisō: Listening to the Weight] (Tokyo: Hakujusha, 1979); Noguchi, DVD book: *Ākaibuzu noguchi taisō – Noguchi Michizō + Yōrō Takeshi* [Noguchi Taisō Archives – Noguchi Michizō + Yōrō Takeshi] (Tokyo: Shunjusha, 2004); Hatori Misao, *Noguchi taisō kankaku koso chikara* [Noguchi Taisō Power from the Sensations] (Tokyo: Hakujusha, 1997); Hatori, *Noguchi taisō shizen jikiden* [Noguchi Taisō Handed Down from Nature] (Tokyo: Hakujusha, 1999); Hatori, *Noguchi taisō nyūmon – karada kara no messēji* [An Introduction to Noguchi Taisō – A Message from the Body] (Tokyo: Iwanami akutibu shinsho, 2003) Hatori, (Tokyo: Shunjusha, 2004); Hatori, *Noguchi taisō kotoba ni kiku* [Noguchi Taisō Listening to Words] (Tokyo: Shunjusha, 2004); Miki Shigeo, *Naizō no hataraki to kodomo no kokoro* [The Work of the Internal Organs and the Spirit of a Child] (Tokyo: Tsukiji shokan, 1982); Miki, *Taiji no sekai* [The World of an Embryo] (Tokyo: Chūkō shinsho, 1983); Miki, *Seimeitaigaku josetsu – kongen keishō to metamorufōze* [An Introduction to Morphology – Fundamental Form and Metamorphosis] (Tokyo: Ubusuna shoin, 1992); Miki, *Umi, kokyū, kodai keishō* [Sea, Breathing, Ancient Form] (Tokyo: Ubusuna shoin, 1992); Miki, *Hito no karada – seibutsushiteki kōsatsu* [The Human Body – A Consideration of the History of Living Things, 1997] (Tokyo: Ubusuna shoin, 1997). The principle texts cited in 'The Reception and Transformation of Hijikata's *Ankoku butō 2*' are as follows: Ishida Hidemi, *Higashiajia no shintai gihō* [East Asian Body Techniques] (Tokyo: Bensei shuppan, 2000); Minamoto Ryōen, *Katachi* [Form] (Tokyo: Sōbunsha, 1989); Minouchi Sōichi, *Tsubo to nihonjin – tōyō dōsagaku e no michi* [The Japanese and Tsubo – The Way to Eastern Movement Studies] (Tokyo: Inaho shobō, 1983); Yuasa Yasuo, *Shintairon – tōyōteki shintairon to gendai* [Body Theory – Eastern Body Theory Today] (Tokyo: Kodansha gakujutsu bunko, 1990); Yuasa, *Shintai – tōyōteki shintairon no kokoromi* [The Body – Attempt at an Easter Body Theory] (Tokyo: Sōbunsha, 1977); Yuasa, *Ki, shugyō, shintai* [Energy, Religious Practice, and the Body] (Tokyo: Hirakawa shuppansha, 1986); Yuasa, *Nihon kodai no seishin sekai – rekishi shinrigakuteki kenkyū no chōsen* [The Spiritual World of Ancient Japan – The Challenge of Historical Psychological Research] (Tokyo: Meicho kankōkai, 1990); Yuasa, *Kyōjisei no uchūkan – jikan, seimei, shizen* [The World-view of Shared Time – Time, Life, and Nature] (Tokyo: Junbunshoin, 1995); Yuasa and others, *Iwanami kōza – tetsugaku 9 shintai kankaku seishin* [Iwanami Lectures – Philosophy 9 Body Sensations Spirit] (Tokyo: Iwanami shoten, 1986); C.G. Jung (Matsushiro Yōichi and Watanabe Manabu trans.), *Jiga to muishiki* [Self and the Unconscious] (Tokyo: Shisakusha, 1984); Shimazu Akira and Matsuda Seishi eds., *Okaruto no shinrigaku – sei to shi no nazo* [Occult Psychology – The Mystery of Life and Death] (Tokyo: Saimaru shuppankai, 1989).

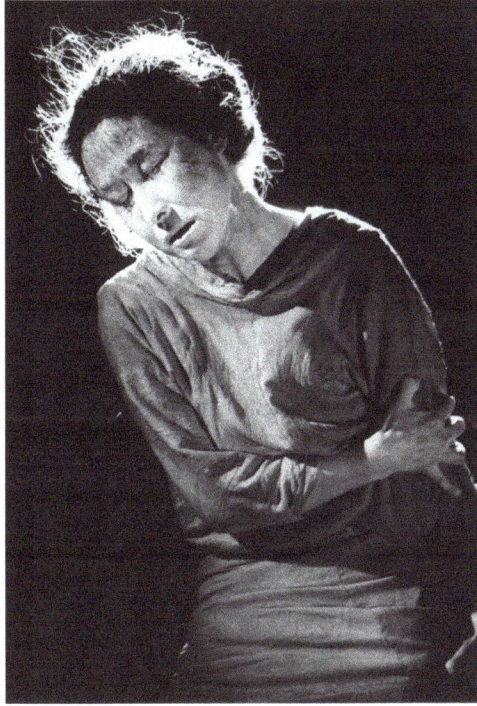

First performance of *Kenka* (1992), by Taniguchi Masahiko

Kenka in Avignon (1993), by André Chambat

Kenka (1993), by André Chambat

With Kudō Taketeru in *Kokuriko* (1998), by Taniguchi Masahiko

Kokuriko (1998), by Taniguchi Masahiko

Torifune Butoh Sha in *Kokuriko* (1998), by Taniguchi Masahiko

While many *butō* dancers and companies have been influenced by Noguchi Michizō's *noguchi taisō* method, Noguchi and the founder of *butō* never actually met. Nor was there any direct connection between Hijikata and Noguchi's contemporary at Tokyo University of the Arts, the anatomist, Miki Shigeo. My own work, however, has been influenced by the work of both Hijikata and Noguchi as teachers, and also by Miki's conception of morphology, as introduced to me by Noguchi.

Hijikata, Noguchi, and Miki all shared in the drive to recover an idea of the human: for Hijikata, the concept of the human being could be expanded through a bodily metamorphosis into all other living things; for Noguchi, a revolution of the human being could be brought about through *taisō* [gymnastic exercise]; and for Miki, a memory-trace of life could be recovered. Their respective approaches to this problem were remarkable. What lay behind them was a critique of modern rationalization, conceptions of objectivity, and a homocentric world-view.

This generation of thinkers were asking anew the questions: 'What am I?' 'What is the human?' They did so through a return to the human body as the grounds for conception and sensation. *Noguchi taisō* had come into being on the arid planes of post-war defeat, *ankoku butō* had arisen through the awakening of an individual and national sensitivity to the flesh body in the context of post-war Westernization, and Miki's subjective approach had grown within the context of conventional science. The ways in which we live as individuals, ethnic groups, and human beings, had become less clear within the context of globalization, rising information technologies, and advancements in medical science – 'I' was becoming an increasingly thin and distant concept. It was with this reality in mind that Hijikata said to me twenty years ago: 'you cannot be made thin by the bite of the mosquito that is information'.

My aim here is to seek out the new reality of the body in the 21st century, through a consideration of the relation between language, body, and image, in the works of Hijikata, Noguchi, and Miki. This is born out of a research project at Kyoto Seika University into the reception and transformation of Hijikata's *butō*.

The State of Butō and Hijikata Research Since 1997

The Publication of Butō-fu and Deciphering the Code of Hijikata's Language

I began my research into Hijikata's *butō* in 1988, having been told by an aesthetician that it was my work to translate Hijikata's words into Japanese. My postgraduate thesis was published in 1991, followed by the initial version of "The Body as a Vessel" in 1993, as the first of its kind. The slow progress of *butō* research partly results from the obscurity of Hijikata's language, and the unavailability of his enigmatic notation '*butō-fu*'. My book was the first publication to make available this *butō-fu*, and to offer an analysis of how it works. The dance critic, Ichikawa Miyabi, commented that my work revealed 'areas of *butō* that are impossible to access', and that it deciphered the code of Hijikata's language.

Since my publication, no significantly new analysis of Hijikata's method has occurred. Kurihara Nanako published translations of Hijikata's work in 2001, which relied heavily on my own decoding of his method [as is outlined in 'The Reception and Transformation of Hijikata's *Ankoku Butō* 2' below], but this did not represent a seriously new contribution to understandings of how the method works. The dissemination of materials relating to Hijikata has nonetheless improved, with the Hijikata Tatsumi Archive opening at Keio University Art Centre in 1998, and a growing number of international symposia focusing on *butō*. In addition to this, Hijikata's disciple, Waguri Yukio, released a CD-ROM containing recordings and analyses of the *butō-fu* that same year. *Butō* research, particularly abroad, continues to grow as a result, though it still remains unclear how *butō* is growing and changing.[1]

Embryological Alchemy: Kawamura Satoru's Theory of 'Yameru maihime' and Kasai Akira's 'Future Butō'

Hijikata famously described *butō* as 'a corpse hanging upright'. This figuring of the *butō* body tore apart existing conceptions of the mind-body connection, and treated the flesh body as an object, estranged from human thought. This raised the problem of the dancer's consciousness in relation to dance forms that conceive of the human body as either doll-like or god-like.

Rehearsal in Brno, Czech Republic (1999)

Both Kawamura Satoru's analysis of *Yameru maihime* in terms of alchemical processes, and Kasai Akira's theory of 'future *butō*' drawn from his work with Rudolf Steiner's Eurhythmy, take Hijikata's *butō* as the transcendence of individual life, through the discovery of the shared life of subjects and objects. Kawamura considers Hijikata's highly enigmatic *Yameru maihime* to be a text of 'recall' rather than 'reminiscence', discovering an 'embryological alchemy' in its final chapter. In Kawamura's reading, the alchemical metamorphosis of the flesh body in Hijikata's work, is like the search for an elixir of life – distilled from an otherworldly chrysalis, as the 'refinement and separation of death'.

Kasai sketches an overview of the history of dance: from the tripartite spirit of ancient temple dances, through the bisected spirit of ballet, to the monism and objectification of contemporary dance. Hijikata's work resists, however, the easy option of objectification, and instead proposes a 'thing-in-itself', treating the 'spirit as a tool' for the expressive act. The *butō* body becomes, then, like 'the codeless form of a corpse'. Hijikata's work is completely committed to preserving this space of the object. It is a 'philosophy of innocence' that urges back through the forces of gravity and time, towards the 'first moment', the embryological space-time. This embryological space-time is prior to the subject-object division – it does not represent a model of monism, but an image of 'a corpse hanging'.[2]

Applying white paint in the dressing room at Brno, Czech Republic (1999)

Tokijikuno Kaguno Konomi (Tachibana Mandarin, 2000), by Tanaka Hideyo

Tokijikuno Kaguno Konomi (Tachibana Mandarin, 2000), by Tanaka Hideyo

The Structural Relation of the Image and the Body: Butō-fu and Butō Workshops

Waguri Yukio and Kobayashi Saga's Reception of Butō-fu

Waguri Yukio trained and performed with Hijikata from 1970 to 1977, during which time the *butō* method was consolidated. The detailed notes Waguri took from this time are organized into seven discrete image-worlds on the 'Butoh Kaden' CD-ROM, beginning from the condition of 'magma': 'World of Abyss', 'World of Neurology', 'World of Flowers', 'World of Birds and Beasts', 'World of Wall', 'World of Burnt Bridge', and 'World of Anatomy'. In total these are made up of 88 *butō-fu*.

Kobayashi Saga also took detailed notes for the duration of her time at Asbestos Studio (1969-74). She has since organized these *butō-fu* around the central form of the 'embryo', as: 'light ball', 'high bird', 'heat haze-state', 'gentlewoman', 'little girl-state', 'plant-state', 'darkness and chaos', 'lizard and earthworm', 'boiled sweets', 'ghost-state', 'old woman-state', 'animal-state'.

Both Waguri and Kobayashi work from ideas of horizontality: the disintegration of 'particles' onto a horizontal plane. Their divisions of the various states of the body are in-line with my systematization of the *butō-fu* in *The Body as a Vessel*. Both propose the idea that Hijikata begins in a possible space, the space of the 'embryo' or 'magma', from which the body can transform into any other thing.

Conception of the Body: Butō Dancers Workshops

The workshops of other *butō* dancers make it possible to get a sense of how *butō* has changed over time, and how it has been received or adapted by subsequent generations.[3]

Ōno Yoshito, who performed with Hijikata during the early 1960s, invites participants in his workshops to become the 'moon', or to 'wring' their bodies out. The importance of the image in his work, and that of his father Ōno Kazuo, allows the individual's emotions and feelings to fall away. Tamano Kōichi, who worked with Hijikata from the late-1960s to the mid-1970s, and then moved to San Francisco, drew particularly on Hijikata's imagery of wind and smells moving the body. His work has also been informed by a knowledge of Martha Graham's use of contraction and release techniques, as well as other forms of American dance. Waguri, who trained with Hijikata throughout the 1970s, focusses on the more formal *butō-fu*, like 'Maya'. He also allows participants to develop their own choreographies based on forms like: 'Bacon's faces', 'Flower', and 'Beast'. The consolidation of Hijikata's technique during the 1970s, and its final form in the 1980s, was passed down to his principle dancer, Ashikawa Yōko, whose workshops I attended in 1989 and 1990.

The third generation of *butō* dancers appeared in the 1990s. An artist like Kudō Taketeru takes as his principle theme an 'interrogation of walking on two legs', and draws on Noguchi's work to build a sequence that moves from the 'embryo', through 'inchworm' and 'beast', towards 'standing'. Kudō places an emphasis on a low centre of gravity, and on the 'necessary emergence of the limbs'. The image, for Kudō, is what allows the necessary to emerge.

Dancers like Kudō or Min Tanaka, and groups like *Sankai Juku* and *Dairakudakan*, have drawn on *noguchi taisō* in their work.[4] They take from Noguchi's work an idea of 'listening to the body', which articulates Hijikata's idea of not using the 'body as a tool for expression'.

With Tamano Kōichi in *Hinomoto* (2001), by Sakauchi Futoshi

"On the road" in the old town of Ljubljana, Slovenia (2002)

"On the road" in the old town of Ljubljana, Slovenia (2002)

"On the road" in the old town of Ljubljana, Slovenia (2002)

"On the road" in the old town of Ljubljana, Slovenia (2002)

Poster for "Bakke" (2003)

A Comparison with Noguchi's Use of Language and the Image

The Reality of the Body and its Language: The Matter of Phonology

For Hijikata, 'a poverty of language meant a poverty of sensation'. This is why *butō-fu* was such an important component of his method. For Noguchi, too, language held the secret to transforming the body's consciousness and to the possibility of creation. Both Hijikata and Noguchi, at the same time, believed that only through 'trying things with the body' could they be understood.

Like Hijikata, Noguchi deployed a large number of coinages and made use of onomatopoeia: 'ash column', 'wind *daruma* [Bodhidharma]', 'head of the anus' (Hijikata), or 'original-life body', 'slipping to sleep', 'hanging up', or 'vel-na (inverse navel)' (Noguchi). These facilitated various transformations of the body. Hijikata's text, *Yameru maihime*, is like a testimony of a child hiding inside the wardrobe, which describes these transformations of the body with unimaginable speed. In the studio, too, Hijikata would fire language at his disciples, sounding like a comic story-teller whose language is constantly shifting between subject and predicate. This was his way of 'deceiving' the body, as the little girl is deceived in the photo series *Kamaitachi*. Hijikata's characteristic speed was also visible onstage, which he treated like a 'live broadcast', in which the dancer's half-awakened body transforms continuously. Hijikata's language could not be divided into parts, it formed a stream of images that worked as a "technique [of] methodological confusion" (Appendix 7). This technique, like an accumulation of *zen kōan*, undermined the conscious control of the body and any sense of individual identity, in order to establish a space for the *reality* of the body. Hijikata, like Noguchi, treated his body as the dwelling place of reality. Even his dying words, recounted to me by his daughter, seem to reflect this peace with the body: 'I am passing away within the light of a God'. Both Hijikata and Noguchi were ultimately searching for this reality of the body through their use of language.

Noguchi understood that there was a gap between language and sensation. His attempt to express the 'sensations that cannot be put into words' *in* words accepted this contradiction: for 'there is no objectivity that exists without subjectivity', 'no sensation that exists without illusion', and 'no understanding that exists without misunderstanding', for Noguchi. His method of 'listening to the body' was like a 'monologue or silent reading', in which the contents of the body changed through 'inner movement'. The origin of language itself could be discovered through this absorption of words into the body. Both the origins of voiced language and the origins of scripted Kanji in ancient Chinese pictographs, could be rediscovered with this new awareness of the origins of human thought. And retracing the distinct sounds that make up the Japanese phonology could afford the possibility of new combinations in language, for Noguchi.

Subjecting the body to language – either through "methodological confusion" or through 'listening to its weight' – both Hijikata and Noguchi overcame dualism, and transformed the body into an object. They were establishing a 'philosophy of the image' and of 'the body'. The possibilities of language, discovered through new word coinages, represented a challenge to the supremacy of the mind, rationality, and objectivity. This made space once again for the potential of the body.

The Body's Inner Sensations Awakened by an Image-Language

In Laban notation, the quality and quantity of movement is decided by the notation of body, force, space, and shape.[5] Considering the shared key-words of Hijikata and Noguchi (time, space, and force), it is possible to characterise their perspective on the body, movement, the human being, and the world.

The 'Water-bag' and 'Ash Column': A Dynamism of Collapse

Hijikata described the compositional treatment of outward space in modern dance as a kind of 'space-phobia', whereas *butō* allowed for 'the creation of space'. *Butō* movement was not reliant on outward space so much as the sensation of inner space-time. The images of a 'water-bag' (Noguchi) and 'ash column' (Hijikata) suggest this sensitivity to the inner space-time. Rather than resist gravity and rely on a contraction of the muscles, the 'water-bag' body relies on the 'secrets of nature' and 'the main energy of weight'. Noguchi fine-tuned the collapse of inner weight in order to position the body between balance and imbalance. This focus on the 'inner', established a deep sensitivity to the muscles, tendons, joints, and internal organs. With the 'water-bag' image, movement is born from within the body through an attention to the body's weight and flow.

Hijikata's image of the 'ash column' figures the body as a mass of tiny particles, barely able to stand, and ready to collapse at the blink of an eye with a sudden gust of wind. This key image in Hijikata's repertoire changes the quality and space of the body by transforming it into floating particles. The closing words of Hijikata's last workshop, just several months before he passed away, reflect this transformation of the body into particles, and the transformation of space that results from it:

> the space full of a field of hydrangea
>
> an ocean of pus
>
> a desolate cornfield
>
> a thick-grown field of dandelions (Appendix 7)

The spinning top that seems to be standing still is actually constantly losing its balance. The constant collapse of the 'water-bag' or the instantaneous collapse of the gravity-less 'ash column', reveal the moment by moment flow of time. This 'collapsing instead of standing' (Hijikata), or dynamism of collapse, inverts the normal starting point of dance: that of standing.

Space and the Periphery of Skin: "Inner Feelers – Outer Feelers" (Appendix 7) and 'Deep Body Sensation'

My body becomes '*me*' through the skin that envelops it. Hijikata worked with images that weakened this periphery of skin ("inner feelers – outer feelers") in his final workshop. When the nerves and mind are able to return to their original form, opening out through this permeable skin, the sensations become receptive and synthetic. Noguchi also sought the receptivity of "inner feelers" in his idea of the sensitivity of inner organs, and 'deep body sensation'. This has a common ground with *nō*, which also used the inner sensations and ideas of multi-directionality to construct ways of standing.[6] Both Hijikata and Noguchi expanded the space of the body through weakening its periphery, conceiving of the inner and outer space as one: for Noguchi, the 'surface world was not clear', and for Hijikata, 'the inside was outside and the outside, inside'. Hijikata's idea of a 'wind *daruma* [Bodhidharma]' and Noguchi's 'theory of the unconscious subject' both indicate this weakening of the individual's periphery in order to enable the body's transformation.

The idea of a 'wind *daruma*' comes from Hijikata's lecture of the same name, *Kaza daruma* (Wind Daruma, 1985). In this lecture he tells a story from the *Nihon ryōiki* (Japanese Miracle Chronicle) of a priest who burns his own body and cries out. Like the monk, the 'wind *daruma*' has been burned up. Telling its story from the doorway, its voice gets lost in the wind and snow, and eventually it, too, dissolves. The 'wind *daruma*' is a body without surround. Like the *Nihon ryōiki*, this is the tale of a near-death-experience: it reflects a kind of sunken consciousness, or 'zero' condition. Noguchi's 'theory of the unconscious subject' similarly articulates an uncontained consciousness that moves towards the world of 'negation' and limitlessness.

San Gettan at Kyoto University's Western Auditorium (2004), by Mashimo Shūhei

San Gettan at Kyoto University's Western Auditorium (2004), by Mashimo Shūhei

San Gettan at Kyoto University's Western Auditorium (2004), by Mashimo Shūhei

Hōzuki (Chinese Lanterns, 2006), by Tanaka Hideyo

Hōzuki (Chinese Lanterns, 2006), by Tanaka Hideyo

Hōzuki (Chinese Lanterns, 2006), by Tanaka Hideyo

Hōzuki (Chinese Lanterns, 2006), by Tanaka Hideyo

With Ōno Yoshito in *Hōzuki* (Chinese Lanterns, 2006), by Tanaka Hideyo

Workshop at Kuro-Kinkaku in Ōiso (2008)

With Tamano Kōichi in *Hinomoto* (2008; in the UK), by Adam Holloway

Hinomoto (2008; in the UK), by Adam Holloway

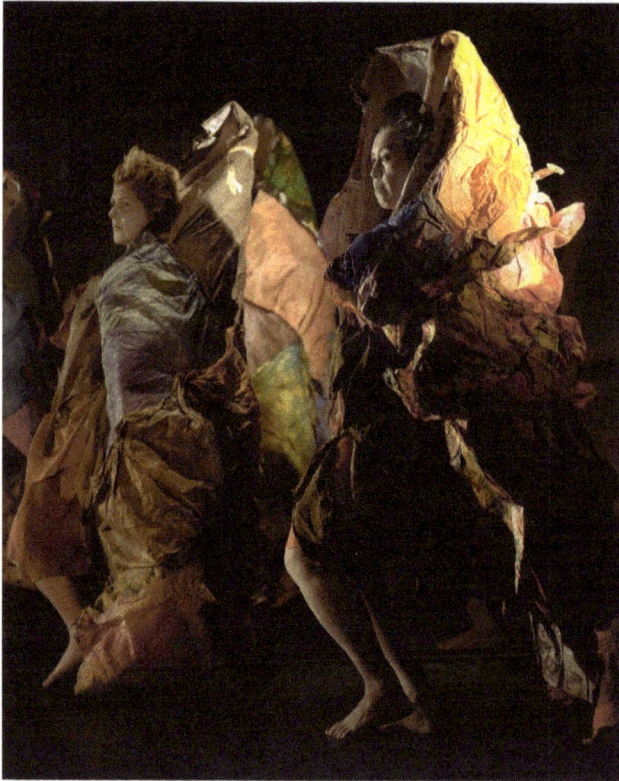

Hinomoto (2008; in the UK), by Adam Holloway

Hinomoto (2008; in the UK), by Adam Holloway

Hinomoto (2008; in the UK), by Adam Holloway

Mikami Kayo in *Hinomoto* (2008), by Sakauchi Futoshi

The Metamorphosis of Continual Transformation: Towards the Source of Life

The world of 'negation' and limitlessness, prior to the subject-object divide, is articulated in Noguchi's idea of an 'original life body', and Hijikata's conception of a 'weakening body'. Noguchi developed the term from the Russian biologist, Alexander Oparin, whose work, *The Concept of Life*, posited the possibility that life developed out of coacervates (the separation of liquid and liquid) forming in the primordial oceans of the earth. This evolutionary theory, for Noguchi, indicated the ultimate relatedness of all life, and suggested a time before the differentiation of beings. The 'original life body' was like the body that 'loosens and relaxes' when it gets into the bath at night, feeling as though it has no concrete substance. This 'original life body' is based on the 'principle of release', which suggests that ever since human beings evolved to walk on two legs and developed a culture using tools, they have sought out forms of mental rest in the state of being unconscious, as well as physical rest.

The 'original life body' and 'theory of the unconscious', and the 'weakening body' and 'wind *daruma*' propose a space in which subject and object are undifferentiated. They establish a condition of the body in which it can transform, or metamorphose, into any other living thing.

Noguchi's idea of the 'secrets of nature' was also the basic principle of Hijikata's 'becoming body': a body fine-tuned to become anything from the wind, to a rock, to a plant, to an animal. Noguchi used more concrete tactility to similarly fine-tune the senses: he would encourage you to touch the many objects and toys in his studio, from spinning tops to *washi*. For both, this related to an idea that in mineral life we might discover human ancestry – either as the origin of life, for Noguchi, or as the deep memory of the dead that lives within us, for Hijikata. These conceptions of the origin of human life on earth, also connect to the appearance of an original culture, with the arrival of the gods. Hijikata's search between light and darkness for the origin of culture, and Noguchi's search for the source of life in images of insects and foetuses, was ultimately grounded through the body.

Original Form and Metamorphosis: Miki's Morphology

The Ancient Memory of Life

Noguchi's theory of our ancestral relation to plants was based on Miki's morphological conception of an ancient memory of life. Miki's theories of anatomy, embryology, and Palaeozoic sciences, drew from the plant theories of Johann Wolfgang von Goethe, the life science theories of Ludwig Klages, and the embryological theories of Ernst Haeckel.

Miki conceived of plant and animal life as stemming from the same origin in water. He figured their divergence at the point where non-photosynthetic life (animal life) was forced to develop the tools for finding food: 'feelers, and the means of movement'. He similarly described the development of the organs in evolutionary terms, and the connection between the human internal organs and the organs of plants. The human body still retains this relationship to plant life, and returns to this 'zero' condition when it is in a state of relaxation. This connects Miki's theory to Noguchi's idea of the 'relaxed' body.

I have been using Noguchi's techniques for relaxation at workshops and in seminars for many years. After a half-year of using these relaxation techniques with a seminar group, they are ready to paint themselves white and perform our 'ancient memory' as amateur *butō* dancers. It can take three hours for them to work through the stages of our 'ancient memory': from an egg, to a fish, to an amphibian, to a reptile, to a human being standing. It requires them to listen to their bodies through a sensitivity to both inner and outer sensation.

Leading this seminar for over five years, I have been surprised by the results. From a training of 'relaxation' it is possible for students to understand what Noguchi termed the 'reward from the gods of nature, that is, the sensation of feeling good'. They begin to understand that the human body, and the human weight can be trusted – that 'weight is energy'. It is a first initiation into an encounter with death. This 'zero' state of relaxation represents a flesh body that can overcome the restrictions of the everyday, and attain a means of standing and walking without aim. The hour it takes for these students to walk down the corridor, followed by the two hours it takes them to move towards the lake, goes by in an instant. Completely relaxed, the students collapse every time they attempt to stand, they become absorbed in minute details – their own hands, far off sounds – and are sometimes moved to tears. One student, crying as we returned to the classroom, said: 'the scariest thing is to encounter yourself'. Their words seemed to echo Hijikata's: 'the furthest thing in the universe is my own flesh body'; and reflect Miki's idea of the 'distant senses'.

Workshop at the Samuel Beckett Centre

Miki considered the human desire to defy gravity to be unnatural when the natural state of plant life is to reach up towards the sun *through* being rooted. He believed we could fine-tune our meditational and universal sensibilities through connecting to the life of plants. Miki's theories represent an opposition to Western modernism, and a release from a logical or egocentric world-view. This is why Eastern ideas became so popular in the 1950s: they proposed another way forward. It is also why a Slovenian university student cried at one of my workshops, saying: 'I've been released from the suffering of my ego'.

In 2004, I received a grant to lead workshops at The Samuel Beckett Centre at Trinity College in Dublin. The participants struggled to just 'do nothing'. In Japan, this time of doing nothing is considered beautiful – as the place to learn from nature. The *nō* master, Zeami, for example, believed expression could only flourish slowly, like the blooming of a flower. Hijikata also proposed a method of 'expressing without expression'. He believed that in 'tying up' the flesh body and consciousness of the *butō* dancer, the mind-body could be truly reunited. Similarly, in *nō*, all obstacles of division were overcome through a commitment to 'form'.

These methods, like Noguchi's theory of relaxation, aimed to return the body to its natural state. Rather than rely on the use of muscles, they attempted to establish a connection between the body and the earth. For Hijikata, this was drawn from the influences of agriculture and folk dances, and connected more to plant life than animal life. He treated the body more like the 'smoke that comes from burning mugwort', than the 'burning of muscle' that fuels most Western dance. This method of becoming like 'smoke' or 'doing nothing' was new to the workshop participants. It represented the peacefulness of becoming a 'thing'. Like the symbol of an egg standing on a single point, a 'thing' exists with a certain peacefulness. This point of balance, for Hijikata, was achieved through the 'sinking' position of *ganimata* [bow-legged], and represented a means to connect more strongly to the earth.

Crying Without Reason: Communicating with the Audience

The paradox of 'expressing without expression' can only be resolved within the experience of the audience. The audience mediate the dancer's body, oscillating between 'distant' and 'proximate sensations' (Miki). Human thought is based on the powers of 'objectivity and the imagination', for Miki, which makes possible this mediation. The evolutionary development of humans, from the breathing of fish ('life breathing') to the breathing of humans ('intentional breathing'), brings both the possibility of thought, and the feeling of suffocation. Only humans are able to feel the forces of happiness and unhappiness. At the same time, it is possible to open up to the world, and to feel the rhythms of universal sensations in the shared world of performer and audience. I have often thought this when foreign audience members claim they 'cry without knowing why', when watching a performance.

This surpassing of the individual through a 'life memory' that is shared and communicated to the audience, overcomes boundaries in the same way Miki's morphology bypassed divisions between inside and outside, or this world and the world after death.

Conclusion: Becoming 'I' from the World of a Foetus

The flavour of an era can change in an instant. The once shocking *butō* has become something of a classic; the cutting-edge didacticism of Noguchi has entered textbooks on educational theory; and the esoteric science of Miki has been taken up by the well-known poet, Yoshimoto Takaaki. It is not so incongruous anymore to find *noguchi taisō* or *ankoku butō*, or any number of Occult traditions relating to 'energy' or '*ki*', discussed in relation to modern science.

Hijikata sought to recover the body's connection to its ancestors and the world through approaching the lives of animals and plants. In this way he hoped to rectify the straying of the institutionalized body. This theory underpins the metamorphic *butō* body, as another configuration of 'becoming *me*' – Noguchi's idea of returning to the 'root' of *I*.

Miki gave preference to the sensations of plant life in order to rediscover a 'natural' time: the time of the meditation in the womb. The plant is interconnected with the earth through the 'distant sensations' of its roots. Human beings, too, can access these 'distant sensations' through becoming aware of their ancestry in plant life. According to this world-view, Hijikata's idea that 'the furthest thing in the universe is my own flesh body' is no longer metaphorical. In Hijikata's last workshop, images of roots extending into the earth, and tree branches extending into the sky featured repeatedly: images of a body connected to the earth, unified with it. For Noguchi, listening to the 'weight' of the body, could equally establish a connection to the earth.

The undifferentiated life that Noguchi articulates in his concept of an 'original life body', is like the achievement of enlightenment described by the Buddhist scholar, Tamaki Kōshirō: where the body gradually evaporates into an encompassing sphere. This expresses the possibility that through evaporating into the universe like nebulae, dancing like foetuses, entering the time of a meditation in the womb, we can experience the reality of a hidden universe.

Hijikata's *butō* was more than just a moment in (or under) history, it remains a history of life, written through our everyday actions – what Miki called the 'manifold diary' of experienced space and time. Hijikata, Noguchi, and Miki, sought to activate our inner awareness within the realm of the everyday – to return us to the 'force of life' that exists within our ancient ancestry and memories of infancy, and to build towards a new understanding of humanity in the future.

Mikami Kayo applying white paint to Eithne McGuinness at Dublin's Samuel Beckett Centre (2004), by Sakauchi Futoshi

Pre-stage open-air performance at Dublin's Samuel Beckett Centre (2004), by Sakauchi Futoshi

"On the road" in Tatton Park, Cheshire (2008), by Adam Holloway

"On the road" in Tatton Park, Cheshire (2008), by Mikami Yukio

"On the road" in Tatton Park, Cheshire (2008), by Adam Holloway

"On the road" in Tatton Park, Cheshire (2008), by Adam Holloway

"On the road" in Tatton Park, Cheshire (2008), by Adam Holloway

Shiawase no Hibi (Days of Happiness, 28 March 2009) by Nakai Hideaki

Gangio Gangioma (2011), by Sakauchi Futoshi

Gangio Gangioma (2011), by Sakauchi Futoshi

Gangio Gangioma (2011), by Sakauchi Futoshi

Gangio Gangioma (2011), by Sakauchi Futoshi

With Ōno Yoshito in Gangio Gangioma (2011), by Onozuka Makoto

Gangio Gangioma (2011), by Onozuka Makoto

With Tamano Kōichi in Gangio Gangioma (2011), by Onozuka Makoto

With Ōno Yoshito in Gangio Gangioma (2011), by Onozuka Makoto

Mikami Kayo in Gangio Gangioma (2011), by Sakauchi Futoshi

The Reception and Transformation of Hijikata's Ankoku Butō 2: The state of Research and the Problem of Academic Misconduct

'*Butō* is already old,' claimed Hijikata, before his death in 1986. 50 years have passed since the creation of *butō*, and around 30 years since it first spread abroad. '*Butō*', or 'Butoh', has become something of a canonised term. 'Butoh' festivals, dancers, and researchers can now be found all over the world – from Europe to Africa. In Japan, all the same, *butō* still occupies a backseat position. With young dancers often traveling abroad to train, *butō* has become another style among the many genres of contemporary dance. This shift in the reception of *butō*, both in Japan and abroad, has been fuelled by a rise in body consciousness and an expansion of the field of the performing arts. It has also been facilitated by the growing interest in Eastern philosophies such as *zen* and qigong, and by the fads for yoga or macrobiotic nutrition that can be seen in places like New York.

The death of *butō* co-founder, Ōno Kazuo, in 2010, at the age of 103, once more raised the question: 'What is *butō*?' The long-standing critic of butō, Gōda Nario, claimed that Ōno was not a *butō* dancer, so much as a modern dancer. Gōda's comment reanimated a consideration of the meaning behind Hijikata's conception of the flesh and its means of expression in *ankoku butō*.

Evaluating developments in *butō* research and performance practices since the turn of the millennium in the light of Eastern body theories, I hope to discover some of the possibilities left open to *butō*.

The State of Butō Research

MA and PhD theses relating to *butō* are being written on subjects like Hijikata Tatsumi, Ōno Kazuo, *Sankai Juku*, and Eiko & Koma, globally. The wider availability of information in the age of the internet has allowed for research knowledge to migrate more quickly abroad. At the same time, this increases the responsibility of universities, publishers, and conference organisers, in establishing the validity of source materials.

In 2001, *The Drama Review* published a special edition on the work of Hijikata Tatsumi and contemporary Japanese performance. The section devoted to Hijikata, 'Hijikata Tatsumi: The Words of Butoh', edited by Kurihara Nanako, provided the first collection of materials by Hijikata translated into English. Despite a number of semblances between Kurihara's commentary on Hijikata and my own in *The Body as a Vessel* – the first monograph on Hijikata, published almost a decade earlier, in 1993 – Kurihara did not cite the publication once. The issue was raised with Kurihara at the International Dance Conference that took place in Gdansk, Poland, in 2009, and then subsequently with the editors of *The Drama Review* and NYU theatre department, where Kurihara had completed her doctorate. It was conceded as a serious breach of academic conduct, but never legally resolved.

More recently, Inada Naomi has published the book *Hijikata Tatsumi – zetsugo no shintai* (Hijikata Tatsumi – A Unique Body, 2008), based on a series of interviews with figures related to Hijikata. Inada writes:

> Towards a body that moves beyond time and space in its expansion, where everything is vague down to the articulation of one part, the inside and outside, the outline... a poetic language of the 'hazy body,' the 'weakening body,' the 'ash column'... Dance criticism and *butō* criticism have to establish a philosophy and theory of dance that shows a body overcoming the flesh and blood body, though it uses that living body as a substance. In other words, they have to analyse the body's consciousness, sensation, and practical technique. [...] I will now proceed to treat this question of Hijikata's own *butō* theory and body theory.[7]

This account paints a false picture. Hijikata's "poetic language" (his *butō-fu*), has in fact been elucidated, as has the "the body's consciousness, sensation, and practical technique," in my own publication, *The Body as a Vessel*. A number of misleading comments along the lines of the one above, feature in Inada's book. This is accompanied by a lack of adequate citation, with *The Body as a Vessel* not even listed in the Selected Bibliography. This concern was later raised with the author, at a Hijikata Research Symposium in 2010 held in Kyōto, and with her publishing house.

I have since presented conference papers addressing these concerns about academic good conduct and intellectual copyright. The response has nonetheless been inadequate, and so these serious problems persist in contemporary research.

The State of Butō Performance

At the 2009 Venice Biennale, of the five Western contemporary dance pieces shown, one would certainly be classed as *butō*, and another showed the clear signs of *butō* influence. These were performers who had taken workshops with *butō* dancers and trained with contemporary dancers with a background in *butō*. In August of that same year, the main work presented at the Avignon Festival – a work drawing on flamenco – contained a physicality comparable to the intensity of *butō* throughout, and even acknowledged a Europe-based *butō* dancer in the programme as the choreographer of one of its vividly *butō*-esque scenes. In the autumn of that year, New York's CAVE space invited 10 foreign *butō* dancers to perform as part of their *butō* festival. These performances raised the question of how *butō* is being received among these dancers?

Nudity, white body paint, a concentration on the body, a focus on the audience staged by the lack of music, slow movements, minutely articulated movements, violent movements, convulsive movements, low wrestling movements, emphasis on the back-body, transformative movements which start with the transformation of each part, hard movements involving the stiffening of the joints. It is often possible to discern what kind of influence these dancers are taking from *butō* based on their uses of these characteristic *butō* movements. Often these dances appear very similar to Japanese *butō* performances. *Butō* has itself absorbed many influences, from ballet to the traditional Japanese martial arts – and, in turn, it has gone on to influence other performance forms: ballet, flamenco, circus, and theatre. Internationally, an idea of *butō* (mainly, as a dance of 'nudity and slow movement') is more commonly known than in Japan.

Since 2005, I have been inviting Japanese and foreign *butō* dancers, folk dancers, actors, and *noguchi taisō* practitioners to assist in running an annual summer workshop entitled 'From the Origins of Japan and the Body, Towards *Butō*'. Participants have included an 80 year-old Japanese *butō* dancer, an Australian physicist, a Portuguese clown, a Mexican actress, a Japanese contemporary dancer based in Paris, and a number of Japanese students who have encountered *butō* whilst abroad. I realized how widespread the influence of *butō* had become, when a Polish participant of a workshop in Gdansk in 2009 informed me they had come across *butō* through a Japanese *butō* dancer based in India.

The Establishment of a Butō Market

This century has seen the world grow narrower, with grass-roots cultural exchanges becoming normalized. When, in the summer of 2009, I went to Hungary to perform along with a handful of traditional Japanese musicians and dancers, I realised the state of *butō* and the degree of institutional support it was receiving abroad had changed. The majority of *butō* performances abroad were supported by major organisations like the Japanese Culture House in Paris, or the Japan Society in New York. Alongside this, *butō* workshops and performances continued to happen at smaller venues like CAVE in New York and TENRI in Paris.

Since the first wave of *butō* dancers traveling abroad to perform in the 1980s (Ōno Kazuo and *Sankai Juku*), a number of dancers have lived or spent long periods abroad in the last 30 years: Murobushi Kō, Carlotta Ikeda, Yumiko Yoshioka, Tamano Kōichi, and Eiko + Koma. And following this, dancers like: SU-EN and Iwana Masaki. Even Japan-based dancers, like Nakajima Natsu and Waguri Yukio, have focused their workshops abroad over the last 20 years. This has begun to look like a *butō* market.[8]

This growth in *butō* demand has meant *butō* dancers not yet performing or offering workshops in Japan might debut their work abroad. It also means *butō* dancers become wanderers, moving from city to city, and country to country. This professionalization and spread of *butō* has also brought with it the uniformity of style that I described earlier, and a new urge for the establishment of a method. The Japanese staff at the TENRI centre in Paris informed me that workshops using the 'Eaten by Insects' *butō-fu* had been held there for the last 10-years. That they understood 'Eaten by Insects' as a foundation for *butō*, something I had attempted to establish in my book, suggested that the analysis I had brought to *butō* was gradually seeping into the field.

The exporting of *butō* by dancers who come to Japan in order to study short-term, shakes the foundation of the *butō* master-disciple system. Training over time is what allows for the 'self-renunciation' necessary to *butō*. Faced by the strictness and challenge of Hijikata's teaching – his demand for a dance that starts from 'the attempt to stand that cannot stand' or that exists in 'the smell of sweat from a shirt behind the studio, on the winding road to Asbestos Studio' – left you wondering what dance was, or what expression was. *Butō* is the technique of pursuing 'life and form', in a tradition that contradictorily claims to reject technique.

Towards 21st Century Butō

Hijikata's Phone Call from Beyond

Just after my father's death in December 1992, a phone call came from the otherworld: 'I'm living, so why can't I?' I thought it was Hijikata. In fact, the phone call came from an old friend who I had met through our daughters when they were at playschool. She had never even seen me dance. Somehow she was able to describe to me an image of two fathers playing together on the bank of a river: one, a laughing man with maggots crawling out of his face, the other a red faced handsome youth. It was Hijikata and my father. She said other strange things about 'not needing a chandelier, only a single light bulb in the *doma*' or that 'everyone peels the four or five eggs left, differently' or about the 'sorrow of losing children.' It was at a time when I was performing and presenting on my research, but inwardly struggling with Hijikata's *butō*. It was important to hear a message from Hijikata at that time. My father and Hijikata told me to dance with the brevity of 'cherry blossom' or transform with the speed of a 'rotating table'. But the description was cut-off midway as my friend came back to herself: 'what was I just saying?'

Hijikata's method is based on poetic phrasings: 'When the paper falls it falls shivering, you can learn from that movement. Nature will teach you. The soles of the feet are important. From the soles on the stones in the riverbed, to the small stones floating in the river, to the sand, to the grass, to the earth... from the soles of the feet the whole body can change. Going into the forest the branches of the timber grow...' Hijikata's message ended with the instruction to dance. It came from the mouth of my friend. She had danced twice in my presence. Once jumping up from the table after drinking she suddenly started to do Hijikata's 'beast' choreography. Exhausted, she stopped and laughed. Then she started to dance again for a second time. After this second dance, she turned to my husband and said, in the tone of Hijikata: 'Mikami, why are you involved in *butō*?'

Following this, I was once lying down and dozing, when I saw a vision of Hijikata by the riverside, calling out to me. He drew me to Ōiso on the other side of the river. Soon after that we built our outdoor stage at Ōiso, where we have since held many performances and summer workshops.

Occultism and the Contemporary Paradigm Shift – The Mind-Body

The scene I just described can be judged as nothing but occult. The philosopher, Yuasa Yasuo, considers a paradigm shift to have occurred through the period of modernity in relation to occultism. The alchemical changes during the renaissance, of alchemist's visions on the one hand and actual changing of chemicals on the other, led to a split between the inner world (as occultism), and the outer world (as the beginning of modern science). This idea of occultism dominated from the 15th to the 20th century. It fed into the establishment of many new fields: research into the spirit and the supernatural, psychology, hypnosis, telepathy, and even played an important role in the conception of Surrealism. According to Yuasa, the spread of occultism cannot be totally separated from the paradigm shift in modern science that occurred during the 21st century. Eastern understandings of occult phenomena, such as inexplicable energy, or 'ki', might indeed pose a challenge to the conceptions of the mind-body that have dominated since Descartes.[9]

Yuasa, influenced by thinkers such as Carl Jung, urged a reconsideration of the mind-body in relation to the subconscious, rather than the ego. This emphasis on the 'universal unconscious' is something that *butō* also shares.

The Methods of 'Falling to the Bottom of the Fleshly Body' and 'Detaching from the Body'

Just two months before Hijikata's death, he gave a final workshop in which images of disintegration surfaced as a means for training the 'nerves' and the 'network of nerves'. Following his death, Hijikata's principle dancer, Ashikawa Yōko took up the idea of the '*butō* dancer's eyes' and the 'awakening body' as central to her understanding of the *butō* method [See 'Chapter 7: The Dissolution of Form' for a further discussion of this]. At one of Ashikawa's workshops I attended, we studied the *butō-fu* of the 'wall' in which the body entering the wall and the body left behind became separated. This 'detaching from the body' resulted in a 'sudden change in the world'. Hijikata had proposed a similar idea of being "the 'double' (the doubled shadow) in the single point of I" (Appendix 7).

This detached body might be figured as the "fourth circuit of the associative body (Nagasawa Yoshi)", described by Yuasa.[10] It might be considered in relation to Yuasa's ideas of meditation and "creative intuition," which occur within a "dark consciousness" of a world in which the "body governs."[11] Or in relation to Minato Ryōen's idea of the *zen* spirit in terms of an "innocence" that is bottomless.[12] But Hijikata's *butō* was also distinct from this: his late disciple Seisaku recalls Hijikata saying 'don't meditate, don't become euphoric, be concrete, be excessive,' 'take courage in falling to the bottom of the flesh body and walking there'. This was Hijikata's way of 'searching for life's true journey' (as his wife Motofuji recalled), in the 'life-posture of hesitation.'

Hijikata's instruction not to 'be made thin by the bite of the mosquito that is information', made me reconsider my position in the world. It returned me to my body as a source of information. The problem of how to be conscious of the body becomes more and more important in dance, for while 'anyone can dance', according to Hijikata, it becomes harder and harder to do so. This is the responsibility of those dancers left behind. For unlike the traditional performing art, *kyōgen*, which "must be protected from the confusion of popularity, even at the expense of dying out," *butō* does not have the protection of a rigid tradition.[13] It is therefore up to the dancers who met Hijikata directly to shape the development of *butō* into the future.

Reviews of Mikami Kayo's Dance

"Japanese Butoh dance is a kind of body spectacle, and Kayo Mikami's *Kenka* (Consecration of Flowers) seemed a perfect balance between introversion and flamboyance. It also renewed my interest in Butoh, which, 15 years after it was first seen in America, seems to get more formulaic [...] *Kenka*, basically a solo, has seven descriptively titled sections that could refer to stages in a life cycle, from the ancestral world to earthly existence and back again to the spirit plane. But that makes the piece sound more narrative than it is. What I remember are intense, disconnected visions.

Mikami crosses the space slowly, bent over with her torso parallel to the ground, her arms fixed, useless. You can't see her face, only the repetitious effort of each step. It takes her 10 minutes to get across, move downstage, then retrace her path. A ghost, I think, condemned to journey forever in the body of a human." (Marcia B. Siegel, 'Butopia', in *The Village Voice*, 10 November 1994)

"'*Kenka*,' which means consecration of flowers, begins with slow chill walks for a bent old woman and gradually picks up speed and intensity. By the end, Miss Mikami does create a strong sense of spiritual turbulence and redemption. And there are quick potent images throughout the piece: a beautifully timed tilt of the head, delayed just a fraction of a moment for full impact, arms reaching out as if to a partner in a wildly cantering waltz, a dress sewn with small gold bells that tinkle as she stomps, and two chalk-white acolytes whose skin appears to shred in places. Another highlight is the interruption of a lilting taped piano rendition of "Plaisir d'Amour" or a cacophonic harmonica solo performed on tape by the dead woman's widower." (Jennifer Dunning, 'The Japanese Art of Speaking in Metaphors', in *New York Times: The Arts*, 12 November 1994)

"The first piece in the programme, *Kenka*, presented nearly one and a half hours of mesmeric movement. The leading dancer of the company, Kayo Mikami, gave a performance that left little doubt as to the nature of purgatory. Portraying a woman who has died young and still pines for her child on Earth, Mikami superbly displayed a lynchpin of Butoh: that transformation of the self into that which is portrayed, with the act of metamorphosis being the key, the mind's movement into a different state. In the various sections of the piece, Mikami displayed utmost physical and mental control in a convincing performance as a body animated not by life but by grief. […] Witnessing such a performance is a transformational experience and I expect, like homeopathy, will continue to alter the consciousness and perception long after the actual dosage. I can't imagine what it must be like to be embroiled in it. Although it requires some sticking power, anyone seriously interested in the performing arts should see and explore this…" (Christine Madden, '*Kenka* and *Kandachime*', in *The Irish Times*, 21 February 2004)

"A Butoh dancer aims at letting go of any sense of self, with the body as a fragile, empty shell. At times the whole body or parts of it freeze, die, then fight to break into movement again. The dancer should not communicate their own persona or any idea at all, but simply act as a vessel for each individual audience members' subjective feelings, thoughts and reactions that it inspires. This poetic freedom of interpretation is helped by the costumes, which bear no reference to everyday reality, often leaving the body almost completely exposed. In Kayo Mikami's performance the pure presence of the body, devoid of any ego, was staggering. Many Irish performers, too, managed to just let their soulless body express what it would and the audience saw some breath-taking visions of withering corpses, each infinitely sad and unique in its precious fragility, contrary to what the logic of war would have us believe." (Riika Jokelainen, 'Torifune Butoh-Sha Visit showcases in the Samuel Beckett Centre, in *Trinity News*, 2 March 2004)

[*Following page:*] Mikami Kayo in Gangio Gangioma (2011), by Onozuka Makoto

Appendices

Note on the Appendices

These appendices comprise a reorganization of notes taken by four of Hijikata's disciples – Akane, Ichiyoshi, Harada and Mikami – according to the systematization of Mikami. The formatting accords as far as possible with Mikami's, which represents a transcription of the original notes. As far as possible, the particularities of Hijikata's language have been retained – including non-equivalent onomatopoeia and culturally specific Japanese words. Italics indicate Japanese words or attempts to render onomatopoeia into English, and square brackets indicate brief explanations of these words.

Appendix 1: Workshop Notes (1977-81): Hijikata's instructive language

On the "Control of Relations"

- with the search for a relational world, there can be no division into parts
- if there were not so many layers, the forest's face could not appear = the materialization of the inevitable / relating to the requirements of the forest's face appearing
- relating to dried out thin things – diffusion and concentration
- white flower, rustling of leaves, branches – increasing the requirements
- the *arabesque* of knowing the things relating in the space behind – the connection of nerves / duck's neck → lotus flower → willow tree (fog, haze) / the duck's neck emerging from within the fog or haze without looking artificial
- relating only to the single ant crawling all over the body
- in a place of inactivity, relating to mould or wind (phantom transformation)
- the control of relations
  / 80% in relation to the rhythm of the head, 20% in relation to the delicate
  form of the lower body (pianissimo)
- the surrounding density increases, frozen and turned to stone / the formation of stone / the looseness of stone / can it be reversed or not (slowdown) relating to that time → unable to reverse completely, became the space of *tanuki* [Japanese racoon dog]
- the density of the stone is at 90%   must pass through the stone's density / continuously relating to the qualities of the material / raw ore as the background requirement
- grappling with the material and growing thin
- dance does not exist as 'this dance or that dance,' dance is to be in relation to the things that run through the interconnected roots of technique, beyond the categories of the body or mind
- relating to the extinction of an existing flesh body   indefinitely expanding the fixed measure
- when some hair has been used, what shape (fast-changing hands) to use
  / 98% in relation to the strands of hair
- 80% in relation to the space behind (the mantle robe)
- passing through the mechanism to which you are related, understand the mechanism and reproduce nature, accurately
- relating to diverging nerves, walking fast
- thought you were relating to OO, but were in fact becoming XX
- creating your own work from the transitions and dislocations within the given material
- when going to do something, it has already happened
  / space transforms and expression becomes strange as a result of relating to the time that runs between each pose
- lagging time, relating – ordering accurately
  / *tara-, doro-, guda-, doro-* [dripping sounds], then allow even the order to melt
- to order time is grotesque
- when seeking a mechanism, each thing becomes equal in time → when you reveal the self in relation, time becomes uniform
- must become rapidly free
- lagging the relations reveals the blurs
- relating to the physical state
- relating mechanically creates an atmosphere   it seems cool, it seems smoky
- twelve aspects – relating to the mechanism of emotion
- the control of nerves – there is a second self

- just unable to do it / just a few nerves in relation / just poor technique
- if you don't feel things constantly from the soles of the feet, the process becomes very unclear
- the final step is important for the relocation of the swaying lotus   but the flesh body yearning towards an end should not anticipate that end
- relating only to the white paper, the bird appears
- presence, the air that birds inhabit
- Mandala of lines → delicately order the ecstasy → though the curve is dismantled, it remains unified, it is a matter of degree
- flower / wave, being tossed around / being tossed around when you try to relate
- the free intervention of nerves / extended, towards the place you want to go

On "Nerves"

- the being of nerves is the pointe of the dancer
- a snake of nerves passing through the body
- nerves seized by a weak electric current
- no longer able to sleep, no longer able to awaken / thunder strikes the mirror of the floor, branch-tip nerves, reverse the flow of capillaries one by one / when all the nerves of the head stand upright   things appear as clues
- nerves even emerge from paper / scrunched, crushed, crumpled (sound)
- chorus girl, one, two, three, four, with branches and leaves of nerves, forward half a step, backwards half a step
- all lagging nerves
- from the tense existence of intending something and doing nothing, being held by a single nerve
- the room is already full of diverging nerves (use them to form relations) (the body wrung into smallness) moved by the nerves   add the divergence of dried grass, walk on stage as you wish
- incredible weakness unreliable nerves, thin nerves
- the nerves of birds – beating wings, hiding, fear, light and shadow, many thousands of nests on the wings
- small bird 1 – each tree branch moves out metres in front and connects to each nerve (strands of hair)
- the nerves of small birds / distant nerves, deviation, layering
- became a bird = certifying the nerves of birds
- adding a dash of thin birds' nerves, the air expands
- there are times when the nerves of birds and a desirous pleasure unify
- the nerves of dried grass   make your body lighter (gutting the entrails)
- diverging nerves of dried grass from the head   how to make them thin

On "Freedom" and the "Movement that Emerges when Pushed Out"

- moving from the spreading of dried grass
- tempted by the smells and walking / if you sniff the various smells you grow weak (decaying)
- change direction with the smell and sound
- the smell is already floating through space
- the smell – moving with uncertain direction
- the density of pollen / if you condense it, the field of vision narrows, if you dilute it, the field of vision widens – perspective
- connecting the relations that exist in sound and in material
- the surrounding density increased, cooled, became stone   repeat with density
- fly, move location – add wind

- eternal connections, that which carries all directions, directions dispersing
- the back of the ear, the great spinning wheel in space   towards the direction of the spinning wheel, towards the spinning direction
- direction chases a direction and becomes sooty   that direction clings to you   losing the aim of the direction in the process, it clings to you
- tufts of hair on the back sway, connecting the forms
- the wind tears   a torn shadow dwells in it   look closer, it was a peacock   no it wasn't, perhaps a phoenix   become the materials of the shadow   sinking into the otherworldly dark
- apply the shadow to the phoenix   in the storehouse, cooling and spreading in the otherworldly dark
- wind, indefinite form, haze, mist, shadow, phoenix, adding the phantom transformation of a peacock
- if you watch the distant fire in the mountains, there are downy hairs around the mouth   dragging her hem behind, the lady becomes sooty – perspective
- magnitude is transmitted through the mesh of the net alone
- magnitude and width accidentally take a form
- eaten by insects   insects are eating those nerves   feel the nerves of those insects
- what does it mean for existence, to be eaten by insects   time / space / self / eaten by insects the moment you want to overcome that thought
- space is itchy, the limit of itchiness bam
- continuation within stasis – a great movement
- itchy space – a state of being related to insects ← being on the edge, where thoughts arise independently
- half able to endure holding the form / eaten by ants – the sickness, the pain, the itchiness, being munched, fear   half able to endure it all   half able to endure the feeling
- made to dance by itchiness
- form is the limit of being eaten by insects
- I itched   and from this itching hair emerged   I became a bird / itching gave rise to friction and from its heat I pursued a lover, became senile, became a bird – flying
- the fluttering of paper carried on an ocean breeze, hairs on the back, disappearing one by one – decrease
- indefinite forms sway   everything appears out of two forms
- if you layer all the colours, pitch-black darkness appears
- things that become like smoke, things that can appear at any moment / dismantled things / hazy bodies, fluttering things, the central thinness and dilution within them
- enter the wall and become a stain mask spreading from the countless gazes becoming a stained body
- if you are made to expand in various directions, you become stuffed – hairs emerging from the pores
- the phantom body is a shadow, light and shadow
- the shadow inside the body, the process of the mountain fire and downy hair – that is the phantom body
- the thing snatched away is a ghost
- the number of horizontal grains increases eternally, many thousand, many million   became a measure / becoming blurred
- Bodhisattva from the state of nothingness (strands of hair + smoke, negated ghost)
- unless you eliminate the dispersing directions, there will be no ending
- dislocations – blurs, spreads > vaporizing

The Butō Dancer's Mind, Body, and Technique

- the state of nothingness preceding dance
- you can't try to do something   and you can't do anything   stand for an instant within the place where either can occur
- thought goes on ahead, and in the act of pursuing it, the true body is made to appear
- subjects of memory in the wind = erasing the self, flashing past in an instant
- fallen   the origin of wind is the place you fell
- dispose of the requirements of being human   please remember that one
- existence is in the instant, the fall – the flight of the spirit
- once caught, made to die, and revived, the dancer is able to talk with winds and grasses
- witnessed a secret   was in the shoes of a dancer who had never landed
- starting out from the moment of being placed
- all existence is a fiction – Bashō (a lie has been told)
- where are the dancing nerves coming from?
- where have they come from – a place of sensitivity
- beginning before the beginning
- original experience / faint / koseki [Japanese family register]
- encountering / fainting – nerves / breaking the pedestal / koseki – being born
- dismantling habits, the koseki of butō
- with no qualifications, the limit place
- questionless – the exposure of existence / dance is that which becomes incompetent, dies once, and is resurrected in a single stroke, landing in the dangerous place of dance
- be captured by the world of innocence
- don't become a beggar of sensations
- clinging to yourself – with low status
- free yourself from the delusion of the ego
- don't cling to yourself, it's better to try existing outside even if you make mistakes
- don't do anything – clinging to that hydrangea / measuring the light and shade of your skin
- the bird cannot dance without continually diving into the sunset, the overcast sky, the wind…
- don't be greedy, isn't the peacock disappearing in light and shade good enough
- don't close your eyes – don't become intoxicated with remaining interior – where are the dancer's eyes?
- thought only remains in the eyeballs, the body is completely eroded
- don't get too stiff   tissue paper is ok   the moment of fainting is ok
- and when you don't know something, a single sheet of paper emerges (entering) from the friction of multiple unknowings
- stretching out – time and space
- can you hide in the place that has been layered so long
- you reach the limit of dance through hiding alone
- pump a single thought through the veins   the depth of that relation, observe the cause of cause and effect!
- surrender, are you trying to hide in the place of surrender / quickly notice the surrender   a wind is blowing there / forbidden things give new life to the known   the mechanism of holding up the hands in surrender is harder
- if it can be concluded with a joke, it's better to conclude it with a joke
- transform immersion to external existence ← taking the body's disabilities as their opposite
- upsetting yourself, losing your dependence on life   that glint in the eyes
- there is always a limit no matter how you experience the dimensions of the everyday   try living it dance-like

- place yourself in a territory where the body cannot move in known ways – it's the same with living
- clearly detail the ambiguity, don't stagnate feelings within the body
- stagnation is important for stasis, but when you're really stuck there's no hiding it
- don't rely on muscles
- encountering something
- observing observation, and what allows it to exist
- sensing the requirements for appearing
- inferring the cause that is prior to the beginning / the little bird – the sky's (unnerving) signs pre-empt needles on the soles of the feet and nape of the neck
- wind blows the dandelion-like things through the void of the inner organs
- drawing and erasing drawing and erasing the image of a fresco   forgetting things once recalled growing thick hair in order to forget
- sobering up with the feeling of smoothly drinking sake
- joining the whole body in prayer   to exist is a prayer
- wanting to dance, made to enter madness   that is also dance / spiritual unity – feet balancing on a ball
- make the lie of an innocent child easily found out   the calculated lie fails
- finished trying to do things, in order to erase the figure (your flesh body)
- mechanically closing in
- technique existing as technique
- the self as the cruelty of technique
- a substance that does nothing – diffusing the space behind you
- the expression of doing nothing – the things you can capture
- quickly go back into the memory of wind   then method is revived (method expires and is revived)
- the inevitability of technique giving rise to technique
- technique is being touched deeply by the primal body of technique
- not the memory of sequence, order   suffocation
- dancing memory and cramping up
- the self being eaten by technique
- the intentionally obscure is enclosed by clarity (clarify) – don't become dazed
- technique is methodological confusion
- the real relief doesn't die   method remains
- precision in the method of losing things, let it blow in the wind (negating the things you are currently doing, something new naturally emerges)
- it is rational to escape controlling things
- the confused state within the depths – that's not confusion   the wriggling movement from inside, disturbance
- caught by a sound   piew–
- disappearing – the wits all burned
- recollection – encountering the untouchable substance
- another time of place / body transference / the object
- yourself united with fiction   there is substance
- if you are watched by an object, enter the object and try seeing from there
- the landscape is reflected in you
- form is chased by life   a nebula, state of suspension / difference, transformation, individuality is that which has appeared to the outside
- taking hold of a clear mechanism, an accurate reproduction of nature
- carry both the image and the physical requirements
- technique without imagination is dull   imagination without technique is risky

- radiation is the foundation of dance   thought goes towards Gotanda and hand towards Meguro / the hydrangea is more particles than transparency, more transparency than paper   gradually spreading / fingers holding the republic of fingers, legs carrying the republic of legs – don't exploit the body
- extremely artisan things / extremely spiritual things – merging radially
- the hand has its own direction / create divided things within the body
- reflected in the water → the shadow of the lotus   existence is dividing
- the precision of nonsense
- the game, things made from the lines of fancy
- the decisive will is betrayed by the flesh = flaccid
- dizzy connections in the head = schizophrenia
- the connection from thin things to thick things
- fluttering things, connections of movement, then congealing things
- the gesture of a hand pulled by the weakness of the body instantly reveals – the string of tears, 12 aspects
- the creation of space – limitation, not like restriction → knees loosening
- numbering the space
- the entire space is being eaten   an extreme   scene
- Mandala of space – not a dandelion (not the anonymity of a dandelion) the afterimage of thought!!
- a single large sheet of paper, swaying radially / the sound of rustle, smooth as space is folded up
- the beginning of dance – trusting in monochrome expressions
- e.g. 1 the neck alone coated in white
-     2 one part coated in white like a bruise
-     3 pulling eight expressions
-     → creating the beginning of an image
- existing within butō, dancing "butō time"
- there are cherry blossoms, there is a fire, there is darkness right at the centre, if you fix a spotlight on it, you can see night cherry blossoms
- if you converse with the things inside a canvas, a picture is drawn as a result   Goya's story

Appendix 2: Collection of Forms

Hijikata employed an image-language (as seen above) to guide the dancer's movement. It operated as a shared code between Hijikata and the dancer. A further selection of this is included in the following section.

Images for Manipulating the Body

The Circuit of Nerves

This shared image-language code was based on the idea that "the being of nerves is the *butō* dancer's *pointe*." Through authentically relating to this image-language sensation and movement could arise. The circuit of relation between the image, its expression in language, and the movement of the dancer, was termed a "circuit of nerves."

The Easy Deception of the Attention

The premise of the "circuit of nerves," is the "easy deception of the attention" – that is, the trickery of the attention into "becoming a cow" instantaneously. This is a matter of believing in images with the innocence of a child. The following section forms a guide to these images. It is divided into: walks, choreographic forms, phrases, and etudes. It is more than a method of bodily manipulation; it also provides a key to Hijikata's understanding of the world around him.

The Walks: Understanding the "Neural Network"

1) Possible Body: Walk of a Measure
2) Speed: Walk of Mesh
3) Pushed Out Movement: Walk by Insects, Walk by Gazes
4) Expansion of the Body: Walk of a Plane
5) Texture of Space: Space of the Hydrangea, Space of the Dandelion
6) Whereabouts: Smoke (Incense, Pipe Smoke, Ventilator Smoke), Slug, Wet Rag, Wet Horse's Neck, Snail, Seal
7) Materials: Stone, Relief, Wall
8) Nerves: Wols, Thousand Branches, Process of Vaporization

1) Possible Body

Walk of a Measure

a)   become a measure and walk
b)   move without walking between heaven and earth
c)   with eyes of glass, place an eye on the forehead
d)   the speed of reflection is faster than that of vision
e)   razor blades on the soles of the feet
f)   a basin on top of the head
g)   joints suspended from spider threads
h)   the desire to walk goes on ahead, and form pursues after
i)   traces of walking hanging in the space before and behind
j)   forest in the molar teeth, threads in the hollows of the body

k) suddenly eyes stop seeing and legs stop walking; at that point, things become walking eyes and walking legs

l) walking requires moments of discontinuity, and urges the expansion of space

2) Speed

Walk of Mesh (Ashikawa Workshop, 1989)

- a weak electric current running through the graph-paper mesh – feeling of the width of two paper sliding doors
- finger on the mesh, instant electric shock – high speed (the knees loosen and height emerges)
- suddenly disappearing
- the opening out of double doors bam – quiver weakening
- capillaries quivering   →
- nerves quivering   → sticking to the mesh
- current under the soles of the feet → (feet naturally separating from the floor)
- the mesh in front
- the mesh behind (the one in front diluting slightly)
- the crunch of the mesh inside the body

    a dentist in the nerve *ouch ouch*, *sharp pain* at the temple, rheumatic joints, *dangly* nerves; where possible, maintain the condition whilst turning. Not just rotating → looking back on yourself as a completely different person.

On the Walk of Mesh
The body is extended and flattened out like graph paper or mesh. This is like a net of nerves. When a current runs through this mesh, vibrations move at high speed, and form appears from this space of vibration. The movement emerges between the mesh placed before and behind the dancer, with no sense of distinction between the self and other.

3) Pushed Out Movement

Walk by Insects

a) an insect on the back of the right hand
b) a second insect crawling down the left side of the nape to the back
c) a third insect crawling up from the right inner thigh
d) a fourth insect crawling down from the left shoulder to the chest
e) a fifth insect wherever you feel it
f) itching here and there   can't stand it   pushed by itchiness
g) 500 insects   beneath the chin   behind the ears   behind the elbows   behind the knees around the belt
h) 5000 insects around the eyes   around the mouth   inside the ears   between the fingers   in all the mucous membranes
i) insects in the hair
j) insects in the pores of the skin pores
k) 30,000 insects   eating from the pores   to the internal organs
l) then continuing to eat   out through the pores   surrounding the body   eating the space
m) then insects eating the insects in space
n) insects eating that situation
o) (500,000,000 insects eating the tree – insides are eaten up)

p)   it is the final moment (the will i.e. insects/the texture of things)

Walk by Gazes (Ashikawa Workshop 1989)

- an eyeball above the head (the big eye of the whirlpool – sinking)
- eyeballs behind (leaning forward – pulled from behind)
- eyeballs on the floor (small eyes of the floor peeking at the inner thighs – the condition of the crotch changes → tightening upwards)
- an eyeball beneath the chin
- two eyeballs (on the floor and behind)
- eyeballs everywhere – can't escape – arms shrinking, standing on one leg

Reference Material for Walk by Gazes

Walk by Gazes (1978)

- gazes from behind – being chased – the advance
- gazes from in front – gazes coercing – the retreat
- gazes from the lower right
- gazes from the lower left
- gazes from above
- o   gazes everywhere – can't escape – arms and legs shrinking, standing on one leg
  ↓
dismantled by countless gazes

Walk by Grains (1978)

- many hundreds and thousands of grains run left, then right
- tens of thousands of millions of grains run horizontally, and increase infinitely
  ↓
becoming hazy

On Walk by Gazes
With the various walks by gazes, movement emerges from sensation.

4) Extension of the Body

Walk of a Plane

- equal planes from the left and right eye threads extending upwards
- equal planes from the left and right ear threads extending upwards
- equal planes from the left and right elbow threads extending upwards
- grasses swaying stirring from the hips down
- damp earth touches the soles of the feet
- four eyes
- a gust of wind through the lips – (lips) part a little
- threads extending from the fingertips down

Hijikata Commentary

Once you enter two-dimensional space, the mind and body become unified, then you disperse eternally, and the customs and habits of three-dimensional life evaporate like ether rising from a can.

On the Walk of a Plane
When a three-dimensional body flattens into two-dimensions, it becomes like thin paper. The lower body sinks with the sensation of grass below the hips and the damp earth beneath the feet, allowing for bodily expressions to emerge, and the texture of space to change. This expression is then erased with the blurred image of four eyes on the front of the face, and the face becomes like a sheet of white paper in a gust of wind from the lips. The perception is diffused both horizontally and vertically by the image of threads extending out from the fingertips.

5) Texture of Space

Space of the Hydrangea – seeping, blurring (Ashikawa Workshop, 1989)

- five roots of the hydrangea (four aims)
- in the rainy season sky, the air dampens, seeps, and blurs
- reflecting in a pond, running in the rain
- (the watercolour painting runs, the colours change)
- the flower rots
- the paints of the painting in the rain
- (colours seep, blur, and run)

Ashikawa Commentary
Walking emerges when the hydrangea's colours blur and seep.

Space of the Dandelion – drifting (Ashikawa Workshop, 1989)

- the dandelion head after the flower has bloomed
- air dries
- soft hairs… around the eyes, around the mouth, beneath the chin, behind the ears. Phwoa–
- drifting feeling (opening behind the head)
- float 30cm off the ground
- the wind is walking

Reference Material for Space of the Dandelion

Dandelion Space (1978)

- a single thread from the forehead
- a second thread from the back of the head
- a third thread from the molar teeth
- leaving these three in place, a fourth to the left
- leaving these four in place, a fifth to the right
- a sixth and seventh thread to the eardrums
- leaving these seven in place, downy hairs of the dandelion, filling the space
- hairs stem from the soles of the feet, the backs of the ears, the waist
- the weak electric current of space

a counter-current from each strand of hair, towards the joints

On the Space of the Hydrangea and the Space of the Dandelion
The body's conditions change with the perception of a hydrangea blurring and seeping, or a dandelion sprouting hairs. The imagery of running and floating causes the body to expand in space, and the space itself becomes textured. Adding humidity, light, and wind to the existing conditions of seeping, floating, and blurring, generates shifts in quality and speed.

6) Whereabouts

Smoke (Ashikawa Workshop, 1989)

i)   Incense
- four thread trails
  (suspended by a thread from heaven, the stomach's thread)
- wind is blowing
- in the end only burned dregs

ii)   Pipe Smoke
- pipe smoke – a single direction

iii)   Ventilator Smoke
- the roomful of smoke goes towards the ventilator
- speed and shade creates a mood
- setting walls and floors at the limit of existing place, *phwoa–*

Whereabouts (1978)

cod roe, eternal connections, filling all directions
slugs, snails, seals…
a single wet mass

i) Slugs
- a slug sliding on the neck

ii) Dust cloth
- a dust cloth full of water, *splosh*
- how far can it be pulled

iii) Whirlpool
- *zoom*, a whirlpool swelling from the hips

iv) Wet Horse's Neck
- the length of the horse's face, *terror*

v) Snail
- the surrounding whirlpool coiled by the shell
- neck emerging *sliding*

vi) Hydrangea
- a lump of flesh *slump* – things filling the whereabouts

On Whereabouts
Things like incense, pipe smoke, or a dishcloth generate different textures in the 'whereabouts.'
The conditions of the 'whereabouts' cause directions to be "pushed out" in unexpected ways.

7) Materials

Stone

- solidification
- lacking arms and neck, the 'negative' condition
- ore, *roughness*, weight, grating
- secrets that don't stray outside (pulling the chin)
- being scraped – over time the face becomes clear
- brought down, particles
- ore, expanding again
- particles plus secrets
- whilst repeating this, the feverous forehead of "stone Hanako" [Japanese girl's name, also a series of sculptures by Auguste Rodin]
- limitation
- being shaven off

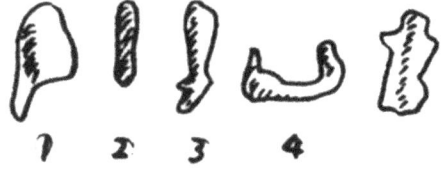

1 right-side being scraped – retracting legs, becoming thin
2 left-side being scraped – becoming taller
3 pulled out sideways (melting)
4 relief   remaining back, being buried
(forehead emerges and stops. The right leg stops a little)

Note
Being shaved off heightens the speed → *roughness*

Relief

- walk inside the relief
1 wall – mud, thickness of the behind
2 diffusion (upwards, sideways) – below is mud
3 petrification – hanging down (appearance of a girl)
4 darkness
5 diffusing sideways – evaporating in an instant (quite brief)

Hijikata Commentary
- Transformation occurs from the material. It's about perceiving the extent to which you can be pushed by something, so it's better to go too far
- Within the layers locate the dried part and the *gloopy* part
- Mud – sticky, running whilst it is held back
- Mud – the slightly dried part is particles

Wall

pressed from behind and in front by wire mesh, mud is drying
plastered wheat grain
stretched into a plane, *help* –
being plastered
stretched, dried, a face like stone
(stone face)

162

Reference Material for Wall

Wall (Ashikawa Workshop, 1989)
- the thickness of the wall, its weight
- perception of the behind – expanding by roughly 3 metres 80 centimetres
- the roughness of the surface

On Materials
The body's perception changes as a result of changing the material – stone, relief, wall, glass, mud, or ceramics. The density changes in accordance with differing degrees of heat, pressure, and humidity. From this, various conditions of heaviness, lightness, dryness and wetness can appear. The form itself can change when it is "scraped down." These shifts in material or form – as well as in speed, direction, heat, density, and humidity – sensitize the perception in a way that allows for the entire condition of the human body to change. This is not only a matter of relating to solid materials, but also liquids and gases.

8) Nerves

Wols – thousands of branches
- sensing thousands of branches
- the branch at the temple breaks   *snap*
- nose becomes an ear
- a thousand birds fly out from the back of the head   *flap flap*
- an insect crawls up from the foot
- crushing the insect whilst walking   *crunch crunch*
- a twitch in the cheek
- the little finger *prick*
- Adam's apple contracts in three stages   *gulp*
- the sound of a spoon falling behind *clank*
- the tree leaves of the skull   *rustle rustle*
- about to walk when   *click* there's a locked room inside
- tooth pain   *suuu suuu*
- the slug sliding from the left nape
- grass-hopper jumping by the foot
- moustache in space
- the horse's neck
- strange smile
- flee like that   bye bye

The Process of Vaporization
- counting the strawberry seeds in the eye
- a rose bloomed in the mouth
- a rose bloomed by the feet
- inhaled the scent of the rose
- completely evaporated

On Wols and Vaporization
Movement is "pushed out" through a continual relation to the image, rather than as an emulation of form. This is the method for fine tuning the senses and developing a "network of nerves."

1) Lotus Flower
2) Orchard
3) Plant
4) Peacock
5) Owl
6) Coutaud's Bird
7) Spectre Bird
8) Duck's Neck
9) Snake of a Shaman
10) Horse
11) Child = Cupid
12) Mad Person Going to a Party
13) Blind Person
14) Sick Person
15) Girl in the Forest
16) Buzzing Person
17) Gentlewoman Pig
18) Hanako of the Reverse-side of the Mask
19) Impaired Face
20) Doll's Hands (Fast-changing Hands)
21) Flower of the Needle
22) Sonnenstern – Flower of the Face
23) Sonnenstern – Horn of Light
24) Michaux – Droplet of Ink
25) Delvaux
26) Redon
27) Ghost
28) Bodhisattva
29) Buddha Mandala
30) Buddha Listening to All Sounds
31) Buddha Pushing Buddhas from his Mouth

1) Lotus Flower – become aware of the stem in the water
- labyrinth of hands – hands in variations of Maya
- reflection on water
- angle upwards right   *phwah–*
- sunken face – pulled downwards from below the hips
- angle upwards right   *phwah–*
- pulled eternally backwards left – sensing smoke from the pores

2) Orchard
- the smell of fruit, *pwah–*
- directions within the body dispersing
  not about the connection of poses
  the smell of the grape orchard   relation towards the landscape

3) Plant
- roots extending from Maya's hands, feet, back
  rustle rustle

- Maya's hand holding the skirt
- fine roots (elbows) extending from Maya's arms and legs
  rustle rustle
- Maya's hand sticks a hair-comb in
- the thickest roots extend from Maya's arms and legs
  rustle rustle
- old woman with Maya's knitting hands
  click click click (hands' nerves)
- Maya's hands intertwine extending upwards
  when the leaves fell the horse's neck appeared

4) Peacock
- *crunch crunch* of the foot (glass high-heel treading on frost)
- *prick prick* of the cockscomb
- *rustle rustle* of feathers from the hips (the long skirt *swishing* in all directions)
- *click click* of the bird's joints
- insects and dust gather in the countless feathers
- thousands of feathers beneath the armpits
- many gazes

1 tips of the distant forest (taller to the left)
2 distant heavy clouds (a little lower to the right)
3 distant horizon, dust cloud *wah–* (advance towards 1, lower *su–*)
4 sinking into the darkness (retreat towards 2)

Ashikawa Commentary
- feet, back, cockscomb neck, gazes diverging
- form emerges from the varying directions and distance of gazes
- gazes pulled by thread – going anywhere you like

5) Owl
- *fluff* of the back
- *rustle* of the armpits
- *tap* of the nails
- *scrunch* of the face
- *prick* of the eyes
- *purse* of the beak

6) Coutaud's Bird
- a bird with a flower on it (the shape and colour of petals)
- *click* of the wings (shoulders)
- *tap* of the nails
- the flower of the face *phwah–*

7) Spectre Bird
- spectre of a chicken reflected on water-covered glass
- *bwah–* the wet world after death
- *oooh – drip drip drip*
- persistence towards life

8) Duck's Neck – a single wire winding within the body
- relating to the nerves of the forehead and back of the head

- a single wire extending from within the body – nerves extend from the soles of the feet
- speed is thinness
- the letter S at a downward-right angle
- leaning the neck to the right-side, a sideways S
- the letter S at a downward-left angle
- the letter S at an upward-right angle

9) Snake of a Shaman
- the thickness of the snake – becoming thin and entering the body
- the torso ascending 20 metres above the head
- hair entering the body
- the snake standing and walking – hair becoming damp   awareness of scales
- the white snake walks holding a candle → watched from above, watched from above after walking

10) Horse
- awareness of the long face
- looking downward-left – three steps (flanks *burn*)
- looking backward-right – three steps
- stretching upwards to place the chin on the upper-left fence – three steps
- body facing sideways, face directed forward
- drawing the S, the chin goes downwards
- looking towards the right-side – three steps
- *drop* towards the back
- stretching towards the front, turning in the direction of backward-right
- reversing the direction, neck left, gaze right, neck right, gaze left
- body sideways, face forward
- letter S – *drop* – letter S – sit
- look to the right-side
- look forward-left
- opening the mouth wide and neighing

Hijikata Commentary – awareness of the cow's weight, its sluggishness, the length of the neck
The awareness of the horse's neck and the length of the face. If the neck of the cow or the horse is used to interrupt the "Walk of a Measure," then the effect is of a 'mysterious figure.' If the same is done with "Maya," then the lower body becomes a statue, whilst the upper body becomes an animal. These are some of the possible movement variations available.

11) Child – Cupid
- child dreaming in its sleep, soft neck
- the neck leans left, a bracelet in the hand
- neck leans right, a ring in the hand

12) Mad Person Going to a Party
- right hand holding the child's hand next to you
- left hand holding a bouquet
- dispersion of gazes
- dispersion of directions
- thin gazes of a mad person

13) Blind Person

No. 1
- a cane in the right hand
- a needle in the left hand
- an eye on the forehead
- nerves extending slightly to the upper-left
- eyes on the soles of the feet, an eye on the nose
- nerves inside the ears
- humidity

No. 2
- hanging the neck
- hand on the opponent's mantle – letting it play

No. 3
- nerves of the back, a blind man caught by gazes, rounded back
- trying to grab the opponent with the right hand – don't lock the elbows
- dispersion of nerves
- the nerves of the back – hunchback

No. 4
- the smiling blind man, looking left, the forehead stares
- laughing, slackening, loose
- hands are playing

No. 5
- *aaah–*, the man who can't be saved, Bosch
- hollow eyes
- towards the sky, *aaah–*
- the right hand grabs the soil

14) Sick Person

No. 1 Handshake with a Doctor
- 100% of the nerves in the right hand
- light on the forehead

No. 2 Girl who was Placed in a Box
- gloominess
- facing forward, whited out eyes
- fingers as a box
- inside the box – nerves going inside, up and down, forward and back, left and right

No. 3 Window
- light rain outside the window to the front-left
- peering forehead as a dead face
- hand permitted to play by the hand

No. 4 Bird, Wind, Light
- bird in the hand   wind through the teeth   light on the forehead
- showing the teeth – slight smile

- forehead forward

No. 5 Flowing
- with the face of No. 4
- thread from the back of the head diagonally upward-right
- straightening the spine

15) Girl in the Forest
- an iron hairband locks to the forehead *click*
- mouth opened wide *gwah* –
- nerves moving across the width of the forehead, whited out eyes
- back of the left shoulder pulling a forest
- to pull the forest, nerves of the nape are made to go upward right

16) Buzzing Person – melting into sensations
- foot tip facing forward
- feathers on the hips
- silver needle in the left hand – don't let it stick to the fingertips
- left hand supporting the horse
- insects surrounding the head   the sound of "buzzing"
- carrying the soles of the feet
- dispersion of nerves – hands, feathers, needle, surrounding sound
- the walk has a feeling of floating from the hips' feathers – dropping the hips

17) Gentlewoman Pig
- 30-watt light bulb on the forehead
- *rustle rustle* of leaves in the left ear
- armrest of the left arm, the wrist *twist* – effortlessly
- the smell of flowers, the smell of gas
- leaves of the head, ribbon

18) Hanako of the Reverse-side of the Mask
- the *rough* feeling of the reverse-side of the mask – pus, scabs
- is the mask a face, or the face a mask
- squished left eye, left face running and drying
- blank right face, right whited out eye turning
- pus and dribble, pus even beneath the soles of the feet

19) Impaired Face (the idiot)

No. 1 Half Idiot
- sticking out the upper teeth with a weak smile
- narrowing the eyes

No. 2 Weak Idiot
- sideways glance (left)
- closing the chin – lower chin pulled upwards – weak smile

No. 3 Great Idiot
- opening the mouth with lips protruding
- whited out eyes

No. 4 Squashed Idiot
- opening the lower chin as wide as possible
- whited out eyes

No. 5 Syphilitic Idiot
- half open mouth, sticking out the tongue, belly *pant pant*
- whited out eyes

20) Hands of the Doll
- made from wood, an object, drying
- insides hollow   light
- moving from being pulled by thread

Hijikata Commentary
Once you understand the "Hands of the Doll," any other movement becomes possible.

21) Flower of the Needle (variation of hands)
- holding a thin needle, there's a beautiful red rose
- unfurled the fine petals with a needle, tried to return them but found the petals were fine pink shells
- forcing open the mouth of the hard-closed shell, and reeling in the fine silk thread

22) Sonnenstern – flower of the face
- weak smile around the mouth
- leaves *rustle rustle*, tendrils extend, tangling
- becoming particles

23) Sonnenstern – horn of light
- horn of light, captured by the sound   *huuu–*

24) Michaux – Droplet of Ink
- drying
- droplet of ink on the left forehead
- droplet running across to the right side of the face
- droplet rising up the back of the nape
- nerve connecting the chin and the foot broke *snap* – chin juts out
- the sound *pi pi* (time)
- made only of nerves

25) Delvaux
- the instant of being captured by something, the thing objectified
- eyes *startle*!! eyes that see nothing *glistening*
- departure of the spirit
- the Delvaux-esque world
- captured by something
- becoming objectified

26) Redon
- rolling back to whited out eyes
- hairs *fluffy* all over the face

- a sunken eye on the forehead
- nerves concentrating in the forehead
- the laughing mouth split to the ears

27) Ghost
- carrying a lantern in the right hand
- teeth like dentures
- background sooty and rotting

ランフを持つ人　　本彩　　灯節

28) Bodhisattva
- lotus flower on the sole of the foot and base of the ear (left foot, left ear)
- flower at the base of the ear stretches backwards
- robe draped from the right arm, a flower in the left hand
- robe fluttering in the wind – thin robe
- everything is evaporating – awareness of smoke

29) Buddha Mandala

便所の天女

- water on the forehead, grain of the Buddha, labyrinth of fingers
- white lotus flower blooming from below, the stem extending, the fountain diverging
- the lotus flower that blooms on the soles of the feet, the knees, the hips, the armpits, the elbows, behind the ears, and on the back of the head
- water droplets dripping down the robe
- the space of Mandala behind, swaying things

30) Buddha Listening to All Sounds
- all the nerves being caught by the sound of a bell ringing inside the skill
- ears angled slightly right, an eye placed on the forehead

Hijikata Commentary – turning when caught by the sound

31) Buddha Pushing Buddhas from his Mouth
- chanting to Buddha, the Buddha chant becomes a string of small Buddhas floating out from the mouth
- the throat closes *gulp*, sick feeling, lower chin juts out
- gaze concentrated on the small Buddhas

Appendix 4: Phrases – Connecting Movements

Girl of Roses
- a rose blooming in the mouth
- dandelions in the ears, Golden Lace flowers on the soles of the feet
- feathers from the hips
- holding a bottle of poison in the right hand

↓

Bird of Light – Heron
- nerves extending above the head parallel to the earth
- nerves extending from the nape to the ceiling
- body bathing in light the heron sung *coo–*

↓

Girl Wearing a Mantle of Light
- a mantle of light on the back, how far can you extend into a plane
- weak girl
- that girl has walked on a net of light

↓

Toyen
- an *obi* of light spreading from the hips to the sky
- the *obi* of light spreading underground, spreads evenly
- a lady wearing lace gloves within the eternally spreading *obi* of light
- from under the girl's nose a butterfly of light *flap flap* soared to the right ceiling

↓

Beardsley

No. 1
- figure made only of nerves
- fine gentlewoman wearing a long trained skirt and thin silk dress
- gaze following the nerve extending from the left fingertip
- a nerve extending from the back of the head to heaven

↓

No. 2
- fine gentlewoman groping along a wall in darkness
- instability underfoot
- eyes attached to the right fingertips feeling along the wall
- nerves extending to the ceiling

↓

Beardsley – gentlewoman Peacock

- fine and beautiful feathers extending from the back of the head
- the long silk skirt (= peacock feathers extending from the hips)
- the gentlewoman turns and her long skirt follows
- the gentlewoman is not turning, the skirt is turning
- from the nape, through the back of the head, nerves extending to the ceiling
- nerves pull the train of the skirt
- turned and gazed at the train of the skirt following behind
- a wind blows from beneath *woosh*
- fine gentlewoman picking up the skirt and half-turning
- just as if there were a deer

↓

No. 4

- gazing over the shoulder at an opponent
- the left hand seeking a handshake
- nerves extending to the ceiling so as not to flee backwards

↓

No. 3
i) a nerve extending from the chin to heaven as if appealing for help
ii) resting hands

↓

Girl of Roses

Phrases of Fluttering Things

Things that transform into smoke; things that can appear at any moment; things that have already passed away; vague substances; lingering things. The weakness and thinness extracted from these things.

Fluttering Buddha
- Buddha in the space of the flower
- pushing out hairs from all of the pores
- wind is blowing
- the sensation of "buzzing person"

↓

Twelve Aspects
- the extracted thinness of a trail of smoke
- seems cool
- seems smoky
- seems sleepy
- seems pitiable
- seems annoyed (strained)
- seems warm

↓

Phantom Transformation
- a formless powerless thing held together by wind
- made of paper
- *flap flap* precisely describe the fluttering thing

No. 1 Flagpole
- trail of wind on the flag
- dispersion of directions

No. 2 Hotpot
- a pot on top of the head
- watched from above
- wind from an accordion

No. 3 The Baboon with Three Faces
- the pot has been removed
- the waving of the baboon's long hair
- curlers on the back of the head

No. 4 Tiger – the letter S tracing the internal organs
- the letter S of the shoulder
- the letter S of the torso

- the letter S of the anus

No. 5 Waving Strands of Hair

No. 6 Fan in the Hand – waving fan in the hand that follows the returning letter S
- hanging neck
↓
Twelve Aspects
↓
Fluttering Buddha
overlaying "Phantom Transformation," "Twelve Aspects," "Fluttering Buddha" = wind blowing in a place of nothingness, the limit of fluttering things

Hijikata Commentary
- the classification of fluttering and tossed about things
- make the technique ambiguous, without becoming confused
- it is impossible to comprehend the uniformity of speed – the speed of wind cannot be uniform.

Space Phrases

Space of *Okame* [round-faced goddess often in *nō*]
- the expansion of *Okame*'s face by 4 metres in 4 directions
- a huge warped space   *bwah–*
- expanding infinitely
↓
Space of *Tengu* [long-nosed red-faced goblin]
- the expansion of a *Tengu*'s face by 4 metres in 4 directions
- a fan in the hand – a wind coming from afar *woosh*
- the long and thick nose
- expanding infinitely
↓
Space of *Okame*
↓
Goya: the Pope of Pus
- pus, saliva, discharge of ears, flesh oozing, darkness
- brain dangling down to the mouth
- elbow brushing the robe of pus
- flesh *zure* [oozing] – here *zure* [ooze] there *zure* [ooze]
- the Pope of Pus sinking into darkness
- controlling the slippage of *zure* [lags] in time = dispersion
↓
Gentlewoman Before the Mirror
- an 80 kilo fat gentlewoman
- armrest of the left arm
- right hand holds a puff
- captivated by the self in the mirror
↓
Vinyl Mantle
- a long vinyl mantle covering from the head
- the cylinder circles the edge of the whirlpool
↓
Skeleton

Appendix 5: Etudes – Butō Image-Language

The longer descriptions Hijikata developed to translate image into movement might be termed 'etudes.' Taking the form of prose-poetry, this language often describes poses that require very little actual movement. In the same way as the necessary requirements of the choreographic forms, the 'etudes' form a communicative medium between Hijikata and his dancers. This language not only cues *butō* movement, but also provides a key to the *butō* worldview. I have entitled these texts as 'etudes,' but they might be thought of more generally as a form of stage direction.

1) Grave-keeper
2) Flamand
3) Flamand – Matière
4) City
5) Canal

Grave-keeper

the season is spring
nothing but sweet scented flowers blooming all around   the out-of-season wind blowing
the blue sky   the ocean of yellow rape blossoms below   the lark soaring higher and higher
rustling in the wind   a conspicuous wave swaying a single white man emerged
holding a birdlime branch in his hand   he approached with a light step
then the man's feet suddenly stopped   even the soaring dust   even the lark in the sky   even the rape blossoms are silenced
just like a painting   the man's eyes are gazing into the empty distance
no   look more closely   they are gazing at some point
it is the bird nest   taking two unnoticed steps forward
a nest on the upper reaches of the high trees   merely gazing
the colour   the call of the fledgling   the size of sweetness
just as though his spirit is captured
carefully taking in each strand   down to the fledgling's downing
to the colour of its beak
just as the child who tries to catch the cicada   and is caught by the cicada
the one gazing at the mirror is the illusion and the one reflected is the reality
nothing but the nest in the man's eyes
squawk the fledgling crying beneath the stone   the secret of why it flies higher
the nest reflected in his eyes   no rather the nest is already formed in his eyes
and then inside his head
his head is full of nests
this is Bosch   this is never truly being saved
the out-of-season wind blew inside his head
summer has passed with the voice of the cicada   rain   like mist hanging all around
at some point   the surroundings completely changed
that was where the spirit was caught   there was a young man soaked through with rain
graveyard   the gravestones are faintly visible in the haze
the young grave-keeper   struck over the head with a blunt thing   there is the gloomy grave-keeper with blood oozing from his nose
and a cleft palate   when the summer passed the man's face   half collapsed with pus
and beneath the side of the collapsed eye a new eye has almost formed
he must have been burned   a fever has completely caught his heart
and so the sound can be heard of flesh boiling *bubble bubble* from the rotten surface of mingling pus and blood

hair soaking wet with rain   stuck to the face of a hunchback
because a summer passed   being caught by the cicada in a dark forest
his back is horribly hunched   his legs draw a curve
in the sludge *slop slop*
the young gloomy grave-keeper fleeing the bark of a small dog
a season came like one never seen

Flamand

he has spent 25 years ailing in a sick bed
the sweetshop owner lying by a roadside   the incompetent
because of that moss and fungi are growing all over his back
the world in a single tatami mat   the dream of the sick   the illusion of the blind
the peculiar reverence and thirst of the blind
the blind man   has more sensitive nerves than the man who sees
the blind man's feelers   nerves   the blind whale   the blind whale shored on a beach
there are many small fish nibbling its body
a fantasy of solitude brought by hunger and fatigue

he is a eunuch   neutralized by castration
that gives rise to a sense of mystery
from the wound left by his severed testicles   pus and blood seep out
a spider's web is stuck to it
the grubby world of a spider's web   meshed with a futon's cotton
he has lost the function of his mouth as a mouth   his eye as an eye   his arm as an arm   his leg as a
leg
chaos
gaze through the inside of a crystal   gaze at the dark interior of the skull   such a strange haunted
house
around you on the tatami there are many things other than floors and walls
like vegetables growing
and the knee joints   the finger joints   the elbow joints   are hoeing the field
things like tomatoes and pumpkins are growing there
there is a room inside your body   a locked room
a language of the flesh that reunites separated things
a language between each finger joint   a kingdom of nerves
for the precise capturing of something vague   you need to find a single tone
the lying figure is not like something neat
nor something slumped   but something in between
you need the strange peace of a trapped place

Flamand – Matière

No. 1

worms entered the anus   the back's fungi
the nape's leeches   the cheek's worms
an ear on the nose   the toes cut the wind *snap*
a finger pricks   listening to an audio illusion
an ear on the nose   a twig in the skull snapped *crack*

No. 2

from the distant forest a girl approaches *tap tap*
your own eyes   watch your own eyes
a huge amoeba in space
a thousand branches
listen to a sound with the back of the ears   hand draws a strange letter
a leg converses with a leg   far off a kite rises *phew*
the body also naturally rises
the doors of the chest and forehead open and close *rattle*
eyeballs on the ends of each hair   an insect crawls up from the foot
a putrid smell in spite of the surround
the knee joints hoe the field *keenly*

No. 3

taking a shit   the shit clinging to the crotch *sticky*   having fled from it
inside the head a spiral swirl turns upwards *sharply*
the head becomes a penis   the legs breathe once then twice *phew*
the leg you intended to lower dropped without asking
was the place it landed a real floor
the face might collapse *slump*
fever   because the hand was on the floor so long it became stuck to the floor
you try to peel it off with the wings on your back
the separation of hands and wings
a trapped blind whale   the blind man's special feelers
chasing invisible things behind eyelids
the immeasurable density   melting   *oozing*
the feeling of picking a scab
a dwarf running in the internal organs
breath in the waist   hands and legs stick to the floor   there's no way to move with ease
the leg longs for a leg's remains
the hand longs for a hand's remains

No. 4

the teeth are a piano's keys   idiot transformation   the convulsing cat leaps and stops in mid-air
insects coming from the anus   a spider's web
eyes behind you   eyes above the head   eyes beneath the chin   eyes inside the abdomen
ears placed on the waist   an ear on the nose
shivering at an unidentifiable pathway
where that harmony reaches its extreme
the right elbow hangs on a thread *phew*
sunflower once twice three times
the hand you intended to lower drops without asking
I want to go to the toilet….
fingers became high-heels
sliding on shit and phlegm *slippery*
gone-off smell   picking the scab   *tearing*
at that moment   a gust of wind blows after 25 years beneath your stomach
somewhere there's a peddler's voice
the neck is so extended it looks completely inhuman
a leech is crawling up the nape   I really want to go to the toilet…   *trickling*
it's fever   meeting the heated counterattack of a tatami   really I can't

obviously I can't   the only thing left is to rub your legs together
you rub and that rubbed leg somehow becomes the face's skin peeling off *flaky*
a strange peacefulness   a fissure in the long sky
a mountain stream running to a river
a single boat is crossing the body of a canal   but then insects come from the anus
the twig at the temple
the letters of the strange fingers will not stop
the incompetent one bedridden   for 25 years

Flamand   what kind of dream can you see
is it a whale eaten by small turtles   or a bateau ivre?
is that a bloody scene of war happening above your head?
what a huge body. The blind whale
a single boat enters the inlet in the back of your eyelid
no   isn't it leaving
density   pus   shit   piss   free-flowing
but the back of the ears are surely listening to some sound
ugh   I want to move   for some reason I want to move
it's the monarch   it's the war   *ugh   peeling*
peeling the skin that is stuck to the floor   *peeling*   Hitler
holding a dagger in the right hand   it's Hitler
there is also the conversation of the legs   the leg dropped by itself
I can't   obviously I can't
the only way is to rub the legs together   a twig above the head *snaps*
what went on really what went on   what happened
in the world of a single tatami   in my world
you are finally standing up Flamand
bedridden for 25 years lying by the roadside   can you stand Flamand
but the hand is not moving as a hand   the leg is not moving as a leg
can you stand Flamand
sagging flesh   skin   creaking bones
collapsing skin *flaking*
the legs and hands aren't listening   each of them moving in any direction they like
from the foot   I was surprised   slug sliding up the leg
birds fly out from the temples *flap flap*
something inside the body *swayed* and collapsed
something must have happened in the kingdom of nerves
can you stand Flamand
the man with shit piss and blood dry *crusty* inside his internal organs
really what does it mean to stand
Flamand
the *crunching* sound of joints
the lowered hips   the expanded chest
the touching of legs after 25 years
what is it really to stand   Flemish
can you stand Flemish
time!!
"comprehend the real meaning of the grotesque"
"the body living only by nerves does not move at all"
can you stand Flemish

City

☆ from ghost and ruins continue towards the investigation of existence
can you continue on to Auschwitz, leprosy, Bresdin, and the city of Ernst
people made of nothing but feelers and particles wander
Fautrier

opened the doors and emerged from the blast furnace   the flesh body with a hand stuck to the leg to
the neck to the chest
twenty stuck lumps of flesh emerged from the furnace
leprosy   scream   only the bone planted white in the stuck lump of flesh   now   the   door   opens
after 20 years of darkness   the Auschwitz victim is bathed in outside light for the first time   softly
collapsing in the light   the turning vision
the Auschwitz leprosy victim just now returned from the city of leprosy emerged with a white-
powdered face   the first season has come   a season like one never seen   the turning vision
everything pales with separation   the separation of flesh and bones   internal organs hanging out of
the body   from separation to rotting   from rotting to digestion   where did that scream go
only hairs and nails grow without relation to personality   the world has completely changed
feelers and particles   feelers are the relatives of insects   insects in space   a person with skin so
weak it flakes at the lightest touch   no   not only the skin
even the inside of the organs are fully dried *flaking* collapsing   the heart is pale as a piece of tin
walking on the thin razor blade   the bloodstained carriage inside a stone   the man with a solidified
right arm   at the moment he decided to walk   the nerves in the forehead broke *snap*   an ear placed
on the nose
birds flew out from the temples   *flap flap flap flap flap flap*   falling leaves inside the head   the
sound of a spoon   wind through the teeth   walking   the walking you is already walking   to the
place where no-one has gone   a slug sliding on the back   an insect crawling up from the foot
eyeballs placed on the ends of hairs   squishing insects with feet soles whilst walking   but that
solidified right arm doesn't sway a single hair   the leaping cat stopped in mid-air   the measure
between heaven and earth is walking this way   stopped *suddenly*   I really wonder how far I have
come   then I realized   I was already in the orchard   the rustling of wind   the whispering of leaves
the foot stung by a prick of grass underfoot   without stopping   it was walking   ripened fruit   that
rich smell   radiating heat   fever   having walked too much on ripened earth   at some point the
solidified right arm moved to a different patch of earth   *galbamejiro* [uncertain meaning]   in the
storehouse   considering entering the storehouse ahead   but there is something pulling you back
who is it!!   It is your self   but of course you still want to enter   the moment you considered entering
the door opened *bang*
old   the stench of mould   a gone-off smell stinging the nose   but going on   a spider's web covers
everything in front   brushed aside and entered   a tray of flesh by the feet *pacing*   the stick in front
of you entered   bent *flop*
its your own tales   the stick escaped slipping away   following it with the eyes   out of sight
a slug sliding on the face
"give me back my money Sasaki" "but I returned it last month" and Maya's hand casually intervenes
the conversation   it transformed unnoticed into a gecko   a gecko stuck to a single plate of glass
stuck out the tongue   plant   Maya's feet   horse's neck   the 5 cm drop of the hips   Bacon Orangutan   flower   waltz   a sheet of the right hand becomes a hook   exhaled   surgeon's horse   that's
the war   that's a rebellion   that's genocide   but the bone horse dances a wild death dance
don't forgive a single flying feather   the surroundings became quiet again   then   many years passed
in that way   many seasons came and went
there was a horse made only of dried feelers and particles
it received the punishment of a great god

Canal

☆ a work bothered by the inner world
movement of the earth   going down the body's canal
that last stage of the work of pouring movement into flesh
the river of oblivion   the pillar of fresh flesh
the world of the ears   until a single goat is born
what is a commemoration photograph

the cow inside the toilet
a single soft beast   there is a cow   a heavy-rain soaked dahlia on the head   a dwarf walking on the
back *tap tap*   the letter S of the back   the waist burning *harshly*   graceful wings on the hips   a red
flag somewhere inside the body   *flap flap*   there is that powerful cow   your own mask is before
you   the mask that is 10 cm from the skin   the flesh is called   and it flees   pulling and being
pulled   a single cow struggles in this ratification   and then going deeper into this extreme a single
moment of vacuum was born   stealing out smoothly as though entering a mirror   and then he
realized there was a strange creature in the palace toilet   a wretched stench   eye-stinging ammonia
drifting steam   not sure what but something mixes with the air rising from beneath   unable to stop
traced the slug's glistening trail on the toilet wall   that's when leaves fell rustling in the head   but
only for a moment   and then the sound of a spoon clinking   a wind entered through the molar teeth
tracing further the slug's trail depends on the sound of that wind   at that moment saw the tray of
flesh by the feet   *scatter*   then whilst thinking *huh* I saw the stick by my left side   thinking
about what it was and realizing it was a stick, it bent *flop*   it was a snake   just your body telling
tales   what does it mean to be straight   the stick *slyly* fled far off again   following its track with
the eyes   going so far it goes out of sight into a dazed place   Macbeth's witches' nails stand up
behind you *prick*   unable to move despite the struggle   the weight intensifies   attempting to grow
taller in stages *gu gu gu gu* but pushed down by something   remaining in that relation   going steadily
upwards   at the limit there is a single yawn   and at that moment someone yawned wide overhead
a ribbon at the compound eyes' focal point   rain fell on the ribbon   heavy wet rag
you notice it and there's a strange sound   it's the sea   the girl with a heavy ribbon on her head
walked on the beach
when you realised that the ribbon and the girl   and everything else   was all the work of the wind an
ear was placed on the nose
huh the hand is also becoming an ear   what sound is it listening to   it was the single slug in the ear
ear discharge   mushy with pus   the gone-off smell of pus
tracing the wall of the ear along a strange curve *sliding*   the unknown shore of an ear where no one
has landed before   the hand traces the wall of the ear by itself   the back is also listening to a sound
by itself   of course there is also an ear on the nose *dribble dribble dribble*
huh what is it   it must be ear discharge and pus coming from you ear
the pus that runs down the nape   *oh* from the armpit and anus too   pus is dribbling out   and there's
pus cooled solid too   and things that have become scabs
it's ear discharge!   the ear's avalanche   and the thing that walks on the back of my ears
trying to climb the wall of the ears   no good   the upper body still wants to go up and up   but an
avalanche of pus falls around the feet *dribble dribble dribble*   the separation of the upper and lower
body   the eternal rising and falling   *dribble dribble dribble* it became harder to breath   it seems
the invisible wall is coming closer   it is getting gradually narrower   entered the ear's recess   where
there was still fresh pus   dribbling   a sea of blood   a room of bright red blood   a room of *gloopy*
and slightly sour blood   a strange smell   can't breathe   somehow can see a white shining door over
there   went towards the door   but unable to move   the whole body coated in pus   stuck in many
places   it hurts   still hard to peel the scabs
ah that's a surprise, isn't my body sinking 1cm at a time   *oozing* just like a bottomless swamp   can't
even struggle

aaah help!!   and then that white door over there rattled a little

a single dandelion bloomed in the ear   *ah* a dandelion has bloomed in the eardrum   it's just that when you break the stem white pus comes out   but for a second   looking closer it's just the same old inner ear   huge ears placed on the waste *crunch*   the ear walking inside the ear that draws a strange curve   the door of the forehead *creaks* and *slams* open and closed   *dribble dribble dribble* and more came out from the inner ear   climbing the wall of the ear   *dribble dribble dribble* slipping out and walking

who is walking inside your ear?   of course it is yourself   isn't that obvious   now you're traveling in the most distant place   *dribble dribble dribble*   insects came out the anus   an ear was placed on the nose   upper and lower body are stretching like sticky rice   the whole body dropped 5 cm   salute cow man became a soldier and returned triumphant from the city of ears   but with a large scab for a face   it's the trace of a valiant war   picking the scab and using it as a mirror to do your make-up the mirror overclouds in an instant   and a memory vividly returns   sediment   smoke   Belmer from that dullness a war trophy of a rhino ornament emerged   *creak* going into the revolving door a season like one never seen before   a bride in the snow seen in a distant land   a *tsunokakushi* [Japanese hood-like bridal veil]   clothes whiter than the snow   carrying a dried fish in the right hand   walking in the snow wearing rubber long boots *crunch crunch*   feet sinking softly   digging the fish in the snow on the left then right side   pointing into the air as though foretelling the coming storm

the next instant   the illusion of the girl passing through a ring of fire like a lion   using a stick to brush off the snow from the body *brush brush*   a distant ringing in the ears   shiverthe ear's mystery sitting in the centre of the eardrum   placing the fish on the earth and playing like a child   like the breath-taking relationship between a girl and old woman who can transform into each other in an instant

the skin that has become as clear-white as snow   just like the wings of a dragonfly   is eaten by insects the whole body is eaten by insects   *crunching* an old woman like a sizzling cuttlefish   to tell the truth it's the girl with a ribbon walking on the beach   the hips dislocate *click*   the flesh of the inner thighs drops and quivers *flap flap* like an octopus   an extreme expression   Bacon

the cuttlefish old woman is walking on the shore of the ears   she stopped abruptly   the trace of a lone finger   then solidified in that state   the death waltz   Holstein [breed of cattle]   returned tracing the ear   or was everything I saw just a single phantom of wind   of course it was just a cow in a toilet   like it had been dazzled by the strong smell   the cow starts to move   persistently fighting with the mask in front   the miraculous and mediated union of animals and plants   the stem extended upwards and leaves scattered

the person with a pipe and the mother with an infant

the old woman playing a *biwa* [Japanese lute-like instrument]   a small bird calls by the feet *co*   it was all the work of the lying old woman   about to sing but check the surround   when discovered like a person crying wolf   no   it must be the dream of the *fukusuke* [round-faced china doll associated with good luck] sitting over there with a head full of 20 litres of water

revealing the back, walk along the line of the ears   look closer   and it is the cloak of pus extending 20 metres ahead   it was a single goat pulling the dress of bright red mauve

looking back *suddenly* with two blurred faces of Bacon   the single goat appeared from the pus polishing the ball of pus   it's the pus candy   the pus jewel   the *kinkatō* [traditional colourful sweets] the *kinkatō* walking in a dark barn   conversing   resting   and hiding behind the column   whilst uttering some secrets   suddenly sunlight flooded the barn *bwah–*   an eye-blinding flash   was this all about a commemoration photograph

look closer and notice the face of the first son who went to war in the yellowed and sooty photograph

Appendix 6: "The Man Like a Firefly Covered with Dust"

For the opening commemoration of *The Kanazawa Dance Theater*, August 26-28, 1977, with Yamamoto Moe and *Kanazawa Butōkan*, recorded by Ichiyoshi Shunzō

(first act)   armour
scene
1 the room of armour squirming – changing panels
2 the birth of the man as a firefly – futon
Yamamoto solo
3 shed-skin
eaten by insects
4 Yamamoto white dress
5 Nishimura red dress

(second act)   sliding door
1 Yamamoto red dress
2 grass seagull
3 duet
4 crow

(third act)   aluminium
1 mask
2 duet – psychology
3 Buddha
4 Nishimura with Buddha
5 Yamamoto white dress
6 finale – male chorus

(first act) armour, third scene, "shed-skin" mantle of pus and petticoat
tiny insects are eating the entire body of the firefly
insects are devouring everything   from the internal organs   the dried out body
the shed-skin of the fireflies which transformed into the firefly man is eaten by insects and collapses
surrounded by insects which are eating the fireflies
those shed-skins   made to move and stand up by insects

(second act) sliding doors, second scene (grass seagull) black dress + grass
firefly man shining pure red attracting strange insects
the grass with seagulls' wings is covering the firefly man
the voice of grass echoes low *oooh*
the landed grasses approaching the firefly man
the frantically running firefly man
the grass seagull sways *rustling*
when the firefly man disappears, the strange grass seagull sticks to the sliding door
rustling, the sound of *rustling* remained as the grass seagull disappeared into the sliding door

(second act) sliding doors, fourth scene "crow" black dress
strange firefly man, crows gather around the scent of his death
no, that's not the crow   that's a crow goblin!!

"crow on the snow, I, II, II"
    ↓

"heron bird of light" two forms

↓

"the duck behind" two forms

↓

"the crow on the cliff" three forms

↓

"crow on the snow"

(third act) aluminium, first scene "mask"
"Hanako of the reverse-side of the mask"

↓

"bottom teeth"

↓

"squashed"

↓

"stretched"

"scorching" induced by the concentration and cramping of nerves

(third act) aluminium, third scene "Buddha"
standing without doing anything

↓

"pomegranate teeth"

↓

"little girl"

↓

"Redon"

↓

"grains of Buddha"

↓

"Small Buddha" the infant Buddha holding a stick in his left hand and sphere in his right
"Heaven and Earth"　　　extending from the tips of the left fingers
　　　　　　　　　　　　a string of light
　　　　　　　　　　　　droplets of water fall from the right hand
　　　　　　　　　　　　the form of the Buddha between heaven and earth
　　　　　　　　　　　　(strangeness of the firefly man in the Buddha's face)
"the Buddha of pomegranate teeth"

↓

"Redon's Buddha"

↓

"grain"

↓

"Fautrier" – sitting
1 *chomp chomp*　　　　　object of plaster, only the jaw moves
　　　chomp chomp jaw moving up and down
2 insect cage　　　　　　holding an insect in the hand.
　　　The entire body of insects that are eaten by insects
3 dwarf　　　　　　　　puffy cheeked face of the dwarf,
　　　pendulum of the right hand

Appendix 7: Hijikata Tatsumi's Last Workshop (November 24-30, 1985)

According to the record of Harada Nanako.

November 24

- figures from the past are walking from within
- when you have "walking eyes," the self disappears
- when the body collapses, form and figure become visible
- everything begins from the choice for self-destruction
- the obscurity of the origin is crucial
- the body is not image but act (function)
- a mysterious journey to my interior, that is *butō*
- the enwrapping of the exterior with the interior

☆ the body suspended by a single thread from the solar plexus
hips lowered as life sinks
walking without feet   the thread from the forehead   the two threads from the molar teeth
the thread from the ears   the thread from the joints   then moved that way by countless threads

☆ <labyrinth of fingers> = (dismantling the family)
the movement of both elbows by the thread guided from 10 metres ahead
the separation of fingers on both hands <the face of Hannya mask [red-horned demonic *nō* character]>
(dismantling the family)

☆ the theatre of faces
<strange smiling mask>   light from the forehead, lower lip slightly projected
                                   80% of behind is darkness
< face with four eyes>   origin of expression and emotion
                                   expression starting from monotone / monotone on the blade
<face of smell>   gauze at the tip of the nose, winter daphne
<gaze into the skull>   face of stone – switch to Hannya mask
<face of porcelain>   pain of the molar tooth inhale smoothly
                                   deer in the forest of the molar tooth
<Redon's single eye>   crumbling teeth
                                   a crushed and trampled Buddha – the idiot boy

※in an instant the faces change one after another

the foot is not a tool to over-stride distance
perceiving the world beneath the sole –

☆ to the forest   sensing the tips of branches transfusing to the sky
the reindeer's antlers / the branch tip of a white birch / the insect's whiskers
the twig of the sole's nerve / the sensation of moistness / the sense of smell
the mushroom / the earthworm underground / the swamp / the bug
※becoming the vacant sky (the shed-skin) inside the forest

- mutual intrusion with the object / here and there
- the primal source of the image in an incision in the body
- when the body is dislocated   the world flourishes
- as the free spirit that does not carry the image…
- the ash disappears and the shape remains
- cloud is the brain of the sky
- before thinking and after thinking is the birthplace of *butō*, *butō* is not born within the process of thought
- as the existence shaken up by existence, like Artaud, like Nijinsky…
- "to appear, or to stop"
  you must decide yourself
- stealthy with heat catch a fly in the air
- become desperate swatting flies

☆ <transparent child in Africa> / countless fly eggs in the eye socket
together with countless flies   together with countless transparent eggs
a boy walking together with countless maggots towards a kingdom of ruin –

☆ diarrhoea – rain – <rotten corpse>
getting close to the strange prototype –
far away from human form –
earthworm playing with the body –

☆ <huge ancient Lion> / its haggard look
the tactiles inside   the feelers outside (whiskers)
the blurring of its figure → the parasitism of maggots – flies → melting and adhesion →
objectification (bleached bones – teeth – box) → < ghost of the lion> (the shadow of disappearing
flesh) → <ghost of a fly>

<Ghost Hannya>

firstly dirty yourself, then take all of the audience's dirt
"*I* is the one dirty thing" towards a place of dirtiness being raised like a monster

☆ falling <rain on the body's illustrated record>, the picture is glued dried and split walking with its
condition

November 26

<dawn   towards the towns of the inner body armed with patience>
tears in the skin = tears in existence / the openings tearing outward
                – the sensation of inner skin and its tears –
mouth   skin's pores   when the countless white downy strands emerge from all the body's openings
I am a dandelion floating on air
doesn't a person with a disability live freely by becoming two people
the measurement between one *zure* [gap] and another – is the source of existence
for example, the mouth on the neck   the nose on the forehead   two vaginas on the back
the "grotesque" is that fakeness born from time
in limitlessness emotion dies / dance stands at the edge of the scope of ordered emotion

<to a self-erasure that relates to mechanism>

☆<hydrangea> / rainy season / dilution
the hydrangea reflected on water / countless hydrangeas proliferating
Bellmer's girl – spreading into space

☆<brushing calligraphy>
a fine brush in the hand – the fine brush 2 metres from the tip of the forehead
the fine brush 2 metres from both ears – the brush of the knee – the brush of the sole
2, 3, 4, 5 brushes at the same time   being written with countless brushes

"the Yamato spirit of Shikishima…"

☆the fading countless brushes of countless cells
　↓
　　mould (dandelion hair on the sole)
dividing in every direction   fragile things in the hand…
"the hand is not doing anything… at that point the hand is dancing by itself"

※the mould will shortly go towards "Bresden's forest" –

wondering if the washed hair lying wet is a fatal disease
the donkey is returning to its own house   but where are you returning to wearing insect feelers?
　　<monomania towards the speed of insect feelers>
not taking responsibility / things without need of meaning
trying to become "1" but becoming "3"

November 27

escaping both legs   towards a primal topology
attaining salvation is the state of a uniform density of space
nirvana occurs when the "golden bell" rings
each of my hands scaling the precipice of the canvas is itself the entire precipice
each moment there is life   and death
oneself as one part of a great arc / myself as an echo of all
<the correspondence of fragment and great arc><the echo far from the centre>
the "double" (the doubled shadow) in the single point of *I*
going afar to become life-size / loving the person afar
a reproduction of Lascaux is not a reproduction
it is the preparatory study and the revisionary study that comes from the call of starvation and hunting
disposing of place-ness / the only place of the human body
the body as the place which circulates the inside and the outside
life and death   the human being as a single blade of grass with twin blossoms
the body is two tears   two stones
the plural picture drawn by water
"although I have forgotten death   I am known by death   when death comes I will offer a sitting
cushion   and together we will drink tea…" (O. Paz)

☆<the walk of a desolate cornfield>
only to sharpen the senses   not to charge with thought
leaving the body to the grass   changing in monochrome

185

countless pieces of withered corn walk alongside you

☆ <the walk of the forest's interior> (the history of Bresden's forest   the history of insects   humus earth)
swamp-land   the road of withered leaves   a brook   ivy   grass
the forest drawn from inside
horn = branch   small animal   sound of stream
the construction of a forest using minute feelers

☆ <stone in the forest's interior> = the magic instrument   the musical instrument
the stone as a flying thing = the space of the stone's interior   that time
the density of interior condensation = eyes towards the interior
the walk of the stone = the feathers of stone
the green through the crack of an iron wheel

☆ the archaeology of gesture
<the stone of Maya><the stone of a crocodile><the fight with a crocodile> =
seven dancing hands
the speed of the centre of Mandala   that standstill

☆ <horse><dinosaur><condor (bird)> dictator
the movement of the letter S
a sky of a hundred forms of waves – Turner (a boy swallowed by sky)

☆ <the dance of birds calling>
collecting air in feathers
the organic transformation of airflow (speed)

☆ <dragon><dead branch><forest><lightning>
whiskers   tusks   scales – fear   thirst   hunger
turning yourself into a crown expanded by daytime
1 a.m.   the return of the dead man

November 28

<escaping from the endurance of a state of continuous time>
- can you eat beef-steak at the slaughter house…
- can you eat a meal beside a dead person….
- "the skin on the man's back continuously peeling off with time" and "the skin peeled and collected from the back of an audience member by the *butō* dancer at a race-track"
- the last empty room in a collecting box – / entering into the empty box
- perfume as the extract (sublimation effect) of the brutal murder of flowers and trees
- the gaze = the sublimation into perfume = catharsis / the back figure (behind) of that man
- the palm and front of a hand   the rest when turning over the palm
- the agreement and incongruity of gazing fixedly at one another
- not retaining the shape   only the repetition of extinction and appearance
- another time within that condensation of a vast expanse of time   that time like the mountain, I change continuously
- between the cloud's skin and the reverse-side of skin
- the neural network on the reverse-side of a single sheet of facial skin
- the face in the mirror and this face

- conversation with my death-mask
- various images from different sources of light / red of the hand, walk of the stone's interior (or the petrifaction of light (condensation))
- "the light of the sun hurting my interior light" – El Greco
- "there is a warbling bird crouching on the marble   saving it with hands of light" – Michelangelo
- the mask of the bare face and the death mask / the actor and the dead

☆ <inner feelers – outer feelers>
peeling the skin off the face / peeling the skin off a cabbage
the bottom's skin being peeled – the neck's skin being peeled – the hand's inside skin being peeled
→ the petals of an enormous rose have been peeled
(towards the expansion of its inner feelers)

◎ the walk of "the inner feelers of small maggots inside facial skin"
↓
stopping as it is   standing on tip-toes   opening the eyes   looking at the mirror
↓ (pure outer feelers – the pure outline of existence)
the fusion of outer feelers – inner feelers
↓
moving back with inner feelers

◎ the blurred focus of inner feelers and outer feelers (the montage of two temporalities)
↓
stopping as it mixed (blurred)   standing on tip-toes reflecting in a sheet of mirror
↓
moving backwards becoming only the inner feelers

◎ <expansion of the space of inner feelers>
expansive space – inner feelers (expanded, diluted, become misty)
↓
reflecting the figure in an expansive mirror <outer feelers>
↓
expansive space – moving backwards with inner feelers

◎ a creeper plant budding from the face's four-corners <inner feelers>
↓
to the front of the mirror <outer feelers>
↓ (flattened –existence of outwardness only (outline))
moving backwards with inner feelers

◎ the inner feelers derived from the creeper plant expanding in space
↓
to the front of the expansive mirror <outer feelers>
↓
moving backwards with expansive inner feelers
↓
returning to the life-size inner feelers

◎ damp with humidity   from within the haze (mist) <simultaneous existence of inner and outer feelers>
↓
in front of the expansive mirror wet with rain (humidity)

187

↓   (the eyes slightly open)
the field of pus outside is in mutual osmosis with inner feelers
↓
moving backwards that way with one clear voice: "go to *Aburamen* and buy soba!"

◎ the facial nerves of inner feelers (the face of F. Bacon)

D
I   distortion of the life-size face
L ↓
U distortion of the 10-metre face (slightly softened distortion)
T ↓
I   distortion of the expansive face (misty dispersion – diluted tiny movements)
O
N
※ facial nerves as the roaming of an enormous Buddhist temple

◎ while peeling the facial skin / while peeling the cabbage
         (inner feelers)   (outer feelers)
while taking the petals → expanding → Bacon's distorted face inside this, is…
※ life-size → 10 times larger → infinitely large → petrified light → Eve   horse

◎ the drying of inner feelers
↓
towards dead grass
↓
towards dead branches

- the continuous return to inner feelers allows for the gain of external freedom
- smoothly leave the point of standstill, smoothly return to inner feelers
- severance   release
- the present as a transition towards explosion
- an expansive city inside the hand

November 29

<total revision>
- standing as a set-measure between the heaven and the earth
- between tension and release
- in one instant to receive a burn   suddenly it "becomes"
- feeling the breathing of the wall   the wall is not merely a plane
- feeling its minute unevenness
- the melting body *gloopy*   desperately trying to stand while supporting itself
- it is cruelty – ignorance – misery
- the flesh body is itself an image   a hand is not a hand
  the *flapping* of torn flesh is important
- you have to lower to the point of an insult
  at that point   you are already right in the middle of the world

<towards the dying forest   towards the dying dance>
<towards light   towards death>   <towards "non-existence">

☆ <the forest's interior> (Bresden's forest)
◎ horn – the extension of outer feelers *crackling*
◎ the mingling of tiny horns and tree branches *crackling*
◎ insect's whiskers (to above   to right   to left)
    (breeze)
◎ the thickly grown hair of white-radish sprouts
the walk of a hundred dried feet
becoming capillary vessels deep underground…
◎ twigs of the tall, tall great tree
minute twigs – transfusion to the sky with capillary vessels
the flow of blood   (towards the sky   towards the earth   counter-current)
◎ <root of the tree> / humidity / insects / soil
the world below the waist
walking on dead leaves
walking in a brook
entering the swamp-land (towards the mud)
◎ the extension of a pine branch = towards the soaring of a dragon
◎ <hydrangea>
spreading as if disappearing / enormous hydrangea → fluttering in the wind → derivation of branches
◎ surrounded by fallen branches
walking on trampled and scattered branches (dead grass)
    ↓
walking on the floor of a "weak electric current"

◎ Bresden's eye disease / the bumpy wall / going the great distance of 1mm
◎ the darkness of inner feelers / the light of outer feelers (outline)
      (the darkness of a 2-metre diameter)
◎ the face of absence (gaunt)
(the hollow of the eye, the groove beneath the nose, the top and bottom of the ear)
    ↓
from the projection of the forehead / blood…→ towards the young grave-keeper

☆ <the face of the person living inside the forest>
iron band on the forehead / hollow of a wide mouth / root of the neck as the root of the tree   thorns
on the head / goose egg on the top of the head
walking ahead with the refrain: "iron band, hollow, root of the neck, goose's egg, iron band, hollow…"
then the branch of a tree is derived and walks in the enormous face of the forest
scent of the forest, corpses of animals, a swarm of flies
when the mist gets thicker and thicker
(the extreme dilution of inner feelers and the extreme minuteness of outer feelers)
– infinitely far – infinitely high –

◎ when he realized he –
<the rugged mountain being pulled>
the space full of   a field of hydrangea
an ocean of pus
a desolate cornfield
a thick-grown field of dandelions

Recorded by Harada Nanako

May 1

discovering the self that is caught
removing the self without conviction from this place
<walk> – take a walk
– why are you walking that way
a. walk
– don't look with eyes   don't listen with ears
walk towards the inside of the body
stand beside the nostalgic things
transcend   stand beside –
A.Y. demonstrates
– don't mistake the measurement
tuck in the chin
relax the shoulders
drop the solar plexus
place an eye on the forehead
carry the measurement –
carry the corpse –
a. imitate
– you can't live only walking
you want to go forward but are pulled back
having just killed a person
and disposed of the corpse –
A.Y., Y.Y., A.K., demonstrate
"someone walking inside my body and gone"
a. split into groups and dance on this theme
– relating as much as possible to the strangeness of the self –
A.Y., Y.Y., demonstrate on stage with lights and music
bathed in too much light becoming dazed

May 2

try doubting you are human
unreasonable ideas are also fine
what is the thing singing inside the body
what is the thing standing listening to it
keeping a creature inside the body
the time of recovery
when a human sleeps for a long time
they move in a way that cannot be thought of as human
"dinosaur neck"
the body made to live
your own body kept by a monster
A.Y. demonstrates
a. imitate
– through the eye of the needle   fall into the pit

pain behind the eyelids, your self leaking out from your anus
the self is melting
a. continue
– if you know well how to be a monster –
improvise <four-legs>
a. improvising – relate as much as possible
a. move as instructed
– facing each other in pairs   look at the opponent as if licking them all over –
– pulling quickly back make the face you just saw –
– the face you saw and the face you are seeing simultaneously –
– try making the animal face at each other –
– try making them both alone
– why are you doing the horse and chicken face

May 3

not trying to express   erasing completely
not trying to move

<Hanako's face> very hot and dazed   swollen face
<child> Japanese child   precocious   pretend to know everything   laugh
<deer's antlers> dividing the space behind and above the head
<little bird> *chirping*   pecking the feed
A.Y. demonstrates
a. imitate
what is an expression
are you learning an expression

May 4

the way to erase the body   wanting to quit being human
butō became visible
<crippled beggar> fold the body
<old woman> become thinner within the hole   become the wall   the wall is trembling
<beheaded><corpse> nape
<ghost>
A.Y. demonstrates
a. imitate
<ghost>
hunch the back
hair pierces the floor
dribble from the mouth
seeing with half-closed eyes
a lantern in the left hand
<light>
the skin is weak   weakening
becoming sensitive in light
1 handshake   listening with the forehead   it's alright
2 rain   cataract eyes   hands as a box
3 wind   slanting neck
4 light from above   light is escaping, overlaying the hands
5 light from above falling intensely   hair become thin   hair of light *phwah–*

191

become the <flower>
small flower   big flower
A.Y. demonstrates
a. imitate
improvise <hospital scenes>
a. split into groups and dance on this theme
– the requirement of life's situation   not change but transformation

July 21

<lotus flower>
not heavy   blooming on the surface of the water   stem within the water
flowers also on the soles of the feet
flower's stamen   petals   stem   colour   flower blooming at 4 a.m.
Buddha's lotus flower
knowing well the formation of the flower
flower – what is the hand   one hand can become a petal
smell   pollen   pain at the moment of blooming
trying to do it with an impairment
flower   mentally – pure
          sensationally – *blushing*
          description – colour – form – light

A.Y. demonstrates
a. imitate

things that are somehow dubious   shady things
when related to uncertain things
the theatre began
pushing forward to become *butō*
what to do in four days
call death and observe it
sleep beside the dead person
there is no individuality
technique is methodological confusion
touching things directly
this is both imagination and substance
the self between the self and otherness
the furthest thing is the self

carrying the voice of the <little bird's *chirp*> soaking into the skull   so as not to let it escape
the forehead knitted   the chin juts out
pursing the lips   closing the eyes
became a <child>   the light laughed   a laugh is the reflection of light
the innocence of being bathed in light
the forehead is enlarged by about 30cm above and below
eyes disperse, diffusion blurs   inclining the face

<monster with one eye>
a large eye on the forehead   the hairs from behind the eyelids   50,000 strands above   the mouth
splits   the nose is squashed
•   to "stand upright" is

192

- to "walk" is

life slanting forward

and the figure following it

< little bird's *chirp*> → <girl> → <monster with one eye> → <idiot>
     light shines

<lotus flower> → <girl > → choreographic form above
     <little girl> → <lotus flower>

why is it not made into form

July 22

description

<blind> man   hand that holds a cane   fingertips   forehead   nose

eyes on the ears   and also on the soles of the feet

relying on the faint light

eyes, mouth hollow

sitting positions   1 2 3 4

<blind – light> sitting positions   1 2 3 4

<Buddha>

1 about 10 Buddhas coming from the throat, [the Buddhist monk] Kūkai
   watching these Buddhas, turning like that

2 grains of the Buddha statue, showing the left palm forward
   slicing the body sideways every 10cms, glass on the forehead
   retreating, as the body retreats it is sliced

3 the Buddha that mummified whilst praying
   orb in the right hand   nerves made to work by all things
   eyes disperse   lip twitches   nape tenses
   stoop   turn

A.Y. demonstrates

a. imitate

<room> improvisation

you can already dance from the methodology

dance using improvisation

– the border between animals and plants   mirror – goldfish – flower – butterfly

not live description   having a perspective on the body

keeping a strange creature within the body

– physical training means relating so far as possible to the necessary requirements in order to know your own body well

– do not think of expressing something   just present an existing condition

a. move as instructed

– facing each other in pairs   out-stare each other –

– seeing as one   uniting this with being seen –

– becoming an object alternately –

– organizing the familiar body –

<walk> carry the measurement
the desire to walk makes you walk
   blades on the soles of the feet
   needles in the heavens
   basin of sulphuric acid on the head

  |

   eyeballs behind   hair behind being pulled up, but unable to stand in that place
   becoming overawed from the front

  |

   entering your own self   blind

A.Y. demonstrates
a. imitate

My *butō* is simplicity, naturalism, mysticism. I want the "now," I don't need tomorrow. *Butō* is something hasty, going from extreme towards extreme, something uncertain, something ambiguous. Recently, I've been thinking things are alright just as they are. It becomes tougher and tougher.

My feelings, my heart, can't possibly be transparent to others. This is because the structure of the creation of the universe is a structure closed off to others. Children seek out the light, not wanting to sleep. Thinking it would be good if there was a fire, they grab the lightbulb.

When emotions, competitive things, or alienating things, swirl in two-dimensions, the self gets completely burnt out. That is why it becomes distant. The emotions rise up from this swirling.

The *butō* dancer is someone who does not surrender themselves to the monotony of sanded out space, even when suffocating. But they are revenged in time.

So, too, is the flesh body.

"The time of fundamental standing" is the theme
     not the experience, but the necessary requirement.

nerves – sensations
1 <mantle of light> 2 <woodcock made of light>
3 <becoming light itself> 4 <tightrope walk on light> <gentlewoman>
necessary requirements
tension and relaxation exist simultaneously
<girl in the mantle of light>   hands   flask almost full of sulphuric acid   rose flower blooming
inside the mouth   soles of the feet in the flowerbed, dandelion flower blooming in the ear
face dazed by the smell   the tension of the hands   wings grow from the hips *phwah–*
<flower girl> → <woodcock of light> → <light itself> → <gentlewoman> → <willow> →
<dryness> → <sky insect>
pouring something as *rough* as concrete into the body
wind cracking   space
pushed to the edge and dried out insect – particle

<willow> the mechanism of extending nerves
eyelids, temples, back of the ears, shoulder joints, hip joints, lower back, ankles, 10, 1 million, 10 million, 100 million, 1 billion nerves extending, space of the willow

- carrying the measurement
- forest in the molar tooth
- ear-line   left   right
  within this thread, combine a clear form
- with yesterday's training
         feelers of nerves
         keeping the nerve-threads of space
  concentration – diffusion – heat

A.Y. demonstrates
a. imitate

why feel that concrete obstacles such as walls are an ending
because there is a wall   but the wall is not only that
there are countless walls in space   approach the wall and merge with it
peeling   and becoming a stain   density emerges
this density begins from the hollow
intentionally drawing out from the self a sense of crisis
the self that can no longer move
where did it begin   the related existence is exposed

a. move as instructed
– getting into a circle, portray a bird or animal in turn
a. do each one – what are they –
a. hedgehog – they're all no good   abstractions
concretely   inside the rabbit
a. looper   become vague
jellyfish   the whole body related to it all at once   etc.
– quickly erase the human body –
a. continue – why can't you relate more delicately –
   – this time individually, do the thing you portrayed along with that of the person next to you
a. jellyfish and hedgehog
   looper and mouse
   cat and penguin   etc.
      – it is the combination of two impossible things –
         – no good –
         – you are still there…
– *butō* can't start that way –
– you are made to dance by the dancing chicken –
the vague portrayal of experience or judgment is no good
by observing observation discover what makes animals exist
have nerves like the surprise of a child

      – merge with the flower – merging further –

a. with the animal   with the plant   entering the physiology
      portrayal of the flower   feelers – colour – smell – sheen – feathers –
      smell – mystery
<room> things you can't understand, inside the room
eye gunge, ear pus

throw away the conditions of the human

195

absolutely don't mistake   things of such degree
but it's not just that
threw many thousand words into this surround
not things that can be taught   only thinking and relating to oneself
think   why the sky comes from the willow

July 25

white make-up   costume   lighting   sound   using these to act on stage as a group

<room>   theme
individually critiquing from the finale seats

Appendix 9: Ashikawa Workshop (May 12-18, 1990)

May 12

the means of 'becoming' – concentration
the work of resembling at full-speed in all instants – *butō* time
the most pitiable time   yearning for an ear of *susuki* [Japanese pampas grass]
the reproduction of *butō* – reproducing life
the air to which an ear of *susuki* is connected by its skin
if you have one soul that closes in on life
<walk of a measure>
correcting the *zure* [slippage] of an adult walking on two legs – returning to the origin
now   or eternity?
reproduce yourself   watch yourself from afar – the soul leads
        ↓
<four eyes – reverse water well>
body of the water well   two eyes on the forehead   two on the cheeks
what's the landscape you see with four eyes?
        ↓
<Buddha walk>
Buddhas on all sides – likewise many Buddhas behind
ten eyes – stain, *zure* [slippage]
<hydrangea>
eyes on the five heads, reflecting in the lake, flowing in the water, the act being drawn, running, blurring
        ↓
<dandelion>
round spores – floating 30 metres above the ground – the wind is walking
where are the *butō* dancer's eyes? their weight? their width?
        ↓
<walk of a measure>
<walk of eyeballs>
eyes gazing from the ceiling – eyes from behind
eyes from the floor – from below the chin…
the distance from yourself   where is yourself
the conversation of the tips of hair
the sensation of the anus   how is the body reflected between the anus and the eyeballs
the condition of a body in the position of being gazed at   naturally changes
the moment by moment transformations of even <hydrangea> and <eyeballs>   there are no pauses

<insect>
the hill of one insect on the hand   eyes are voids (perhaps like water wells)
gradually the insect disappears

May 13

the time of the condition of 'becoming'
caught in the everyday   a point being divided vertically   *bam* it comes out
continuous hesitation = a thread for forgetting   and not forgetting
the substance of standing
a trace of walking – the first step

the time of a stone (stone Buddha)
the old person's sense of inner and outer things stopping 30cm ahead
you're conscious of the things beside you, but it would be great to see them – like the one-thousand-year old man of candy
reproducing the figure that lives at the full-speed of a stone   Ksitigarbha [Bodhisattva] materializes the dream
most anti-nature   most anti-everyday   don't peel your eyes from it – trace
don't need anything below the knees – the paper   don't need a face   bow down with your hands there
an eye on the forehead (easy to understand) the feet are difficult
the fastest thing in the universe is the flesh body
no legs   the bones go into the paper – the sensation of sleeping – the sensation of the paper's thickness
the most unsettling thing – the body as it is (original size)
where are the *butō* dancer's eyes placed?   inside or outside of the water well?
old man sitting – *daze*   eyes everywhere
ending at a 30cm circumference   suddenly ends just before dancing.
the things that exist here are difficult.
like the sensibility of a blind person's skin – the body's condition changes when it loses an ability
eyes can be placed here and there (they become the audience's eyes from anxiety)
the consciousness of a more natural everydayness
eyes over here that see two other eyes   another enveloping eye – the sensation of 30cm
life – working endlessly to live for an instant
try searching to stroke the place of the body (where's the pelvis? the knees?)
the speed of the slice of an <eye>
eyeballs gazing from the ceiling (existing directionality)   ...behind (the body's condition)
things that lose direction from being mixed go *gucha–*
the current condition gets displaced (slipped, blurred, as though the joints have been dislodged... one, two)
consider how your eyeballs can face another eyeball
the place where the body has slipped, blurred   is where the eyeballs are   things like laughing (not emotion)

<dead body hanging in the eaves>
walking body carrying something on its back   memory of weight   return of weight
paper made of wood   light things become heavy
can't move   lightness of being hung   measuring the weight of the hips in one go

<the arbour – walk>
divergence of branches (back of ears, joints, temples...) – continued slicing = expansion of the body
eye on the forehead   eyeballs on the root-tips of the arbour   back   eyeballs beneath the crotch
eyeballs on the knees
the time of being 'here'   moving at a great speed

<stain on the wall>
the body that can't become singular gazed at from all directions   tracing the underground waterways going somewhere
bodily fluids   water seeps from the underground waterways   this becomes the earth
three eyes   four eyeballs   go towards the wall's interior   the eyeballs are detached 30cm from each other
at the moment of detachment   become a shadow   transform rapidly as a shadow
time transforms rapidly as the water that has seeped into the wall (what's the remaining skeleton and body?)

the time of detachment is still confronting the eyeballs   the sensation of the distance between the
eyeballs and the body
what is the space between the wall and the body?
the thing being detached is a shadow   the time that turned around
can you see the world as totally changed from your dead body?
air of sulfuric acid   razor blades   on the ceiling, walls, and floor   nothing lukewarm remains
I am harbouring the obstinate wish   of living nowhere but here – the awakening body –

May 14

looking at the paper   I want to dance the ghost   coming and going between darkness and reality
it takes three years to stand – gaze of a cat – gradually stopped dancing from your own thinking
back   the visualization of the words: 'eyeballs beneath the feet' – no choice but to be deceived
awakening an attentiveness to being easily deceived – the eyes behind become a reality
the sleep of a *butō* dancer who can never sleep – somnambulism without walking
at the same time as walking on the floor making a parallel time of walking   while floating
the descent of a waterfall that could be rising or falling
the rhythm of speed   that time passing through the body – the body becomes transparent
becoming, is the condition of repetition for your bodily condition – this is the mirror
the time of looking in the mirror   the consciousness is no longer split as you become one

<the arbour>
eyes on the root-tips, and on the self that is wood   two eyes *zure* [blur]   this is the condition of
wood
the body is perhaps the point – at which imagination becomes reality

<wall>
eyes behind   eyes on the floor   your own two eyes   the blurred body of four eyes
lightning – *flash* – in the crack between the body and the wall   come unstuck
is the person who looked back a dead person?   what's the body's condition at that moment?

<four eyes>
tobacco smoke from the knees, the condition of being drawn blurred in crayon
   ↓
<dandelion>
the floating sensation of being on the edge of not knowing where you fly
   ↓
<hydrangea>
seeping into the wall behind
   ↓
<Portuguese man-of-war from the wall>

dismantling the flesh body (nerves joints remain) – nerves   the image dissects the body
the feeling of substance induces movement   force
no-one is watching the dancing body   they are watching the space   there is no need for flesh
 – that person's condition of electrical discharge   space expands and contracts from the vector of
energy
when you moved   the entire wall behind was pulled   collapsed   a dust cloud rose
inducing the next movement
movement is incidental: the continual encounter with unknown things   one method is using razors

as above – the deformation of skin – only the sensation of skin metamorphosing
just enough surrounding air and shed-skin

<wall – net>
the net of two sliding doors, before, behind, in the centre of the body
electric current through the net (or lightning, ink pot)
capillary vessels of Asian ginseng   razors in the nerves
   ↓
<arbour> → <cow> → electric current through the roots of the <arbour> → <five variants of peacock> → <particles of darkness> → <hydrangea> → <stain on the wall> → <submerged from the hips down> → <shadow peacock>
able to go anywhere
first   dismantling the flesh body – I want to do the material
crack in the glass   I want to dance a cross-section of the millennia-old eternal landslide
this world-view

May 15

start to see where threads are attached to your body – this is not a method
become a reality   it's not 1   it's the hollow of the vector between 1 and 10
the transparent body – the receptacle into which time and space enter

<the tableau of darkness>
for the sake of an easy image, limit yourself to the darkness of a single panel
– and also the shadow that watches you do this
the space of a carried tableau   the black painting depicted on a dark tableau
carried in turn beneath a 60-watt light bulb
the frequency and density of light and darkness blending
erasing things done by yourself – e.g. being laughed at by a shadow

<shed-skin>
covered by a horse   on top of that soggy paper
the space of paper-entities and discarded body-entities, moves

<powder>
the powder quietens *gently*
the condition of steam rising from the lid of an iron pot
like the mathematician counting the number of insects eating

<space of hair>
paper wet with water (the lower body is submerged in water)
eyes beneath the floor, there are two floors

<four eyes>
you don't need your eyes, just ask the shadow where to place them
→ <dandelion> → <hydrangea> → <wooden door> →floating hair of <dead person> → <half close-eyed smile>
you set to work, it's with Buddhas and light particles → <wall – net> → <arbour> → <dinosaur> → <shed-skin> → lightning strikes the <arbour> → <dinosaur> → <shed-skin> → the shadow laughs

the cause of language – is not the drama of making into form
entering and exiting the inside/outside of the body   things that measure distance
keeping what the body depicts
eyes of the *butō* dancer – the shadow laughs, where are your eyes placed?
the self-consciousness you can only attain as a three-year-old, however you try to dance
the space of the void is being *ganimata* [bow-legged]
roots of the arbour
↓
space of the dinosaur   a matter of the water well

<ears beside ears>
the 'double', half-submerged in the surface of the lake
gazed at by the eyeballs beneath the floor   beneath the hips
seaweed entangled beneath the feet   the fingertips
from the knees   to the calf   to the shin   to the crotch   circular canals   ears of the floor (curve of
the shed-skin)
pus of the ears   scabs

<shed-skin> → <pipe smoke> → <smoke filling the room>
even with only the five senses   the endless condition of distortion will transform
the child that *quietly* enters the condition

<wall – net>
electric current → <crack in the glass> → <ink pot>
splash of ink → distant <lightning>
electrical discharge from hairs – overlapping divergences
I want to get the feeling of the substance from the shock alone
there will be no infinite reality until it comes through the reality of the body
interrogating nothing but the raw materials
the condition of becoming – the continuation of a divided condition – extending into infinity no matter
where it began
pressure of a wall – cells – pressure to the very end of capillary vessels

May 17

sending a thread from the body   the expansion of the body and space   entering the interior, entering
the capillary vessels
the imagination as the struggle to arrive somewhere
by asking the body   the body's threads diversify   extend
eyes on the body   attaching threads   a single step – the difficult step out into the world
the condition of the form that approaches as you throw out gazes from over here
you don't acquire that form   having that condition inside your body is the shadow
the direction of hesitation, walking with the condition of mottled Buddha portraits on all sides
even when walking, and at the same time expanding
you can't tell where the divergence starts
the divergence of directions – the body feels like it's half left behind and half gone
make the body into a vacuum, as the reverse water well – smoke blocking up the straw   make a hole
continue as the smoke comes out   it comes out where it likes, as the holes quickly shift

<shed-skin> → <smoke of incense>

<'double' of darkness> → <submerged from the hips down> → <eyes beneath the feet> → <ears beside ears> → <room of ears>
yellow pus   scabs
closing in on the reality of ears
obstinately clinging onto the shape of ears   blurring   multiplying arbitrarily
it's not the multiplication of the image   the becoming multiplies the becoming
gradually entering the place where it's impossible to stop

<flowing neck> <incense> <half close-eyed smile>
<costume of the shed-skin> <Buddha>
gold dust *rustling* from the hand   candlestick in the right hand   ball in the left hand

<guardian Deva kings from the wall> – three layers of the wall of net
the eyes are clearly sealed   in that moment produce the Deva kings as a single fiction
eyeballs facing the wall enter it   two eyeballs are sealed at 30cm away
gap in the wall – distant lightning
seeping into the wall – the passage of darkness – smashing the pelvis   breaking the spine   piercing the internal organs
isn't there the feeling of an earthworm slithering   in the remaining body and wall
waking up the things that live in darkness one by one
they start to peel off – the *tearing* of eyes
Deva kings – an eye on the forehead, a staff in the hand, throne of the lotus, eyes on the small Buddhas all around
the feel of peeled-off red and blue material
the problem is how much you passed through the darkness
the blaze of war damages   a voice of someone attempting to escape   a cloud of dust... as the backdrop
dappled sunlight   the material receiving... half-light   weight
the condition of being torn apart
that condition both inside and outside the body   the surround is the subject and the body resembles the outside
the form of Deva kings is made by the surrounding resemblance (about ten arms coming from the back)
a crack in the existence of the Deva kings   death peeling off
the impression of things occurring outside being regenerated as they enter the body
the impression of cells and capillary vessels
a single condition seems to display multiple transformations
it doesn't matter when it starts   make it dark once
don't make it using the face, feelings, or sensations, become innocent
dissecting your own body   it's purity – the *butō* body
it's not the Deva kings you want to see   but the landscape carried on their backs
the ability to be deceived develops inside you   once the body can become detached
multiplying with the same sensation and your own body   do it up to there

May 18

eyes behind – from this relationship to eyes, the bodily sensations...
the possibility of disappearing freely like mist.... – is clearly the wish for release
this is not the exhibition of process
the minute detachment of flesh when   even the bounds are absurdly off
free once the eyes are blocked up   not free at first
the feeling of raw material – when that person cried out   Ksitigarbha [Bodhisattva] turned into stone

202

the *rapid* breathing of an African child refugee desperate for life
reflecting that figure – it's not empathy   the irresponsible act = a single cry solidifies
the feeling of raw material = the density of stone
the moment of opening the mouth was not a call for aid   but perhaps a call for beatitude
walking body – various conditions
the energy that grows concentrated while diffusing – 'becoming'
thoughts and feelings dividing somehow equally, 1 over there, 1 over here (unite easily)
the energy that diffuses while condensing –
it's not the imitation of movement   the condition of the body when it 'becomes' is different
can you become stone from the <gaze of the skull>
<the garden of stones>
<hole – fish>
boundless, endless → <meteor>
you cannot break the body without becoming the wall, staring eyes
at some point absorbed → <gaze of the skull> → <stone>
yaa → <peacock> → the <stone column> walked this way

<sleep>
the body that slept – vessel (shed-skin)   powder of sleep   how much liquid can be collected
what's the light on the face?
walking as a peacock inside the dream – don't leave sleep behind   without it you can't see the dream
the moment of waking and sleeping   you can't enter it through form   drawing on the electric current
beneath the feet
transforming from a far off distance – the hairs   by the feet (it's *sudden* when you transform at
proximity)
<shed-skin>
using the ears   ears seep into the floor   ears crawl on the floor (seep into the wall) – ears on the
head and back

<king of ears>
the costume of pus
meat soup, dribble, soaking in – various patterns on the floor
it's more interesting that you soaked in instead of moving   gradually unable to stop moving
the space between the body and the floor is like a dwelling place   many layers of floor
your eyes drop down   the thread half hanging from the legs
hanging with the thread of the hairs – cat's cradle
there is no single place where the body doesn't dance

imagined provisional title
<garden of stone columns>
<king of ears>
do the painting   can you see it in the garden
the single theme until yesterday – the condition of sleep, four eyes, paper
it's fine to enter it from sleep, the expansion of the flesh body, being scattered   in the beautiful
garden
the shed-skin gets wet   goes down the stairwell of the ears   the king of ears   the knees and elbows
are ears
my dwelling place is a conch shell, the palace of the ears
collapsing with the erosion of ivy, moss, and water   the stone columns already gone
crack in the ears   change the sensation of the raw material
even though there's no regeneration   become the same raw material   this transformation is
what *butō* should nurture with increasing regression.
both the person looking and the person dancing, leaving a trace like the imprint of a slug

Classification of "Form" Titles

From rehearsal notes, 1978-81

- ❖ Plants
  - ➢ Plant
  - ➢ Orchard
  - ➢ Tree Knot
  - ➢ Dried Leaves
  - ➢ Tree Leaves
  - ➢ Willow
  - ➢ Hydrangea
  - ➢ Plum Blossom
  - ➢ Cattleya
  - ➢ Daffodil Head
  - ➢ Lotus Flower
  - ➢ Cluster Amaryllis
  - ➢ Lily
  - ➢ Flower of the Needle
  - ➢ *Kondō* Flower
  - ➢ Dandelion
- ❖ Animals / Fish
  - ➢ Cow
    - ▪ Cow's Neck
  - ➢ Horse
    - ▪ Horse's Neck
    - ▪ Horse Gallop
  - ➢ Fox
  - ➢ Reindeer Horns
  - ➢ Pig
  - ➢ Wild Cat
  - ➢ Goat
  - ➢ Orangutan
  - ➢ Gecko
  - ➢ Seal
  - ➢ Snail
  - ➢ Slug
- ➢ Dinosaur's Neck
- ➢ Snake
  - ▪ Snake's Neck
  - ▪ Gooseneck
  - ▪ Snake of a Shaman
  - ▪ Nijinsky Snake
  - ▪ Snake of Nerves
- ➢ Fish
- ➢ Shellfish
- ➢ Cod Roe Shellfish
- ➢ Rotten Fish Eyes
- ❖ Birds
  - ➢ Domestic Duck
  - ➢ Crow
    - ▪ Crow on a Clifftop
    - ▪ Crow on the Snow
    - ▪ Upside-down Crow
  - ➢ Duck's Neck
  - ➢ Flying Seagull
  - ➢ Peacock
  - ➢ Sandpiper
  - ➢ Crane's Neck
  - ➢ Chicken
  - ➢ Collared Dove
  - ➢ Chick
  - ➢ Owl
  - ➢ Flying Bird
  - ➢ Coiffured Bird
  - ➢ Carrier Pigeon
- ➢ Phantom Chick
- ➢ Bird B
- ➢ Bird of Light – Heron
- ➢ Spectre Bird
- ➢ Daddy Longlegs
- ➢ Fossilized Bird
- ❖ Religion / Death
  - ➢ Skeleton
  - ➢ Snake Shedding Scales
  - ➢ Ghosts
    - ▪ Ghost Ascending Stairs
    - ▪ Ghost Become a Stick
  - ➢ Phantom Transformation
  - ➢ Three Variations of Buddha
    - ▪ Fluttering Buddhas
    - ▪ Lotus Flower Buddha
    - ▪ Wood Grain Buddha
  - ➢ Buddha Listening to all Sounds
  - ➢ Buddha Pushing Buddhas from his Mouth

- ➤ Mummified Buddha
- ➤ Buddha Mandala
- ➤ Little Buddha
- ➤ Bodhisattva
- ➤ Deva Kings
- ➤ *Hannya* [red-horned demonic *Nō* character]
- ➤ Ghoul
- ➤ Demon Head
- ➤ Deity of Plagues
- ➤ Allah Prayer
- ➤ Allah Deity
- ➤ Fallen Angel 1 to 4
- ➤ Angel
- ➤ Maya
  - ▪ Maya's Hands
- ➤ Madonna Maria
- ➤ *Oshira-sama* [*Tōhoku* deity of the home]
- ❖ Tools and Other Forms
  - ➤ Puppet Form
  - ➤ Puppet Hands
  - ➤ Mask
  - ➤ *Nō* Mask
  - ➤ Japanese Battledore
  - ➤ Mannequin
  - ➤ Pipe
  - ➤ Crayons
  - ➤ Gas Lamp
  - ➤ Guitar Strings
  - ➤ Dust cloth
  - ➤ Strip of Bamboo
  - ➤ Flower Mirror

- ➤ Writing Brush
- ➤ Vinyl Mantle
- ➤ Limestone Cave
- ➤ Oriental
- ➤ G
- ➤ Tornado
- ➤ Sky
- ➤ Wave
- ➤ Ruins of a Fire
- ➤ Wall
- ➤ Smoke
- ➤ Stone
- ➤ Relief
- ❖ People / Parts of the Body
  - ➤ *Kotarō*
  - ➤ Boy Attacked by Light
  - ➤ Rotten Boy
  - ➤ Fat Man
  - ➤ *Hanako*
  - ➤ *Hanako* of the Reverse-side of the Mask
  - ➤ Girl of Roses
  - ➤ Girl in the Mantle of Light
  - ➤ Blind Girl
  - ➤ Schizophrenic Girl
  - ➤ Girl of Dried Leaves
  - ➤ Girl of Stars
  - ➤ Girl of the Horse Carriage
  - ➤ Girl of Smells
  - ➤ Girl of Bones
  - ➤ Girl of Insects
  - ➤ Hey Girl
  - ➤ Girl Returning from School
  - ➤ Girl with Half a Face

- ➤ Church Choir Girl
- ➤ Little Girl Smiling with Half-closed Eyes
- ➤ Princess *Kaguya* with a 12-Layer Kimono
- ➤ Soaked Woman
- ➤ Gentlewoman Pig
- ➤ Woman in the Garden
- ➤ Buzzing Person
- ➤ Person Being Hung on Weighing Scales
- ➤ Old Woman of Rumours
- ➤ Okinawan Old Woman
- ➤ White Old Woman
- ➤ Old Woman Being Kissed
- ➤ Old Woman with a Fan
- ➤ Resting Old Woman
- ➤ Old Woman of Cabbages
- ➤ Old Woman of Tristan
- ➤ Child = Cupid
- ➤ Sleeping Child
- ➤ Captured Child
- ➤ Fox Old Person

- Mad Person Going to a Party
- Beggar
- Sick Man
- Disintegrating Leper
- Sick Person Leaning on a Wall of Light
- Face of the Person with a Disability (Fool)
- Step of the Person with a Disability
- Woman Sitting on a Chair
- The Back of the Hair of the Lady of the House
- Gentlewoman Before a Mirror
- Gentlewoman Holding an Infant
- Woman in the Forest
- Gentlewoman Cut Out of Paper
- Gaze of the Skull
- 12 Aspects
- Face in the Forest
- Stone Face
- Head Rolling
- Dancing Neck
- Four Eyes
- Illusion of Hands

- Hand Signals
- Shapes of the Fingers
- String of Tears
- Eye Techniques
  - Old Woman's Raisins
  - Fish of the Space
  - Light Sphere
  - Cicada's Eyes
  - Concentric Circles
  - Thin Thread
- Blindness
- Assassin
- Hostage
- Official
- Grave-keeper
- Actress
- Courtesan
- Lady *Tokiwa* [Heian noblewoman]
- Three Versions of Menace
- Three Versions of Steam

❖ Forms with Other Aspects Added or Combinations of Forms
- *Kondō* Flower Reflected in Water
- Pomegranate Lotus
- Cod Roe Lotus
- Flower Gorilla

- Lily Peacock Snake
- Crazy Horse
- Wet Horse's Neck
- Lily Peacock
- Flower Peacock
- Steam Peacock
- Phantom of Mould
- Smoke Phantom
- Lotus Eaten by Insects
- Ghost Peacock
- Decapitated Peacock
- Giant Peacock
- Itchy Peacock
- Decaying Three-Dimensional Peacock
- Peacock Walk
- Peacock Divergence
- Stone *Hanako*
- Itchy Fox Old Person

❖ Things Derived from Forms or Spaces (Including Phrases)
- Space of the Hydrangea
- Space of the Divergent Flower
- Space of *Tanuki* [racoon dog]
- Space of *Okame* [round-

faced deity often in *Nō*]
- Space of *Tengu* [long-nosed red-faced goblin]
- Space of the Skull
- Space of Turner
- Space of the Ear Inside the Ear (Whereabouts)
- Space of the Dandelion
- Space of the Lotus Flower
- Space of Wings
- Space of a Saint
- Space of Eyes
- Space of Moreau
- Goya Face
- ❖ Things Prefixed by the Names of Artists and Other Forms
  - Beardsley – Gentlewoman Peacock
  - Beardsley – No. 1 to No. 5
  - Beardsley En Face
  - Bellmer
  - Michaux
    - The Figure of Light
    - Droplet of Ink
    - Three Faces

- Michaux – The Figure of Glass
- Goya – The Pope of Pus
- Delvaux
- Theresia
- Ophelia – White Face
- The Flower Garden of Bresdin
- The Marsh of Bresdin
- Bacon Face
- Pool Edge, Rubber
- Director
- Sycophant and Others
- Bosch – Face of the Unsaved
- New Munch
- Modigliani – Figure of the Fine Gentlewoman
- Moreau
- Redon Eyeballs
- Fautrier
- Toyen
- Picasso's Horse
- Delvaux – *Kinkatō* [traditional colourful sweets]
- Blake's Beard
- John The Baptist's Face
- Queen Elizabeth
- Boccaccio
- Nijinsky

- Wols
- Figures in Ukiyo-e
- Glass / Mosquito Net
- Grass / Umbrella
- Ekin's Burden
- Delaunay
- Picabia's Face
- Picasso
- Spoon, Pope
- Old Woman Knitting
- Fool Looking Upwards
- Great Fool
- Goya's Bat Old Woman
- Gogh Holding a Letter
- Coutaud's Laughing Flower
- Coutaud's Bird
- Coutaud's Fine Gentlewoman on the Shore
- Chagall's Bird
- Sonnenstern – Horn of Light
- Sonnenstern – Flower of the Face
- Turner – Girl Playing the Piano
- Turner – Storm

Classification of "Form" Conditions

Arranging the language – from rehearsal notes, 1978-81

- ❖ Materials
  - ➢ Solid
    - ▪ Hard
      - • Sharpness
        - ◆ Needle
        - ◆ Spear
        - ◆ Sword
        - ◆ Japanese Sword
        - ◆ Halberd
      - • Fineness
        - ◆ Wood Grain
        - ◆ Steel
      - • Weight
        - ◆ Iron Hair
        - ◆ Band
        - ◆ Stone
      - • Whiteness
        - ◆ Bones
        - ◆ Marble
        - ◆ Plaster
      - • Shininess
        - ◆ Gold
        - ◆ Mirror
      - • Curviness
        - ◆ Cherry Blossom Shell
        - ◆ Shell
      - • Straightness
        - ◆ Stick
        - ◆ Board
      - • Roughness
        - ◆ Sand
        - ◆ Gold Dust
        - ◆ Particles
        - ◆ Pumice Stone
        - ◆ Ore
        - ◆ Grains
    - ▪ Soft
      - • Curviness
        - ◆ Mantle
        - ◆ Skirt
        - ◆ Obi of Light Cloth
        - ◆ Petticoat
        - ◆ Thread of Light
        - ◆ Ribbon
        - ◆ Cloth
        - ◆ Flag
        - ◆ Vinyl
        - ◆ Rope-String
        - ◆ Mane
        - ◆ Cord
        - ◆ Candle
      - • Lightness
        - ◆ Cotton
        - ◆ Down
        - ◆ Fur
        - ◆ Wings
        - ◆ Fur on a Peach
        - ◆ Flower Petals
        - ◆ Front-side of Paper
        - ◆ Paper
        - ◆ Tissue Paper
        - ◆ Paper Flowers
        - ◆ Tree Leaves
        - ◆ Feather Pattern
        - ◆ Sheets
      - • Heaviness
        - ◆ Futon
      - • Thinness
        - ◆ Thin Membrane
        - ◆ Book Pages
        - ◆ Gold Leaf
      - • Wet or Dry
        - ◆ Stuffed Thing
        - ◆ Fish Scales
        - ◆ Mud
        - ◆ Earth
    - ▪ Shape
      - • Straightness
        - ◆ Shelves
        - ◆ Wood
        - ◆ Anchor
        - ◆ Cane
        - ◆ Basket
        - ◆ Insect Cage

- Scissors
- Window Frame
- Foundations
- Curviness
  - Pendulum
  - Cotton Reel
  - Spider's Web (+Thinness)
  - Kaleidoscope
  - Spinning Wheel
- Clothes
  - Dress
  - Silk Gloves
  - Hat
  - Bracelet
  - Ring
  - Artificial Flowers
  - Waistcoat
  - Fan
  - Bouquet
  - Brooch
  - Puff
  - Knitted Material
- Shelter/Tools
  - Shutter
  - Wickerwork Chair
  - Lightbulb
  - Armchair
  - Bowl
  - Stew pot
  - Pedestal
  - Lantern
  - Accordion
  - Banner
  - Bellows
  - Sphere
  - X-Ray
  - Fireworks

> Liquid
  - Water Droplet
  - Water
  - Rain
  - Fountain
  - Ink
  - Strong Poison
  - Soup

- Paint
- Droplet

> Gas
  - Phosphorus
  - Ether
  - Gas

❖ Living Creatures
  > Animals
    - Land Animals
      - Baboon
      - Dwarf
      - *Amanojaku* [folkloric demon]
      - Parts
        - Tail (1)
        - Tusks
        - Tail (2)
        - Horns
    - Aerial Animals
      - Bird
      - Hawk
      - Parts
        - Cockscomb
        - Beak (Bird's Nerves)
    - Water Animals
      - Stingray
    - Mixtures of the Above
      - Grasshopper
      - Beetle
      - Tortoise
      - Snake
      - Flea
      - Insect
      - Mosquito
      - Daddy Longlegs
      - Butterfly
      - Foetus
      - Parts
        - Gooseneck
        - Spiral
        - Feelers of Light
  > Plants
    - Vegetation
      - Figs
      - Grapes
      - Strawberries
      - Leaves

- ◆ Grass
- ◆ Dead Tree
- ◆ Mould
- • Parts (including Movements)
  - ◆ Twigs
  - ◆ Stem
  - ◆ Roots
  - ◆ Creeper
  - ◆ Ivy
  - ◆ Leaf Veins
  - ◆ Wood Grain
- ▪ Flowers
  - ◆ Rose
  - ◆ Dahlia
  - ◆ Dandelion
  - ◆ Golden Lace Flowers
  - ◆ Iris
  - ◆ Thistle
  - ◆ Winter Daphne
  - ◆ Lotus Blossom
  - ◆ Flower
  - • Parts (including Movements)
    - ◆ Flower Head
    - ◆ Pollen
    - ◆ Petals (1)
    - ◆ Petals (2)
    - ◆ Nerves of Dried Grass
    - ◆ Tracks of Plants
- ➢ Indications for Body Parts
  - ▪ Head
    - ◆ Skull
    - ◆ Back of Head
    - ◆ Forehead
    - ◆ Temples
    - ◆ Ears
    - ◆ Earlobes
    - ◆ Back of Ears
    - ◆ Eyes
    - ◆ Beneath the Eyes
    - ◆ Nose
    - ◆ Beneath the nose
    - ◆ Mouth
    - ◆ Around the Mouth
    - ◆ Molars
    - ◆ Edge of the Lips
    - ◆ Upper lip
    - ◆ Top Teeth
    - ◆ (Lower) Jaw
    - ◆ Beneath the Chin
    - ◆ Neck
  - ▪ Limbs
    - ◆ Elbow
    - ◆ Hand
    - ◆ Back of Hand
    - ◆ Fingertips
    - ◆ Nails
    - ◆ Knee
    - ◆ Sole of Foot
  - ▪ Trunk
    - ◆ Left side
    - ◆ Armpits
    - ◆ Hips
    - ◆ Anus
    - ◆ Bottom
  - ▪ Hair
    - ◆ Body Hair
    - ◆ Downy Hair
    - ◆ Pores
    - ◆ Back of Hair
    - ◆ Black Hair
    - ◆ Grey Hair
    - ◆ Hair of Light
    - ◆ Head Hair
    - ◆ Electric Hair
    - ◆ Eyebrows
    - ◆ Beard of Light
    - ◆ Beard of Metal
    - ◆ Rubber Eyebrows
  - ▪ Bodily Functions
    - ◆ Bones
    - ◆ Nerves
    - ◆ Internal Organs
    - ◆ Joints
    - ◆ Capillaries
    - ◆ Skin
    - ◆ Brain
  - ▪ Expressions and Other Forms
    - ◆ Face of Dead Person
    - ◆ Sooty Face
    - ◆ Flowing Face
    - ◆ Intelligent Face
    - ◆ Proud Face

- ◆ Heavy Face
- ◆ Red Tongue
- ◆ Swelling
- ◆ Frown
- ◆ Whited Out Eyes
- ◆ Four Eyes
- ◆ Gaze
- ◆ Thinness of the Lips
- ◆ Cleft Palate
- ◆ Puckered Lips
- ◆ Looking Inside Yourself
- ◆ Corpse
- ◆ Pigeon Breast
- ◆ Thin Smile
- ◆ Clothes of Flesh
- ◆ Folds
- ◆ Lines from Fingers
- ◆ Dribble
- ◆ Ear Discharge
- ◆ Eye Discharge
- ◆ Nosebleed
- ◆ Snot
- ◆ Pus
- ◆ Scab
- ◆ Flesh *Zure* [oozing]
- ◆ Rotten Flesh
- ◆ Cramp
- ◆ Burn
- ◆ Blood Vomit
- ❖ Natural Phenomena
  - ▪ Wind and Rain
    - ◆ Rain
    - ◆ Snow
    - ◆ Haze
    - ◆ Mist
    - ◆ Sea Breeze
    - ◆ Thunder
    - ◆ Air
    - ◆ Wind
    - ◆ Wave
    - ◆ Whirlpool
    - ◆ Drizzle
    - ◆ Fog
  - ▪ Light
    - ◆ Moonlight
    - ◆ Sunlight
    - ◆ Light
    - ◆ Darkness
    - ◆ Shadow
    - ◆ Fading of Light
    - ◆ Westerly Light
    - ◆ Curtain of Light
  - ▪ Phenomena
    - ◆ Smoke
    - ◆ Droplets
    - ◆ Dust
    - ◆ Cracks
    - ◆ Phenomena
    - ◆ Foam
    - ◆ Air
    - ◆ Electric Current
    - ◆ Sandpit
    - ◆ Mesh of Net
    - ◆ Sleep
- ❖ Emotional Elements
  - ➢ Emotions
    - ▪ Shade
      - ◆ Unsettled
      - ◆ Startled
      - ◆ Malice
      - ◆ Regret
      - ◆ Hatred
      - ◆ Resentment
      - ◆ Unpleasantness
      - ◆ Hesitation
      - ◆ Indecision
    - ▪ Light
      - ◆ Too Many Emotions
  - ➢ Descriptions of People's Characters
    - ▪ Shade
      - ◆ Introverted
    - ▪ Light
      - ◆ Kindness
      - ◆ Nobility
      - ◆ Gracefulness
  - ➢ Eros
    - ◆ Licentious
    - ◆ Lewd
    - ◆ Fickleness
    - ◆ Ecstasy
    - ◆ Intoxication
  - ➢ Sickness

- ◆ Suffering
- ◆ Dryness
- ◆ Itchiness
- ◆ Dullness
- ◆ Agony
- ◆ Sickness
- ◆ Feeling of Sickness
- ◆ (Sensation)

- ◆ Quarrel
- ◆ Feelings of the Buzzing Person
  - ▪ Forms
    - ◆ Brevity
    - ◆ Length
    - ◆ Square
    - ◆ Curviness
    - ◆ Outline
    - ◆ Shape
    - ◆ After-Image
    - ◆ Periphery
    - ◆ Undefined
    - ◆ Radial Lines
    - ◆ Height
    - ◆ Depth
  - ▪ Colours
    - ◆ Whiteness
    - ◆ Cloudy White
    - ◆ Hues
    - ◆ Colour
    - ◆ Blocks of Light
  - ▪ Temperature
    - ◆ Cold
    - ◆ Chilly
    - ◆ Heat
    - ◆ Fever
  - ▪ Humidity
    - ◆ Humidity
- ❖ Sensation Elements
  - ▪ Sounds
    - ◆ Sound of Big Bell
    - ◆ Sound of Little Bell
    - ◆ Sound
    - ◆ Buddhist Prayer
    - ◆ Voice
    - ◆ Soprano
    - ◆ Alto

- ◆ Humming
- ◆ Sound of Insect Buzzing
- ◆ Moment When You Listen to the Sound of Beeping
  - ▪ Quality (Sensations)
    - ◆ Sooty
    - ◆ Rotten
    - ◆ Weakening
    - ◆ Soft
    - ◆ Hardness
    - ◆ Strong Density
    - ◆ Light and Shade
    - ◆ Fineness
    - ◆ Density
    - ◆ Transparent
    - ◆ Groaning
  - ▪ Volume (Sensations)
    - ◆ Weight
    - ◆ Levity
    - ◆ Thinness
    - ◆ Dilution
    - ◆ Fineness
    - ◆ Number of Sheets
    - ◆ Thickness Behind
    - ◆ Spreading Out
    - ◆ Condition of 0°
  - ▪ Light
    - ◆ Light and Dark
    - ◆ Darkness
    - ◆ 30 Watts
    - ◆ Ghostly Shade
  - ▪ Smells
    - ◆ Odour
    - ◆ Unpleasant Smell
    - ◆ Pungent Smell
    - ◆ Fragrance
    - ◆ Perfume
  - ▪ (Sensing)
    - ◆ Sign
    - ◆ Vacuum
    - ◆ Space
    - ◆ Space Behind
    - ◆ Perspective
    - ◆ Phenomena
    - ◆ Hairless

212

- - ◆ Sickness
  - ◆ Rumours
  - ◆ Heaven and Earth
  - ◆ Mandala of Space
  - ◆ Miraculous
  - ◆ Artificial
  - ◆ Void
  - Directions
    - ◆ Sensation of Directions
    - ◆ Angle
    - ◆ Iteration of Waves
    - ◆ Waving (of Hair)
    - ◆ Trail (of Smoke)
    - ◆ Direction (of Wind)
    - ◆ Letter S
    - ◆ Winding of a Spiral
    - ◆ Whereabouts
    - ◆ Tracks
    - ◆ Infinity of the Character 8
    - ◆ Winding
    - ◆ Twist
    - ◆ Connection
  - Strength
    - ◆ Strength
    - ◆ Stagnation
  - Power
    - ◆ Centripetal Force
  - Rhythm
    - ◆ Vibrations
    - ◆ Ornamental Sounds
- ❖ Movements Guiding Forms
  - ➢ (Disappearing) Movements
    - Disappearing
      - ◆ Becoming Gas
      - ◆ Becoming Smoke
      - ◆ Becoming Nothing
      - ◆ Becoming Particles
    - Spreading
      - ◆ Dissemination
      - ◆ Dispersion
      - ◆ Expansion
      - ◆ Divergence
      - ◆ Separation
    - Shrinking
      - ◆ Compression
      - ◆ Concentration
  - - ◆ Dryness
    - Floating
      - ◆ Floating
      - ◆ Combination
      - ◆ Dismemberment
      - ◆ Fusion
    - Dynamics
      - ◆ Toss About
      - ◆ Vibration
      - ◆ Concentration
    - Space
      - ◆ Append
      - ◆ Circumference
      - ◆ Refraction
      - ◆ Intervention
    - Time
      - ◆ *Bure* [blur]
      - ◆ Over There
      - ◆ *Zure* [slippage]
      - ◆ Over Here
      - ◆ Appear and Disappear
      - ◆ Stratification
      - ◆ Stagnation
      - ◆ Peeling Off
      - ◆ Becoming a Skeleton
      - ◆ Encounter
      - ◆ Hazy Body
      - ◆ Reflection
      - ◆ Dislocation
      - ◆ Becoming a Physical Body
- ❖ Movement (Verbs)
  - ➢ Movement
    - ◆ Descending Three Steps
    - ◆ Pushing Upwards
    - ◆ Pushing Through
    - ◆ Chasing
    - ◆ Pitching forward
    - ◆ Being Engraved
    - ◆ Pulling
    - ◆ Entering
    - ◆ Falling
    - ◆ Being Ravished
    - ◆ Wailing
    - ◆ Retreating
    - ◆ Entangling

213

- Being Reflected
  - Flying / Turning
    - Leaping
    - Rotating
    - Hanging
    - Flying
  - Stop
    - Stopping
    - Dam
    - Painting
    - Hitting
- Flowing
  - Flowing Backwards
  - Hovering
  - Whirlpool
  - Fluttering
  - Waving
  - Trembling
  - Flowing
  - Being Blown
  - Being Tossed About
  - Hanging
  - Dangling
  - Incontinence
  - Slackening
  - Quivering
  - Loosening
  - Being Spun
  - Being Centralized
  - Being Fanned
- Spreading
  - Stretched out
  - Extending
  - Expanding
  - Contracting
  - Being Enfolded
  - Becoming Rough
- Surface Erosion
  - Collapsing
  - Rising Up
  - Being Crushed
  - Standing on End
  - Being Hooked
  - Being Buried
  - Being Scrubbed
  - Painting Over
  - Floating Up
  - Being Imprinted
  - Being Shaved
  - Being Peeled
- Quality Sensations
  - Wet
  - Transparent
  - Sooty
  - Dried
- Time/Space
  - *Bureru* [blurring]
  - *Zureru* [slipping]
  - Warping
  - Melting
  - Permeating
  - Misting up
  - Disappearing
  - Being Crushed
  - Cramps
  - Fading Out
- (Mental) State
  - Becoming Senile
  - Being Captured
- ❖ Onomatopoeia[†]
  - Movements
    - *Berobero*
    - *Kotsukotsu*
    - *Tsurutsuru*
  - Sounds
    - *Kyu'*
    - *Gobo'*
    - *Buu*
    - *KaranKoron*
    - *Pari'Pari'*
    - *GachaGacha*
    - *Gashaa*

[†] Onomatopoeia in Japanese often carries semantic meaning, though not always, and not always a singular one. Where onomatopoeia seemed to indicate some clear meaning in the Appendix, an equivalent was given in italics. Not all of the list given here, however, are reducible to semantic content – at times onomatopoeia works as a rhythmic or vague sensory indicator in Hijikata's notation – so the original sounds have been transcribed according to the Japanese.

- *Gashi'*
- *HakiHaki*
- *KakunKakun*
- *Bari'Bari'*
- *Geee*
- *Uwaa*
- *KuchaKucha*
- *Pachi'*
- *Kyu*
- *GuchaGucha*
- *GaraGara*
- *BataBata*
- *Bon*
- *Suu'*
- *KaranBachi*
- *KaranBo'*
- *PachiPachi*
- *PoppoKara*
- *Zun*
- *Hyuu*
- *ChakiChaki*

> Qualities

- *ZaraZara*
- *KasaKasa*
- *Kasa'*
- *TsuruTsuru*
- *GasaGasa*
- *DoroDoro*
- *NumeNume*
- *GushuGushu*

> Conditions

- *Buwaa*
- *HooHoo*
- *PoPoPoo*
- *Fuwaa*
- *PokoPoko*
- *Pouu*
- *HyuuDoroDoro*
- *KyuKyuKyuTaraa*
- *BariBariBari*
- *GiraGira*
- *YuraYura*
- *HaaHa*

- *WasaWasa*
- *HiraHira*
- *Taraa*
- *HeraHera*
- *Kuru'*
- *MokoMoko*
- *BoyaBoya*
- *BaraBara*
- *NumeNume*
- *Bowaa*
- *Guwaa*
- *Pichaa*

> Cries

- *Kuu*
- *Ku'Ku'*
- *GyuuGuuKu'Ku'Ku'*
- *KuuKu'KuKuKuKu*
- *Gwa'*
- *Abuu*
- *Kaa*

Notes

Preface

1. Hijikata's last stage performance was as a guest dancer in *Dairakudakan*'s *Tenputenshiki: Yōmotsu Shintan* [Tenputenshiki: Story of the Phallus God].

1. Introduction: Themes & Methodology

1. Gunji Masakatsu ed., *Nihon buyō jiten* [Glossary of Japanese Dance] (Tokyo: Tōkyodō shuppan, 1977), 21.
2. "Zen'ei Butō-ka: Hijikata Tatsumi san shikyo" [Avant-garde Dancer: Death of Hijikata Tatsumi], *Asahi Shimbun* (January 22, 1986), 23.
3. Kamizawa Kazuo, *21-seiki e no buyōron* [Dance Theories for the Twenty-First Century] (Tokyo: Taishukan shoten, 1996), 22, 231.
4. Kamizawa, *20-seiki no buyō* [Twentieth Century Dance] (Tokyo: Miraisha, 1990), 220, 221.
5. Gunji, "'*Buyō' to iu hanashi*" [On 'Dance'], *Tsubouchi Shōyō kenkyū shiryō* 7, ed. Shōyō Kyōkai (Tokyo: Shinjusha, 1977), 3. Also see *Gunji Masakatsu sakuteishū* [Collected Works of Gunji Masakatsu] (Tokyo: Hakusuisha, 1991), 43-47.
6. Yamaguchi Masao, "*Ashi kara mita sekai*" [World Seen from the Feet], *Bessatsukoku bungaku* (Tokyo: Gakutōsha, 1985), 140.
7. Motofuji Akiko, *Hijikata Tatsumi to tomo ni* [Together with Hijikata Tatsumi] (Tokyo: Chikuma shobō, 1990), 140.
8. Gunji ed., *Nihon buyō jiten*, 21.
9. Okuno Takeo, "*Engeki kakumei no ankoku kyōso*" [The Charisma of Darkness of the Revolution in Theatre], *Asubesutokan tsūshin 4* (July 1987), 2.
10. Mishima Yukio, "*Junsui to wa*" [What is Purity], in *Hijikata Tatsumi to tomo ni*, 96.
11. Shibayama Mikio, "'*Jappu' kara ichiban tōi hito*" [Nothing Like a Nip], *Asubesutokan tsūshin 7* (April 1988), 1, 12.
12. Kuniyoshi Kazuko addresses this lack of research in "*Hijikata Tatsumi o meguru futatsu no shimpojiumu*" [Two Symposiums on Hijikata Tatsumi], *Buyō gakkai 10* (March 1987), 36-44.
13. Hasegawa Roku describes it as such in "*Ai no chigiri koso – Hijikata Tatsumi tsuitō kōen 'Yameru maihime'*" [A Vow of Love – Hijikata Tatsumi 'Ailing Danseuse' Memorial Speech], in *Shingeki* (Tokyo: Hakusuisha, 1987), 89.
14. Mark Holborn, "Tatsumi Hijikata and the Origins of Butoh", *Asubesutokan tsūshin 4*, 27.
15. Matsuyama Shuntarō, "*Intabyū, marugoto nazo no hito – tensaiteki de naku tensai de atta*" [Interview with an Enigma – Not Having Genius but being Genius Itself], *Asubesutokan tsūshin 9*, (November 1988), 29.
16. Gōda Nario, "*Hijikata butō' sakuhin nōto 1*" ['Hijikata Butō' Work Note 1], *Asubesutokan tsūshin 2* (January 1987), 34.
17. Gōda cites Hijikata as saying "life turns to form, and form turns to life," in "*Jikan o yadosu nikutai – Hijikata Tatsumi no butō-reki*" [Time Conceived Body – Hijikata Tatsumi's Butō History], in *BODY ON THE EDGE OF CRISIS (Kiki ni Tatsu Nikutai)*, (Tokyo: PARCO, 1987), 85.
18. *Ibid.*, 87.
19. Hijikata Tatsumi, "*Hijikata Tatsumi – kijin to hanashita hi*" [Hijikata Tatsumi – The Day I Spoke to a Demon God], *Asubesutokan tsūshin 6* (January 1988), 8.
20. Hijikata, "*Hijikata Tatsumi – kijin to hanashita hi*," 7.
21. Deborah Jowitt, "Made in Japan", *The Village Voice* (November 1992).

22. Anna Kisselgoff, "Dance That Startles and Challenges Is Coming From Abroad", *New York Times* (October 13, 1985).
23. Kisselgoff, "A Speeded-Up Butoh, Without the Gloom", *New York Times* (October 1992).
24. Kisselgoff, "The Dance: Montreal Festival," *New York Times* (September 1985).
25. Tobi Tobias, "Human Interest", *New York Magazine* (December 1993).
26. Kisselgoff, "A Speeded-Up Butoh, Without the Gloom."
27. *Ibid.*
28. Jack Anderson, "The Dance: Sankai juku", *New York Times* (May 1986).
29. Kisselgoff, "A Speeded-Up Butoh, Without the Gloom."
30. Suzanne Asselin, "Pina Bausch et Natsu Nakajima: deux façons de <recoudre nos peaux>", *Le Devoir* (September 1985).
31. Andrea Rowe, "Eastern dance an intense, fragile study of life", *Ottawa Citizen* (September 1985).
32. Kisselgoff, "Japanese Distillation in 3 Works at the Joyce", *New York Times* (April 1990).
33. Kisselgoff, "The Dance: Montreal Festival", *New York Times* (September 1985).
34. Kisselgoff, "A Speeded-Up Butoh, Without the Gloom."
35. Jowitt, "Made in Japan."
36. Marcia B. Siegel, "Glistening Stones," *The Village Voice* (October 1985).
37. *Ibid.*
38. Rowe, "Eastern dance an intense, fragile study of life."
39. Siegel, "Glistening Stones."
40. Rowe, "Eastern dance an intense, fragile study of life."
41. Tobi Tobias, "Human Interest."
42. *Ibid.*
43. Kisselgoff, "A Speeded-Up Butoh, Without the Gloom."
44. Siegel, "Glistening Stones."
45. Jowitt, "Made in Japan."
46. Siegel, "Glistening Stones."
47. Bonnie Sue Stein, "Butoh: Twenty Years Ago We Were Crazy, Dirty, and Mad", in *Moving History / Dancing Cultures: A Dance History Reader*, eds. Ann Dils and Ann Cooper Albright (Durham: Wesleyan University Press, 2001), 376.
48. Ichikawa Miyabi, "*Pōsuto–modan dansu to butō*" [Post-Modern Dance and Butō], in *Buyō no cosumorojī* (Tokyo: Keisō shobō, 1983), 137.
49. Watanabe Moriaki, *Gekijō no shikō* [Thoughts on Theatre] (Tokyo: Iwanami shoten, 1984), 40.
50. Ichikawa "*Pōsuto–modan dansu to butō*", 134.
51. Amagasaki Akira ed., *Geijutsu toshite no shintai* [The Body as Art] (Tokyo: Keisō shobō, 1988), 18.
52. Shibusawa Tatsuhiko, *Tenbō*, cited in *Asubesutokan tsūshin 5* (October 1987), 26.
53. Ichikawa, *Kōi to nikutai* [Act and Body] (Tokyo: Tahata shoten, 1972), 33.
54. Ichikawa, "*Erosu to 'tsuchi' no kyōen*" [Feast of Eros and Earth], in *Buyō no cosumorojī*, 163-4.
55. Gunji, "*Butō to kinki*" [Butō and Taboo], *Gendaishi techō* (May 1985), 89.
56. Suzuki Tadashi, "*Kozetsu no shi o ayumu*" [Walking in Isolated Death], *Bijutsu techō* (February 1973), 146.
57. Takechi Tetsuji and Tomioka Taeko, *Dentōgeijutsu to wa nanna no ka* [What is Traditional Art] (Tokyo: Bijutsu shuppansha, 1973), 146.
58. Kobayashi Masayoshi, "*Chi no buyō*" [Dance of the Earth], *Bijutsu techō* (February 1973), 127.
59. Yamaguchi Takeshi, "*Toboshiki jidai no shijin no keiji*" [Revelation of a Youthful Poet], Bijutsu techō (February 1973), 136.
60. Suzuki Shiroyasu, "'*Hangidaitōkan' goku shiteki kansō*" [Private Impressions of the Burnt Offerings], Bijutsu techō (February 1973), 125.
61. Matsumoto Koshirō, "*Nikutai to hihyō no abangyarudo – Hijikata Tatsumi no shi*" [The avant-garde of Criticism and the Body – the death of Hijikata Tatsumi], *Gendai shisō*, (May 1987),

248.

62. Ichikawa, *Kōi to nikutai*, 33.

63. Matsumoto, "*Nikutai to hihyō no abangyarudo – Hijikata Tatsumi no shi*", 248.

64. Tōno Yoshiaki, *Gurotta no gakka* [Painters of the Grotesque] (Tokyo: Bijutsu shuppansha, 1965), 205.

65. Yamaguchi Masao, "*Hirakareta shintaisei e*" [To the Open Body], *Gendaishi techō* (May 1985), 79.

66. Gunji "Butō to kinki", 88.

67. *Ibid*.

68. Tōno, *Gurotta no gakka*, 11, 45.

69. Kobayashi Yasuo, "*Buyō to sono bunshin*" [Dance and its Other], *Gendaishi techō* (May 1985), 124.

70. Tōno, *Gurotta no gakka*, 206.

2. A Portrait of Hijikata's Youth and his Native Landscape

1. Ichikawa, "*Erosu to 'tsuchi' no kyōen*", 176.

2. Yoshimoto Takaaki, "'*Hai-imēji ron*' Butō Ron 1, 2" ['High Image Theory' Butō Theory 1, 2], *Kaien* (April 1989), 170-179, (May 1989), 222-232.

3. Hijikata, "*Kyokutanna gōsha: Hijikata Tatsumi-shi intabyū*" [Extreme Luxury: an Interview with Hijikata Tatsumi], *W-Notation 2* (July 1985),17.

4. *Ibid.*,18.

5. *Ibid.*, 23.

6. Hijikata in dialogue with Uno Akira, "*Kurayami no oku e tōnoku seichi o mitsumeyo*" [Gazing at a Sacred Land as it Fades into the Deepest Dark], *Koritsusha-tachi no taiwa* (Yamanashi: Yamanashi shiruku sentā shuppan, 1969), 104.

7. Hijikata, "*Hito o nakaseru yōna karada no irekae ga watashitachi no senzo kara tsutawatte iru*" [Replacements of Bodies that Move us, Passed on from Ancestors], in *Bibō no aozora* [Beautiful Blue Sky] (Tokyo: Chikuma shobō, 1987), 83.

8. Hijikata, "*Hijikata Tatsumi to ankoku butō-ha*", 86-87.

9. Hijikata, *Inu no jōmyaku ni shitto suru koto kara* [From Being Jealous of a Dog's Vein] (Tokyo: Yukawa shobō, 1976), 7.

10. Hijikata in dialogue with Uno Akira, '*Kurayami no oku e tōnoku seichi o mitsumeyo*', 107.

11. Motofuji, *Hijikata Tatsumi to tomo ni*, 77.

12. Hijikata, cited in *Hijikata Tatsumi to tomo ni*, 81.

13. Hijikata, *Inu no jōmyaku ni shitto suru koto kara*, 4.

14. Hijikata, "*Hijikata Tatsumi to ankoku butō-ha*", 4.

15. Tanemura Suehiro, postscript to *Bibō no aozora* [Beautiful Blue Sky], 252.

16. Gōda, "*Monogoshi no jiritsusei*" [Independence of Manner], *Gendaishi techō* (April 1977), 96.

17. Nakamura Fumiaki, "*Butō – sono shitashimi e no oku no te*" [Butō – A Last Hand to Friendship], *Ekoda bungaku 17* (January 1990), 17.

18. Uno Kuniichi, "*Hijikata Tatsumi no dimenshon*" [Dimensions of Hijikata Tatsumi], *W-Notation 2*, 62, 69.

19. Uno Kuniichi, "*Sai to shintai*" [Difference and Body], *Ekoda bungaku 17*, 30.

20. Miyoshi Toyoichirō, "*Korishō*" [The Enthusiast], cited in *Asubesutokan tsūshin 10* (July 1989), 38.

21. Nishitani Osamu, "*Butō suru kotoba no mure*" [Crowd of Dancing Words], *W-Notation 2*, 90-92.

22. Hijikata, *Inu no jōmyaku ni shitto suru koto kara*, 3.

23. Hijikata, *Yameru maihime* [Ailing Danseuse] (Tokyo: Hakusuisha, 1983), 7.

24. *Ibid.*, 4.
25. *Ibid.*, 189.
26. Hijikata, *"Kyokutanna gōsha: Hijikata Tatsumi-shi intabyū"*, 23.
27. Hijikata, *"Shizukana ie: zenpen / kohen"* [Quiet House: First/Second Half], *Bibō no aozora* [Beautiful Blue Sky] (Tokyo: Chikuma shobō, 1987), 98.
28. Hijikata, *"Kaza daruma"* [Wind Daruma], *Gendaishi techō* (May 1985) 76.
29. *Yameru maihime*, 103.
30. *Ibid.*, 63.
31. *Ibid.*, 67.
32. *Ibid.*, 52.
33. *Ibid.*, 195.
34. *Ibid.*, 53.
35. Hijikata, *"Kaza daruma"*, 73.
36. Hijikata, *"Sen ga sen ni nitekuru toki – Takiguchi Shūzō"* [When a Line Resembles a Line – Takiguchi Shūzō], *Bibō no aozora* [Beautiful Blue Sky], 126.
37. Hijikata, *"Kaza daruma"*, 74.
38. Hijikata, *Yameru maihime*, 90.
39. *Ibid.*, 89.
40. Uno, *"Hijikata Tatsumi no dimenshon"* 70.
41. Hijikata, *"Kaza daruma"*, 72.
42. Hijikata, *Yameru maihime*, 5-6.
43. *Ibid.*, 8.
44. *Ibid.*, 27.
45. *Ibid.*, 60.
46. *Ibid.*, 16.
47. *Ibid.*, 19.
48. *Ibid.*, 4.
49. *Ibid.*, 8.
50. *Ibid.*, 53.
51. *Ibid.*, 41.
52. *Ibid.*, 12.
53. *Ibid.*, 13-14.
54. *Ibid.*, 48.
55. *Ibid.*, 14.
56. *Ibid.*, 5.
57. *Ibid.*, 13-14.
58. Hijikata, *"Kaza daruma"*, 73.
59. Shibusawa, *"Hijikata Tatsumi ni tsuite"* [On Hijikata Tatsumi], commentary in *Yameru maihime*, 231.
60. Hijikata, *Yameru maihime*, 15.
61. *Ibid.*, 27-29.
62. *Ibid.*
63. *Ibid.*
64. *Ibid.*, 160-161.
65. *Ibid.*, 4.
66. Hijikata, *"Amaetagatte ita"* [Wanted to be Spoiled], *Bibō no aozora* [Beautiful Blue Sky], 112-113.
67. Hijikata, *Yameru maihime*, 7.
68. *Ibid.*, 159-162.
69. *Ibid.*, 23.
70. *Ibid.*, 51-52.

71. *Ibid.*, 55.
72. *Ibid.*, 4.
73. *Ibid.*, 7.
74. *Ibid.*, 62.
75. *Ibid.*, 37-38.
76. *Ibid.*, 55-56.
77. *Ibid.*, 45.
78. *Ibid.*, 91-92.
79. *Ibid.*, 5.
80. *Ibid.*, 11.
81. *Ibid.*, 61-62.
82. Hijikata, "*Kyokutanna gōsha: Hijikata Tatsumi-shi intabyū*", 16.
83. Uno Kuniichi, "*Mada odori tsuzukeru hito ni*" [To the One Who Can Keep Dancing], *Asubesutokan tsūshin 10* (July 1989), 44-45.
84. Hijikata, "*Kyokutanna gōsha: Hijikata Tatsumi-shi intabyū*", 11.

3. Hijikata's Historical Context and the Development of his Ideology

1. Hijikata, "*Ajia no sora to butō taiken*" [The Asian Sky and Butō Experience], *Bibō no aozora* [Beautiful Blue Sky], 59.
2. Motofuji, "*Hijikata Tatsumi to tomo ni 2 – shōwa no kodomo*" [Together with Hijikata Tatsumi 2 – Shōwa's Child", *Asubesutokan tsūshin 2* (January 1987), 36.
3. Ichikawa, *Kōi to nikutai*, 26.
4. Hijikata, "*Ankoku butō*" [Ankoku butō], *Bibō no aozora* [Beautiful Blue Sky], 38.
5. Hijikata, "*Hijikata Tatsumi to ankoku butō-ha*", 82.
6. *Ibid.*
7. See Kamizawa, *20-seiki no buyō*.
8. Hijikata, "*Naka no sozai / sozai*" [Inside Material / Material], *Bibō no aozora* [Beautiful Blue Sky], 29.
9. Motofuji, "*Hijikata Tatsumi to tomo ni 2 – shōwa no kodomo*", 45.
10. Yoneyama Mamako cited in "*Hijikata Tatsumi o meguru futatsu no shimpojiumu*", 43.
11. Hijikata, "*Naka no sozai / sozai*", 29.
12. Hijikata, "*Hijikata Tatsumi to ankoku butō-ha*", 83.
13. *Ibid.*
14. Hijikata, "*Naka no sozai / sozai*", 30.
15. Hijikata, "*Keimusho e*", 40.
16. *Ibid.*
17. Hijikata, "*Naka no sozai / sozai*", 33.
18. Hijikata, "*Keimusho e*", 47.
19. Hijikata, "*Naka no sozai / sozai*", 32.
20. See Ishifuku Tsuneo, *Buyō no rekishi* [The history of Buyō] (Tokyo: Kinokuniya shoten, 1974).
21. Hijikata, cited in "*Hijikata Tatsumi to tomo ni 2 – shōwa no kodomo*", 47.
22. *Ibid.*
23. Hijikata, "*Naka no sozai / sozai*", 32.
24. *Ibid.*
25. *Ibid.*, 33.
26. *Ibid.*, 32.
27. *Ibid.*, 30.
28. Hijikata, "*Hijikata Tatsumi to ankoku butō-ha*", 84.
29. Hijikata, "*Naka no sozai / sozai*", 30.

30. Hijikata, "*Hijikata Tatsumi to ankoku butō-ha*", 84.

31. Hijikata, "*Keimusho e*", 42.

32. *Ibid.*

33. *Ibid.*, 47.

34. *Ibid.*, 45.

35. *Ibid.*, 47.

4. Hijikata's Principal Works and the Methodology of his Technique

1. This study accords with Gōda's and Nakamura's divisions of Hijikata's work into periods. As opposed to Furusawa Toshimi, who subdivides the Middle Period, and Ichikawa and Shibusawa, who both subdivide the Early Period.

2. Ichikawa, "*Erosu to 'tsuchi' no kyōen*", 161.

3. Shibusawa, "*Hijikata Tatsumi ni tsuite*", 227-228.

4. Gōda, "*Jikan o yadosu nikutai – Hijikata Tatsumi no butō-reki*", 86.

5. Ichikawa, "*Erosu to 'tsuchi' no kyōen*", 163.

6. Gōda, "'*Hijikata butō' sakuhin nōto 4*" ['Hijikata Butō' Work Note 4], *Asubesutokan tsūshin 7* (April 1988), 23.

7. Gōda, "'*Hijikata butō' sakuhin nōto 2*" ['Hijikata Butō' Work Note 2], *Asubesutokan tsūshin 5* (April 1987), 38-41.

8. Gōda, *BODY ON THE EDGE OF CRISIS*, 85.

9. Gōda, cited in "*Erosu to 'tsuchi' no kyōen*", 162.

10. Gōda, "*Ankoku-butō ni tsuite*" [On Ankoku-Butō], *Butō – nikutai no shūrurearisutotachi* [Butō – Surrealists of the Flesh] (Tokyo: Gendai shokan, 1983), 121.

11. Haniya Yutaka, "'*Dō to sei no rizumu' yori*" [From 'The Rhythm of Movement and Stillness'], *W-Notation 2* (June 1985), 77-78.

12. Shibusawa, "*Hijikata Tatsumi ni tsuite*", 224.

13. Motofuji Akiko, "*Hijikata Tatsumi to tomo ni 6*" [Together with Hijikata Tatsumi 6], *Asubesutokan tsūshin 6* (January 1988), 55-56.

14. Shibusawa, "*Hijikata Tatsumi ni tsuite*", 228.

15. Motofuji, "*Hijikata Tatsumi to tomo ni 6*", 59-60.

16. Tanaka Ikkō, "*Zen-ei to anchi-moraru*" [Avant-garde and Anti-morals], *Bijutsu techō* (May 1986), 54.

17. Motofuji, "*Hijikata Tatsumi to tomo ni 7*" [Together with Hijikata Tatsumi 7], *Asubesutokan tsūshin 7* (April 1988), 40.

18. Yoshimura Masunobu, "*Hai-reberuna supekutoru*" [High-level Spectrum], *Bijutsu techō* (May 1986), 56.

19. Ōno Kazuo, cited in "*Pōsuto–modan dansu to butō*", 134.

20. Gunji, "*Butō to kinki*," 86-89.

21. Gunji, "*Shironuri jigoku kō*" [White-painted Inferno], *Gunji Masakatsu sakuteishū*, 262.

22. Tanigawa Kōichi, "*Buta to kirisuto*" [Christ and the Pig], *Bijutsu techō* (May 1986), 52.

23. Motofuji, "*Hijikata Tatsumi to tomo ni 7*", 40.

24. Motofuji, "*Hijikata Tatsumi to tomo ni 8*" [Together with Hijikata Tatsumi 8], *Asubesutokan tsūshin 8* (August 1988), 41.

25. Yokoo Tadanori, "*Totsuzen hen'i no posutā*" [Poster of Mutation], *Bijutsu techō* (May 1986), 55.

26. Hijikata in dialogue with Uno Akira, "*Kurayami no oku e tōnoku seichi o mitsumeyo*", 103-106.

27. Hijikata, *Ibid.*, 104-106.

28. Gōda, "*Jikan o yadosu nikutai – Hijikata Tatsumi no butō-reki*", 86.

29. Hijikata, cited in *Hijikata Tatsumi to tomo ni*, 101.

30. Motofuji, "*Hijikata Tatsumi to tomo ni 9*" [Together with Hijikata Tatsumi 9], *Asubesutokan tsūshin 9* (October 1988), 52.
31. Gōda, "*Jikan o yadosu nikutai – Hijikata Tatsumi no butō-reki*", 86.
32. *Ibid.*
33. Gōda, "*Monogoshi no jiritsusei*", 55-56.
34. Gōda, "*Jikan o yadosu nikutai – Hijikata Tatsumi no butō-reki*", 86.
35. Ichikawa, "*Erosu to 'tsuchi' no kyōen*", 165.
36. Gōda, *BODY ON THE EDGE OF CRISIS*, 86.
37. Nakamura, "*Butō – sono shitashimi e no oku no te*", 16.
38. Hijikata, "*Hito o nakaseru yōna karada no irekae ga watashitachi no senzo kara tsutawatte iru*", 87.
39. Gōda, "*Jikan o yadosu nikutai – Hijikata Tatsumi no butō-reki*", 87.
40. Ibid., 86-87.
41. Suzuki, "'*Hangidaitōkan' goku shiteki kansō*", 125.
42. Gunji, "*Shi to iu koten butō*" [Classical Butō as Death], *Bijutsu techō* (February 1973), 122-123.
43. Nakamura, "*Butō – sono shitashimi e no oku no te*", 17.
44. Gōda, "*Jikan o yadosu nikutai – Hijikata Tatsumi no butō-reki*", 87.
45. Shibusawa, "*Hijikata Tatsumi ni tsuite*", 229.
46. Gōda, "*Jikan o yadosu nikutai – Hijikata Tatsumi no butō-reki*", 87.
47. *Ibid.*, 87.
48. Furusawa Toshimi, "*Hisanna yami o hikisaku eishō*" [Aria that Tears Through the Dreadful Dark], *Ekoda bungaku 17*, 90.
49. Furusawa, "*Hijikata Tatsumi Hangidaitōkan*", *Ekoda bungaku 17*, 99.
50. Nakamura, "*Butō – sono shitashimi e no oku no te*", 13.
51. Ichikawa, "*Nikutai no busshitsusei, busshitsu no nikutaisei*" [Body Material Body, Material Body], *Bijutsu techō* (February 1973), 29-40.
52. *Ibid.*
53. *Ibid.*
54. Ichikawa, "*Erosu to 'tsuchi' no kyōen*", 170.
55. Gōda, "*Monogoshi no jiritsusei*", 54.
56. Gōda, "'*Hijikata Butō' sakuhin nōto 1*", 34-35.
57. Gōda, "*Nikutai no busshitsusei, busshitsu no nikutaisei*", 56.
58. Nakamura, "*Butō – sono shitashimi e no oku no te*" ,13-14.
59. Furusawa, "*Sei Hijikata Tatsumi*" [Saint Hijikata Tatsumi], *Ekoda bungaku 17*, 94.
60. Gōda, "'*Hijikata Butō' sakuhin nōto 1*", 29.
61. Motofuji, "*Hijikata Tatsumi tsuitō kōen 'Yameru maihime' panfuretto*" [Hijikata Tatsumi Memorial Event '*Yameru maihime*' Pamphlet] (Tokyo: Sezon gekijō, August 1987).
62. *Ibid.*

5. The Fundamentals of Hijikata's Ankoku Butō Technique

1. Hijikata, "*Nikutai no fuan ni tatsu ankoku buyō*" [Ankoku butō in the Anxiety of the Body], cited in *Asubesutokan tsūshin 5*, 24.
2. Gōda, "*Hijikata Tatsumi o itamu*" [In Memory of Hijikata Tatsumi], *Asahi Shimbun* (January 1986).
3. Ichikawa, "*Erosu to 'tsuchi' no kyōen*", 173.
4. Hijikata, "*Hijikata Tatsumi to ankoku butō-ha*", 84.
5. Hijikata, *Inu no jōmyaku ni shitto suru koto kara*, 12.
6. Hijikata, cited in "*Hijikata Tatsumi to tomo ni 6*", 58.

7. Hijikata, "*Hito o nakaseru yōna karada no irekae ga watashitachi no senzo kara tsutawatte iru*", 80.
8. Ichikawa, *Kōi to nikutai*, 71.
9. Hijikata, "*Hijikata Tatsumi to ankoku butō-ha*", 84.
10. Hijikata, "*Kyokutanna gōsha: Hijikata Tatsumi-shi intabyū*", 19.
11. Konparu Kunio, *Nō e no izanai* [Invitation to Nō] (Tokyo: Tankosha, 1980), 203.
12. Gunji, *Odori no bigaku* [Aesthetics of Dance] (Tokyo: Engeki shuppansha, 1957), 186.
13. Hijikata, *Inu no jōmyaku ni shitto suru koto kara*, 3.
14. Hijikata, "*Keimusho e*", 44.
15. Hijikata, "*Kyokutanna gōsha: Hijikata Tatsumi-shi intabyū*", 7.

6. Modes of Walking and Choreographic Forms

1. Hijikata, "*Ankoku no butai o odoru majin*" (Interview), in Mainichi Gurafu (February 1969), 13.
2. Hijikata, "*Kaza daruma*", 73.
3. Hijikata, *Inu no jōmyaku ni shitto suru koto kara*, 7.
4. Gunji, *Odori no bigaku*, 18.
5. Hijikata, "*Kyokutanna gōsha: Hijikata Tatsumi-shi intabyū*", 16.
6. Gōda, "*Monogoshi no jiritsusei*", 57.
7. Gunji ed., *Nihon buyō jiten*, 21.
8. Takashina Shūji, *Kindai kaiga-shi* [The History of Modern Painting] (Tokyo: Chūkō shinsho, 1975), 8.
9. Sakazaki Otsurō, *Roman-ha geijutsu no sekai* [The World of Romantic Art] (Tokyo: Kōdansha gendai shinsho, 1976), 145.
10. Takashina, *Kindai kaiga-shi*, 13.
11. Sakazaki, Roman-ha geijutsu no sekai, 145.
12. Ibid., 28.
13. Ibid.
14. Takashina, *Seiki-matsu geijutsu* [Fin de Siècle Art] (Tokyo: Kinokuniya shoten, 1981).
15. Hijikata, *Inu no jōmyaku ni shitto suru koto kara*, 6.
16. Ibid.
17. Hijikata, cited in "*Hijikata Tatsumi to tomo ni 2 – shōwa no kodomo*", 47.
18. For Hijikata's notion that "stuffed" bodies are more able to fly, see "*Ketsujo toshite no gengo = shintai no kasetsu / butai kūkan e no purosesu*" [Language as Absence = Makeshift Body / the Process of Stage Space], *Gendaishi Techō* (April 1977), 124-125.
19. Hijikata, "*Kyokutanna gōsha: Hijikata Tatsumi-shi intabyū*", 8.
20. Hijikata, "*Kaza daruma*", 75.

7. The Dissolution of Form

1. Hijikata, "*Ankoku no butai o odoru majin*", 13.
2. Gōda, "*Butō no dōshi 12*" [Butō Verb 12], *Gendaishi techō* (May 1985), 125.
3. Hijikata, "*Ketsujo toshite no gengo = shintai no kasetsu / butai kūkan e no purosesu*", 124.
4. Shibusawa, "*Hijikata Tatsumi ni tsuite*", 231.
5. Hijikata, "*Kyokutanna gōsha: Hijikata Tatsumi-shi intabyū*", 11.
6. Hijikata, "*Ketsujo toshite no gengo = shintai no kasetsu / butai kūkan e no purosesu*", 120.
7. Hijikata, "*Kaza daruma*", 74.

8. Conclusion

1. Hijikata, "*Asobi no retorikku*" [Rhetoric of Play], *Bibō no aozora* [Beautiful Blue Sky], 95.

2. *Ibid.*, 93.
3. Tōno, *Gurotta no gakka*, 46.
4. Hijikata, cited in "*Hijikata Tatsumi to tomo ni 2 – shōwa no kodomo*", 47.

9. Afterword

1. Recent publications related to Hijikata's *butō* include: Ōno Kazuo butō kenkyūsho ed., *Ōno Kazuo – keiko no kotoba* [Ōno Kazuo – Workshop Words] (Tokyo: Firumuātosha, 1997); Ōno Kazuo and others, *Ōno Kazuo* [Ōno Kazuo] (Tokyo: Shoshi seijusha, 1997); *Hijikata Tatsumi zenshū I, II* [Hijikata Tatsumi Complete Works I, II] (Tokyo: Kawadeshobō shinsha, 1998); *Geijutsu shinchō – seiki-matsu ni kōrinsuru butō no 'majin' Hijikata Tatsumi* [Geijutsu Shinchō – Hijikata Tatsumi, the 'Devil' of Late-twentieth Century Butō] (Tokyo: Shinchōsha, 1998); Hijikata Tatsumi ākaibu ed., *Hangidaitōkan shiki no tame no nijūnana-ban* [Hangidaitōkan Twenty-Seven Nights for Four Seasons] (Tokyo: Keio daigaku āto sentā, 1998); Waguri Yukio CD-ROM, *Butō kaden* [Butoh Kaden] (Tokyo: JustSystems, 1998); Ōno Yoshita, Ōno Kazuo butō kenkyūsho ed., *Ōno Kazuo – tamashii no kate* [Ōno Kazuo – Food for the Soul] (Tokyo: Firumuātosha, 1999); Sondra Fraleigh, *Dancing into Darkness: Butoh, Zen and Japan* (Pittsburgh: University of Pittsburgh Press, 2000); Hijikata Tatsumi ācaibu ed., *Hijikata Tatsumi 'butō' shiryōshū daiippo* [A First Step in Releasing Materials on Hijikata Tatsumi's Butō] (Tokyo: Keio daigaku āto sentā, 2000); Nakamura Fumiaki, *Butō no mizugiwa* [The Waterside of Butō] (Tokyo: Shichōsha, 2000); Tanemura Suehiro, *Hijikata Tatsumi e – Nikutai no 60-nendai* [Towards Hijikata Tatsumi – The 60s of the Flesh] (Tokyo: Kawadeshobō shinsha, 2001); Ōno Yoshito and Ōno Kazuo butō kenkyūsho, DVD: *Ōno Kazuo – bi to chikara* [Ōno Kazuo – Beauty and Power] (Tokyo: NHK Software, 2001); Odette Aslan and Beatrice Picon-Vallin eds., *BUTO(S)* (Paris: CNRS Editions, 2002); Kawamura Satoru, *Nikutai no aparishon – katachi ni narikirenu mono no shutsugen to shōmetsu – Hijikata Tatsumi 'Yameru maihime' ron* [The Apparition of the Flesh – The Appearance and Disappearance of Formless Things – On Hijikata Tatsumi's *Yameru maihime*] (Tokyo: Kureriēru shuppan, 2002); Shimizu Masashi, *Hijikata Tatsumi o yomu – bōsei to kaosu no ankoku butō* (Tokyo: Chōeisha, 2002); Kawasaki-shi Okamoto Tarō bijutsukan, Keio daigaku āto-sentā eds., *Hijikata Tatsumi no butō – nikutai no shururearisumu shintai no ontorojī* [Hijikata Tatsumi's Butō – Surrealism of the Flesh, Ontology of the Body] (Kawasaki: Kawasaki-shi Okamoto Tarō bijutsukan, 2003); Nakatani Tadao, *Hijikata Tatsumi butō sekai – Nakatani Tadao shashinshū* [The World of Hijikata Tatsumi's Butō – Collected Photographs of Nakatani Tadao] (Tokyo: Mediapurodakushon, 2003); Harada Hiromi, *Butō taizen – ankoku to hikari no ōkoku* [Butō Encyclopedia – The Empire of Darkness and Light] (Tokyo: Gendaishokan, 2004); Kasai Akira, *Mirai no buyō* [Future Butō] (Tokyo: Dansuwākusha, 2004); Shimizu Masashi, *Ankoku butō ron* [Ankoku butō Theory] (Tokyo: Chōeisha, 2005); Kobayashi Saga, *Ume no sasō – butō no kotoba* [The Dream Sand-flower – The Words of Butō] (Tokyo: Atoriesādo, 2005); Yamada Setsuko, *Sokudo no hana* [Flower of Speed] (Tokyo: Goryū shoin, 2005).
2. Ōno Kazuo also centres his dance on the image of a foetus. See: Ōno Kazuo, *Ōno Kazuo* [Ōno Kazuo] (Tokyo: Shoshi seijusha, 1997).
3. The *butō* workshops referenced here are: Tamano Kōichi (Terpsichore, Tokyo, July 2003); Torifune Butoh Sha, Ōno Yoshito, and Kudō Taketeru (for *Kuroinkaku* performance, 2005); and Waguri Yukio (Kyoto Arts Centre, 2005).
4. Odette Aslan and Beatrice Picon-Vallin eds. (listed above) indicate this connection between the practice of *butō* and *noguchi taisō*.
5. Rudolf von Laban (Kamizawa Kazuo trans.), *Shintai undo no shūtoku* [The Mastery of the Body's Movement] (Tokyo: Hakusuisha, 1985).
6. Watanabe Moriaki, *Gekijō no shikō* [Thoughts on Theatre] (Tokyo: Iwanami shoten, 1984), 22.
7. Inada Naomi, *Hijikata Tatsumi zetsugo no shintai* [Hijikata Tatsumi – A Unique Body] (Tokyo:

Nihon hōsō shuppankyōkai, 2008), 543-544.

8. The spread of *butō* is reflected in the rising field of *butō* studies, with recent publications including: Inada Naomi, *Hijikata Tatsumi zetsugo no shintai* [Hijikata Tatsumi – A Unique Body] (Tokyo: Nihon hōsō shuppankyōkai, 2008); Morishita Takashi, *Hijikata Tatsumi butō-fu no butō – kigō no sōzō, hōhō no hakken* [Hijikata Tatsumi's Butō of Butō-fu – The Construction of a Symbol, the Discovery of a Method] (Tokyo: Keio daigaku āto-sentā, 2010); Stephen Barber, *Hijikata Revolt of the Body* (London: Creation Books, 2007); Sondra Fraleigh and Nakamura Tamah, *Hijikata Tatsumi and Ohno Kazuo* (New York: Routledge 2006).

9. Yuasa Yasuo, *Kyōjisei no uchūkan – jikan, seimei, shizen* [The World-view of Shared Time – Time, Life, and Nature] (Tokyo: Junbunshoin, 1995), 7-35.

10. Yuasa, *Shintairon – tōyōteki shintairon to gendai* [Body Theory – Eastern Body Theory Today] (Tokyo: Kodansha gakujutsu bunko, 1990), 273-6, 369.

11. Ibid., 273-6.

12. Minamoto Ryōen, *Katachi* [Form], 148.

13. Harada Kaori ed., *Kyōgen o tsugu – Yamamoto Tōjirō-ka no oshie* [Following Kyōgen – The Teachings of Yamamoto Tōjirō] (Tokyo: Sanseidō, 2010), 2.

Works Cited

Amagasaki Akira ed., *Geijutsu toshite no shintai* [The Body as Art]. Tokyo: Keisō shobō, 1988.

Anderson, Jack, "The Dance: Sankai juku", *New York Times*, May 1986.

Aslan, Odette and Beatrice Picon-Vallin eds., *BUTÔ(S)*. Paris: CNRS Editions, 2002.

Asselin, Suzanne, "Pina Bausch et Natsu Nakajima: deux façons de <recoudre nos peaux>", *Le Devoir*, September 1985.

Barber, Stephen, *Hijikata Revolt of the Body*. London: Creation Books, 2007.

Furusawa Toshimi, "*Hisanna yami o hikisaku eishō*" [Aria that Tears Through the Dreadful Dark], *Ekoda bungaku 17*, January 1990.

————"*Sei Hijikata Tatsumi*" [Saint Hijikata Tatsumi], *Ekoda bungaku 17*, January 1990.

————"*Hijikata Tatsumi Hangidaitōkan*" [Hijikata Tatsumi Hangidaitōkan], *Ekoda bungaku 17*, January 1990.

Geijutsu shinchō – seiki-matsu ni kōrinsuru butō no 'majin' Hijikata Tatsumi [Geijutsu Shinchō – Hijikata Tatsumi, the 'Devil' of Late-twentieth Century Butō]. Tokyo: Shinchōsha, 1998.

Gōda Nario, "*Ankoku-butō ni tsuite*" [On Ankoku-Butō], in *Butō – nikutai no shūrurearisutotachi* [Butō – Surrealists of the Flesh]. Tokyo: Gendai shokan, 1983.

————"*Butō no dōshi* 12" [Butō Verb 12], *Gendaishi techō*, May 1985.

————"*'Hijikata butō' sakuhin nōto* 1" ['Hijikata Butō' Work Note 1], *Asubesutokan tsūshin 2*, January 1987.

————"*'Hijikata butō' sakuhin nōto* 2" ['Hijikata Butō' Work Note 2], *Asubesutokan tsūshin 5*, April 1987.

————"*'Hijikata butō' sakuhin nōto* 4" ['Hijikata Butō' Work Note 4], *Asubesutokan tsūshin 7*, April 1988.

————"*Hijikata Tatsumi o itamu*" [In Memory of Hijikata Tatsumi], *Asahi Shimbun*, January 1986.

————"*Jikan o yadosu nikutai – Hijikata Tatsumi no butō-reki*" [Time Conceived Body – Hijikata Tatsumi's Butō History], in *BODY ON THE EDGE OF CRISIS (Kiki ni Tatsu Nikutai)*. Tokyo: PARCO, 1987.

————"*Monogoshi no jiritsusei*" [Independence of Manner], *Gendaishi techō*, April 1977.

Gunji Masakatsu ed., *Nihon buyō jiten* [Glossary of Japanese Dance]. Tokyo: Tōkyo-dō shuppan, 1977.

Gunji Masakatsu, "*Butō to kinki*" [Butō and Taboo], *Gendai-shi techō,* May 1985.

————"*Buyō' to iu hanashi*" [On 'Dance'], *Shōyō Tsubouchi kenkyū shiryō 7*, ed. Shōyō Kyōkai. Tokyo: Shinjusha, 1977.

————*Gunji Masakatsu sakuteishū* [Collected Works of Gunji Masakatsu]. Tokyo: Hakusuisha, 1991.

————*Odori no bigaku* [Aesthetics of Dance]. Tokyo: Engeki shuppansha, 1957.

————"*Shironuri jigoku kō*" [White-painted Inferno], in *Gunji Masakatsu sakuteishū* [Collected Works of Gunji Masakatsu]. Tokyo: Hakusuisha, 1991.

————"*Shi to iu koten butō*" [Classical Butō as Death], *Bijutsu techō*, February 1973.

Haniya Yutaka, "'Dō to sei no rizumu' yori" [From 'The Rhythm of Movement and Stillness'], *W-Notation 2*, June 1985.

Harada Hiromi, *Butō taizen – ankoku to hikari no ōkoku* [Butō Encyclopedia – The Empire of Darkness and Light]. Tokyo: Gendaishokan, 2004.

Harada Kaori ed., *Kyōgen o tsugu – Yamamoto Tōjirō-ka no oshie* [Following Kyōgen – The Teachings of Yamamoto Tōjirō]. Tokyo: Sanseidō, 2010.

Hasegawa Roku, "Ai no chigiri koso – Hijikata Tatsumi tsuitō kōen 'Yameru maihime'" [A Vow of Love – Hijikata Tatsumi 'Ailing Danseuse' Memorial Speech], in *Shingeki* (Tokyo: Hakusuisha, 1987), 89.

Hijikata Tatsumi, *Bibō no aozora* [Beautiful Blue Sky]. Tokyo: Chikuma shobō, 1987.

————"Hijikata Tatsumi – kijin to hanashita hi" [Hijikata Tatsumi – The Day I Spoke to a Demon God], *Asubesutokan tsūshin 6*, January 1988.

————"Hijikata Tatsumi no butō shisō" [Hijikata Tatsumi's Butō Philosophy], in *BODY ON THE EDGE OF CRISIS (Kiki ni Tatsu Nikutai)*. Tokyo: PARCO, 1987.

————*Hijikata Tatsumi zenshū I, II* [Hijikata Tatsumi Complete Works I, II]. Tokyo: Kawadeshobō shinsha, 1998.

————*Inu no jōmyaku ni shitto suru koto kara* [In Being Jealous of a Dog's Vein]. Tokyo: Yukawa shobō, 1976.

————*"Ketsujo toshite no gengo = shintai no kasetsu / butai kūkan e no purosesu"* [Language as Absence = Makeshift Body / the Process of Stage Space], *Gendaishi Techō*, April 1977.

————*"Kyokutanna gōsha: Hijikata Tatsumi-shi intabyū"* [Extreme Luxury: an Interview with Hijikata Tatsumi], *W-Notation 2*, July 1985.

————*"Kurayami no oku e tōnoku seichi o mitsumeyo"* [Gazing at a Sacred Land as it Fades into the Deepest Dark] (conversation with Uno Akira), *Koritsusha-tachi no taiwa*. Yamanashi: Yamanashi shiruku sentā shuppan, 1969.

————*Yameru maihime* [Ailing Danseuse]. Tokyo: Hakusuisha, 1983.

Hijikata Tatsumi ācaibu ed., *Hangidaitōkan shiki no tame no nijūnana-ban* [Hangidaitōkan Twenty-Seven Nights for Four Seasons]. Tokyo: Keio daigaku āto sentā, 1998).

————*Hijikata Tatsumi 'butō' shiryōshū daiippo* [A First Step in Releasing Materials on Hijikata Tatsumi's Butō]. Tokyo: Keio daigaku āto sentā, 2000.

Holborn, Mark, "Tatsumi Hijikata and the Origins of Butoh", *Asubesutokan tsūshin 4*, July 1987.

Ishida Hidemi, *Higashiajia no shintai gihō* [East Asian Body Techniques]. Tokyo: Bensei shuppan, 2000.

Ishifuku Tsuneo, *Buyō no rekishi* [The history of Buyō]. Tokyo: Kinokuniya shoten, 1974.

Ichikawa Miyabi, *"Erosu to 'tsuchi' no kyōen"* [Feast of Eros and Earth], in *Buyō no cosumorojī*. Tokyo: Keisō shobō, 1983.

————*Kōi to nikutai* [Act and Body]. Tokyo: Tahata shoten, 1972.

————*"Nikutai no busshitsusei, busshitsu no nikutaisei"* [Body Material Body, Material Body], *Bijutsu techō*, February 1973.

————*"Pōsuto–modan dansu to butō"* [Post-Modern Dance and Butō], in *Buyō no cosumorojī*. Tokyo: Keisō shobō, 1983.

Jowitt, Deborah, "Made in Japan", *The Village Voice*, November 1992.

Jung, C.G., *Jiga to muishiki* [Self and the Unconscious], Matsushiro Yōichi and Watanabe Manabu trans. Tokyo: Shisakusha, 1984.

Kamizawa Kazuo, *21-seiki no buyō* [Twenty-First Century Dance]. Tokyo: Taishukan shoten, 1996.

————*20-seiki no buyō* [Twentieth Century Dance]. Tokyo: Miraisha, 1990.

Kasai Akira, *Mirai no buyō* [Future Butō] (Tokyo: Dansuwākusha, 2004); Shimizu Masashi, *Ankoku butō ron* [Ankoku butō Theory]. Tokyo: Chōeisha, 2005.

Kawamura Satoru, *Nikutai no aparishon – katachi ni narikirenu mono no shutsugen to shōmetsu – Hijikata Tatsumi 'Yameru maihime' ron* [The Apparition of the Flesh – The Appearance and Disappearance of Formless Things – On Hijikata Tatsumi's *Yameru maihime*]. Tokyo: Kureriēru shuppan, 2002.

Kawasaki-shi Okamoto Tarō bijutsukan, Keio daigaku āto-sentā eds., *Hijikata Tatsumi no butō – nikutai no shururearisumu shintai no ontorojī* [Hijata Tatsumi's Butō – Surrealism of the Flesh, Ontology of the Body]. Kawasaki: Kawasaki-shi Okamoto Tarō bijutsukan, 2003.

Kisselgoff, Anna, "A Speeded-Up Butoh, Without the Gloom", *New York Times*, October 1992.

———— "Dance That Startles and Challenges Is Coming From Abroad", *New York Times*, October 13 1985.

———— "Japanese Distillation in 3 Works At the Joyce", *New York Times*, April 1990.

————"The Dance: Montreal Festival," *New York Times*, September 1985.

Kobayashi Masayoshi, "Chi no buyō" [Dance of the Earth], *Bijutsu techō*, Feb. 1973.

Kobayashi Saga, *Ume no sasō – butō no kotoba* [The Dream Sand-flower – The Words of Butō]. Tokyo: Atoriesādo, 2005.

Kobayashi Yasuo, "Buyō to sono bunshin" [Dance and its Other], *Gendaishi techō*, May 1985.

Konparu Kunio, Nō e no izanai [Invitation to Nō]. Tokyo: Tankosha, 1980.

Kuniyoshi Kazuko, "Hijikata Tatsumi o meguru futatsu no shimpojiumu" [Two Symposiums on Hijikata Tatsumi], *Buyō gakkai 10*, March 1987.

Laban, Rudolf von, *Shintai undo no shūtoku* [The Mastery of the Body's Movement], Kanzawa Kazuo trans. Tokyo: Hakusuisha, 1985.

Matsumoto Koshirō, "Nikutai to hihyō no abangyarudo – Hijikata Tatsumi no shi" [The avant-garde of Criticism and the Body – the death of Hijikata Tatsumi], *Gendai shisō*, May 1987.

Matsuyama Shuntarō, "Intabyū, marugoto nazo no hito – tensaiteki de naku tensai de atta" [Interview with an Enigma – Not Having Genius but being Genius Itself], *Asubesutokan tsūshin 9*, November 1988.

Miki Shigeo, *Naizō no hataraki to kodomo no kokoro* [The Work of the Internal Organs and the Spirit of a Child]. Tokyo: Tsukiji shokan, 1982.

————*Taiji no sekai* [The World of an Embryo]. Tokyo: Chukō shinsho, 1983.

————*Seimeitaigaku josetsu – kongen keishō to metamorufōze* [An Introduction to Morphology – Fundamental Form and Metamorphosis]. Tokyo: Ubusuna shoin, 1992.

————*Umi, kokyū, kodai keishō* [Sea, Breathing, Ancient Form]. Tokyo: Ubusuna shoin, 1992.

Miki, *Hito no karada – siebutsushiteki kōsatsu* [The Human Body – A Consideration of the History of Living Things, 1997]. Tokyo: Ubusuna shoin, 1997.

Minamoto Ryōen, *Katachi* [Form]. Tokyo: Sōbunsha, 1989.

Minouchi Sōichi, *Tsubo to nihonjin – tōyō dōsagaku e no michi* [The Japanese and Tsubo – The Way to Eastern Movement Studies]. Tokyo: Inaho shobō, 1983.

Mishima Yukio, "Junsui to wa" [What is Purity], in *Hijikata Tatsumi to tomo ni* [Together with Hijikata Tatsumi]. Tokyo: Chikuma shobō, 1990.

Motofuji Akiko, *Hijikata Tatsumi to tomo ni* [Together with Hijikata Tatsumi]. Tokyo: Chikuma shobō, 1990.

————"Hijikata Tatsumi to tomo ni 2 – Shōwa no kodomo" [Together with Hijikata Tatsumi 2 – Shōwa's Child", *Asubesutokan tsūshin 2*, January 1987.

————"Hijikata Tatsumi to tomo ni 6" [Together with Hijikata Tatsumi 6], *Asubesutokan tsūshin 6*, January 1988.

————"Hijikata Tatsumi to tomo ni 7" [Together with Hijikata Tatsumi 7], *Asubesutokan tsūshin 7*, April 1988.

————"Hijikata Tatsumi to tomo ni 8" [Together with Hijikata Tatsumi 8], *Asubesutokan tsūshin 8*, August 1988.

————"Hijikata Tatsumi to tomo ni 9" [Together with Hijikata Tatsumi 9], *Asubesutokan tsūshin 9*, October 1988.

————"Hijikata Tatsumi tsuitō kōen 'Yameru maihime' panfuretto" [Hijikata Tatsumi Memorial Event 'Yameru maihime' Pamphlet], Tokyo: Sezon gekijō, August 1987.

Nakamura Fumiaki, *Butō no migiwa* [The Waterside of Butō]. Tokyo: Shichōsha, 2000.

————"Butō – sono shitashimi e no oku no te" [Butō – A Last Hand to Friendship], *Ekoda bungaku 17*, January 1990.

Nakatani Tadao, *Hijikata Tatsumi butō sekai – Nakatani Tadao shashinshū* [The World of Hijikata Tatsumi's Butō – Collected Photographs of Nakatani Tadao]. Tokyo: Mediapurodakushon, 2003.

Nishitani Osamu, "Butō Suru Kotoba no Mure" [Crowd of Dancing Words], *W-Notation 2*, July 1985.

Noguchi Michizō DVD book: *Ākaibuzu noguchi taisō – Noguchi Michizō + Yōrō Takeshi* [Noguchi Taisō Archives – Noguchi Michizo + Yōrō Takeshi]. Tokyo: Shunjusha, 2004.

————*Genshoseimeitai toshite no ningen* [Human Beings as Original Life Bodies]. Tokyo: Mikasashobō, 1972).

————*Noguchi taisō karada ni kiku* [Noguchi Taisō: Listening to the Body]. Tokyo: Hakujusha, 1977.

————*Noguchi taisō omosa ni kiku* [Noguchi Taisō: Listening to the Weight]. Tokyo: Hakujusha, 1979.

Okuno Takeo, "Engeki kakumei no ankoku kyōso" [The Charisma of Darkness of the Revolution in Theatre], *Asubesutokan tsūshin 4*, July 1987.

Ōno Kazuo butō kenkyūsho ed., *Ōno Kazuo – keiko no kotoba* [Ōno Kazuo – Workshop Words]. Tokyo: Firumuātosha, 1997.

Ōno Kazuo and others, *Ōno Kazuo* [Ōno Kazuo]. Tokyo: Shoshi seijusha, 1997.

Ōno Yoshito and Ōno Kazuo butō kenkyūsho, DVD: *Ōno Kazuo – bi to chikara* [Ōno Kazuo – Beauty and Power]. Tokyo: NHK Software, 2001.

————*Ōno Kazuo – tamashii no kate* [Ōno Kazuo – Food for the Soul]. Tokyo: Firumuātosha, 1999.

Rowe, Andrea, "Eastern dance an intense, fragile study of life", *Ottawa Citizen*, September 1985.

Sakazaki Otsurō, *Roman-ha geijutsu no sekai* [The World of Romantic Art]. Tokyo: Kōdansha gendai shinsho, 1976.

Shibayama Mikio, "'Jappu' kara ichiban tōi hito" [Nothing Like a Nip], *Asubesutokan tsūshin 7*, April 1988.

Shibusawa Tatsuhiko, "Hijikata Tatsumi ni tsuite" [On Hijikata Tatsumi], commentary in *Yameru maihime* [Ailing Danseuse]. Tokyo: Hakusuisha, 1983.

Siegal, Marcia B., "Glistening Stones," *The Village Voice*, October 1985.

Stein, Bonnie Sue, "Butoh: Twenty Years Ago We Were Crazy, Dirty, and Mad", in Ann Dils and Ann Cooper Albright eds., *Moving History / Dancing Cultures: A Dance History Reader*. Durham: Wesleyan University Press, 2001.

Suzuki Shiroyasu, "'Hangidaitōkan' kyoku shiteki kansō" [Private Impressions of the Burnt Offerings], *Bijutsu techō*, February 1973.

Suzuki Tadashi, "Kozetsu no shi o ayumu" [Walking in Isolated Death], *Bijutsu techō*, February 1973.

Takashina Shūji, *Kindai kaiga-shi* [The History of Modern Painting]. Tokyo: Chūkō shinsho, 1975.

————*Seiki-matsu geijutsu* [Fin de Siècle Art]. Tokyo: Kinokuniya shoten, 1981.

Takechi Tetsuji and Tomioka Taeko, *Dentōgeijutsu to wa nanna no ka* [What is Traditional Art]. Tokyo: Bijutsu Shuppansha, 1973.

Tanaka Ikkō, "Zen-ei to anchi-moraru" [Avant-garde and Anti-morals], *Bijutsu techō*, May 1986.

Tanemura Suehiro, *Hijikata Tatsumi e – Nikutai no 60-nendai* [Towards Hijikata Tatsumi – The 60s of the Flesh]. Tokyo: Kawadeshobō shinsha, 2001.

————'Postscript' to *Bibō no aozora* [Beautiful Blue Sky]. Tokyo: Chikuma shobō, 1987.

Tanigawa Kōichi, "Buta to kirisuto" [Christ and the Pig], *Bijutsu techō*, May 1986.

Tobias, Tobi, "Human Interest", *New York Magazine*, December 1993.

Tōno Yoshiaki, *Gurotta no gakka* [Painters of the Grotesque]. Tokyo: Bijutsu shuppansha, 1965.

Uno Kuniichi, "Hijikata Tatsumi no dimenshon" [Dimensions of Hijikata Tatsumi], *W-Notation 2*, July 1985.

————"Sai to shintai" [Difference and Body], *Ekoda bungaku*.

————"Mada odori tsuzukeru hito ni" [To the One Who Can Keep Dancing], *Asubesutokan tsūshin 10*, July 1989.

Waguri Yukio CD-ROM, *Butō kaden*. Tokyo: JustSystems, 1998.

Watanabe Moriaki, *Gekijō no shikō* [Thoughts on Theatre]. Tokyo: Iwanami shoten, 1984.

Yamada Setsuko, *Sokudo no hana* [Flower of Speed]. Tokyo: Goryū shoin, 2005.

Yamaguchi Masao, "Ashi kara mita sekai" [World Seen from the Feet], *Bessatsukoku bungaku*. Tokyo: Gakutōsha, 1985.

————"Hirakareta shintaisei e" [To the Open Body], *Gendaishi techō*, May 1985.

Yamaguchi Takeshi, "Toboshiki jidai no shijin no keiji" [Revelation of a Youthful Poet], *Bijutsu techō*, February 1973.

Yokoo Tadanori, "Totsuzen hen'i no posutā" [Poster of Mutation], *Bijutsu techō*, May 1986.

Yoshimoto Takaaki, "'Hai-imēji ron' Butō Ron 1" ['High Image Theory' Butō Theory 1], *Kaien*, April 1989.

————"'Hai-imēji ron' Butō Ron 2" ['High Image Theory' Butō Theory 2], *Kaien*, May 1989.

Yoshimura Masunobu, "Hai-reberuna supekutoru" [High-level Spectrum], *Bijutsu techō*, May 1986.

Yuasa Yasuo, *Ki, shugyō, shintai* [Energy, Religious Practice, and the Body]. Tokyo: Hirakawa shuppansha, 1986.

————*Kyōjisei no uchūkan – jikan, seimei, shizen* [The World-view of Shared Time – Time, Life, and Nature]. Tokyo: Jinbunshoin, 1995.

————Nihon kodai no seishin sekai – rekishi shinrigakuteki kenkyū no chōsen [The Spiritual World of Ancient Japan – The Challenge of Historical Psychological Research]. Tokyo: Meicho kankōkai, 1990.

————Shintai – tōyōteki shintairon no kokoromi [The Body – Attempt at an Easter Body Theory]. Tokyo: Sōbunsha, 1977.

————Shintairon – tōyōteki shintairon to gendai [Body Theory – Eastern Body Theory Today]. Tokyo: Kodansha gakujutsu bunko, 1990.

Yuasa and others, Iwanami kōza – tetsugaku 9 shintai kankaku seishin [Iwanami Lectures – Philosophy 9 Body Sensations Spirit]. Tokyo: Iwanami shoten, 1986.

"Zen'ei Butō-ka: Hijikata Tatsumi san shikyo" [Avant-garde Dancer: Death of Hijikata Tatsumi], Asahi Shimbun, January 22 1986.

Index

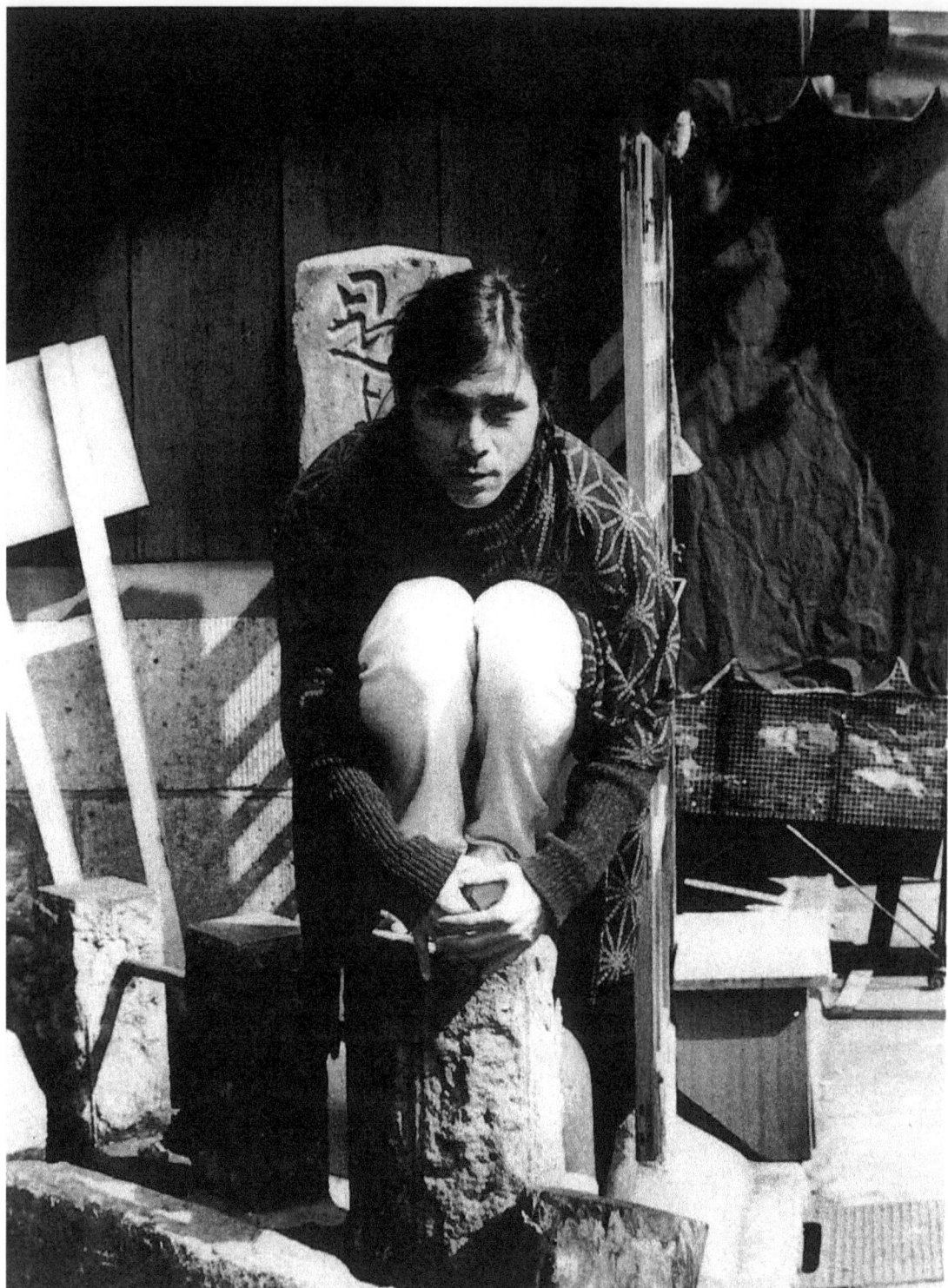

Hijikata in front of the Aburamen Jizō in Meguro (1967), by Sekine Kaoru

Other publications from Ōzaru Books

Ichigensan
– The Newcomer –
David Zoppetti

Translated from the Japanese by Takuma Sminkey

Ichigensan is a novel which can be enjoyed on many levels – as a delicate, sensual love story, as a depiction of the refined society in Japan's cultural capital Kyoto, and as an exploration of the themes of alienation and prejudice common to many environments, regardless of the boundaries of time and place.

Unusually, it shows Japan from the eyes of both an outsider and an 'internal' outcast, and even more unusually, it originally achieved this through sensuous prose carefully crafted by a non-native speaker of Japanese. The fact that this best-selling novella then won the Subaru Prize, one of Japan's top literary awards, and was also nominated for the Akutagawa Prize is a testament to its unique narrative power.

The story is by no means chained to Japan, however, and this new translation by Takuma Sminkey will allow readers world-wide to enjoy the multitude of sensations engendered by life and love in an alien culture.

"A beautiful love story" (Japan Times)

"Sophisticated... subtle... sensuous... delicate... memorable... vivid depictions" (Asahi Evening News)

"Striking... fascinating..." (Japan PEN Club)

"Refined and sensual" (Kyoto Shimbun)

"quiet, yet very compelling... subtle mixture of humour and sensuality...the insights that the novel gives about Japanese society are both intriguing and exotic" (Nicholas Greenman, amazon.com)

ISBN: 978-0-9559219-4-0

Sunflowers
– Le Soleil –
Shimako Murai

A play in one act
Translated from the Japanese by Ben Jones

Hiroshima is synonymous with the first hostile use of an atomic bomb. Many people think of this occurrence as one terrible event in the past, which is studied from history books.

Shimako Murai and other 'Women of Hiroshima' believe otherwise: for them, the bomb had after-effects which affected countless people for decades, effects that were all the more menacing for their unpredictability – and often, invisibility.

This is a tale of two such people: on the surface successful modern women, yet each bearing underneath hidden scars as horrific as the keloids that disfigured Hibakusha on the days following the bomb.

"a great story and a glimpse into the lives of the people who lived during the time of the war and how the bomb affected their lives, even after all these years" (Wendy Pierce, goodreads.com)

ISBN: 978-0-9559219-3-3

The Call of Cairnmor
Sally Aviss

Book One of the Cairnmor Trilogy

The Scottish Isle of Cairnmor is a place of great beauty and undisturbed wilderness, a haven for wildlife, a land of white sandy beaches and inland fertile plains, a land where awe-inspiring mountains connect precipitously with the sea.

To this remote island comes a stranger, Alexander Stewart, on a quest to solve the mysterious disappearance of two people and their unborn child; a missing family who are now heirs to a vast fortune. He enlists the help of local schoolteacher, Katherine MacDonald, and together they seek the answers to this enigma: a deeply personal journey that takes them from Cairnmor to the historic splendour of London and the industrial heartland of Glasgow.

Covering the years 1936-1937 and infused with period colour and detail, The Call of Cairnmor is about unexpected discovery and profound attachment which, from its gentle opening, gradually gathers momentum and complexity until all the strands come together to give life-changing revelations.

"really enjoyed reading this – loved the plot... Read it in just two sittings as I couldn't stop reading." (P. Green – amazon.co.uk)

"exciting plot, not a book you want to put down, although I tried not to rush it so as to fully enjoy escaping to the world skilfully created by the author. A most enjoyable read." (Liz Green – amazon.co.uk)

"an excellent read. I cannot wait for the next part of the trilogy from this talented author. You will not want to put it down" (B. Burchell – amazon.co.uk)

ISBN: 978-0-9559219-9-5

Changing Tides, Changing Times
Sally Aviss

Book Two of the Cairnmor Trilogy

In the dense jungle of Malaya in 1942, Doctor Rachel Curtis stumbles across a mysterious, unidentifiable stranger, badly injured and close to death.

Four years earlier in 1938 in London, Katherine Stewart and her husband Alex come into conflict with their differing needs while Alex's father, Alastair, knows he must keep his deeper feelings hidden from the woman he loves; a woman to whom he must never reveal the full extent of that love.

Covering a broad canvas and meticulously researched, Changing Times, Changing Tides follows the interwoven journey of well-loved characters from The Call of Cairnmor, as well as introducing new personalities, in a unique combination of novel and history that tells a story of love, loss, friendship and heroism; absorbing the reader in the characters' lives as they are shaped and changed by the ebb and flow of events before, during and after the Second World War.

"I enjoyed the twists and turns of this book ... particularly liked the gutsy Dr Rachel who is a reminder to the reader that these are dark days for the world. Love triumphs but not in the way we thought it would and our heroine, Katherine, learns that the path to true love is certainly not a smooth one." (MDW – amazon.co.uk)

"Even better than the first book! A moving and touching story well told." (P. Green – amazon.co.uk)

"One of the best reads this year ... can't wait for the next one." (Mr C. Brownett – amazon.co.uk)

"One of my favourite books – and I have shelves of them in the house! Sally Aviss is a masterful storyteller [... She] has obviously done a tremendous amount of research, judging by all the fascinating and in-depth historical detail woven into the storyline." ('Inverneill' – amazon.co.uk)

ISBN: 978-0-9931587-0-4

Where Gloom and Brightness Meet
Sally Aviss

Book Three of the Cairnmor Trilogy

When Anna Stewart begins a relationship with journalist Marcus Kendrick, the ramifications are felt from New York all the way across the Atlantic to the remote and beautiful Scottish island of Cairnmor, where her family live. Yet even as she and Marcus draw closer, Anna cannot forget her estranged husband whom she has not seen for many years.

When tragedy strikes, for some, Cairnmor becomes a refuge, a place of solace to ease the troubled spirit and an escape from painful reality; for others, it becomes a place of enterprise and adventure – a place in which to dream of an unfettered future.

This third book in the Cairnmor Trilogy, takes the action forward into the late nineteen-sixties as well as recalling familiar characters' lives from the intervening years. Where Gloom and Brightness Meet is a story of heartbreak and redemptive love; of long-dead passion remembered and retained in isolation; of unfaltering loyalty and steadfast devotion. It is a story that juxtaposes the old and the new; a story that reflects the conflicting attitudes, problems and joys of a liberating era.

"the last book in Sally Aviss's trilogy and it did not disappoint ... what a wonderful journey this has been ... cleverly written with an enormous amount of research" (B. Burchell – amazon.co.uk)

"I loved this third book in the series ... the characters were believable and events unfolded in a beguiling way ... not too happy ending for everyone but a satisfying conclusion to the saga" (P. Green – amazon.co.uk)

ISBN: 978-0-9931587-1-1

Reflections in an Oval Mirror
Memories of East Prussia, 1923-45
Anneli Jones

8 May 1945 – VE Day – was Anneliese Wiemer's twenty-second birthday. Although she did not know it then, it marked the end of her flight to the West, and the start of a new life in England.

These illustrated memoirs, based on a diary kept during the Third Reich and letters rediscovered many decades later, depict the momentous changes occurring in Europe against a backcloth of everyday farm life in East Prussia (now the north-western corner of Russia, sandwiched between Lithuania and Poland).

The political developments of the 1930s (including the Hitler Youth, 'Kristallnacht', political education, labour service, war service, and interrogation) are all the more poignant for being told from the viewpoint of a romantic young girl. In lighter moments she also describes student life in Vienna and Prague, and her friendship with Belgian and Soviet prisoners of war. Finally, however, the approach of the Red Army forces her to abandon her home and flee across the frozen countryside, encountering en route a cross-section of society ranging from a 'lady of the manor', worried about her family silver, to some concentration camp inmates

"couldn't put it down... delightful... very detailed descriptions of the farm and the arrival of war... interesting history and personal account" ('Rosie', amazon.com)

"excellent, light and cheerful in the main, with wonderfully evocative photographs of a lost age, but always there is the sense of menace not far away ... leaves one wondering at the spirit and hardiness of the author and her family and friends" (Mr Joseph Eddington, amazon.co.uk)

ISBN: 978-0-9559219-0-2

Carpe Diem
Moving on from East Prussia
Anneli Jones

This sequel to "Reflections in an Oval Mirror" details Anneli's post-war life. The scene changes from life in Northern 'West Germany' as a refugee, reporter and military interpreter, to parties with the Russian Authorities in Berlin, boating in the Lake District with the original 'Swallows and Amazons', weekends with the Astors at Cliveden, then the beginnings of a new family in the small Kentish village of St Nicholas-at-Wade. Finally, after the fall of the Iron Curtain, Anneli is able to revisit her first home once more.

ISBN: 978-0-9931587-3-5

Skating at the Edge of the Wood
Memories of East Prussia, 1931-1945… 1993
Marlene Yeo

In 1944, the thirteen-year old East Prussian girl Marlene Wiemer embarked on a horrific trek to the West, to escape the advancing Red Army. Her cousin Jutta was left behind the Iron Curtain, which severed the family bonds that had made the two so close.

This book contains dramatic depictions of Marlene's flight, recreated from her letters to Jutta during the last year of the war, and contrasted with joyful memories of the innocence that preceded them.

Nearly fifty years later, the advent of perestroika meant that Marlene and Jutta were finally able to revisit their childhood home, after a lifetime of growing up under diametrically opposed societies, and the book closes with a final chapter revealing what they find.

Despite depicting the same time and circumstances as "Reflections in an Oval Mirror", an account written by Marlene's elder sister, Anneli, and its sequel "Carpe Diem", this work stands in stark contrast partly owing to the age gap between the two girls, but above all because of their dramatically different characters.

ISBN: 978-0-9931587-2-8

Turner's Margate Through Contemporary Eyes
The Viney Letters
Stephen Channing

Margate in the early 19th Century was an exciting town, where smugglers and 'preventive men' fought to outwit each other, while artists such as JMW Turner came to paint the glorious sunsets over the sea. One of the young men growing up in this environment decided to set out for Australia to make his fortune in the Bendigo gold rush.

Half a century later, having become a pillar of the community, he began writing a series of letters and articles for Keble's Gazette, a publication based in his home town. In these, he described Margate with great familiarity (and tremendous powers of recall), while at the same time introducing his English readers to the "latitudinarian democracy" of a new, "young Britain".

Viney's interests covered a huge range of topics, from Thanet folk customs such as Hoodening, through diatribes on the perils of assigning intelligence to dogs, to geological theories including suggestions for the removal of sandbanks off the English coast "in obedience to the sovereign will and intelligence of man".

His writing is clearly that of a well-educated man, albeit with certain Victorian prejudices about the colonies that may make those with modern sensibilities wince a little. Yet above all, it is interesting because of the light it throws on life in a British seaside town some 180 years ago.

This book also contains numerous contemporary illustrations.

"profusely illustrated... draws together a series of interesting articles and letters... recommended" (Margate Civic Society)

ISBN: 978-0-9559219-2-6

The Margate Tales
Stephen Channing

Chaucer's Canterbury Tales is without doubt one of the best ways of getting a feel for what the people of England in the Middle Ages were like. In the modern world, one might instead try to learn how different people behave and think from television or the internet.

However, to get a feel for what it was like to be in Margate as it gradually changed from a small fishing village into one of Britain's most popular holiday resorts, one needs to investigate contemporary sources such as newspaper reports and journals.

Stephen Channing has saved us this work, by trawling through thousands of such documents to select the most illuminating and entertaining accounts of Thanet in the 18th and early to mid 19th centuries. With content ranging from furious battles in the letters pages, to hilarious pastiches, witty poems and astonishing factual reports, illustrated with over 70 drawings from the time, The Margate Tales brings the society of the time to life, and as with Chaucer, demonstrates how in many areas, surprisingly little has changed.

"substantial and fascinating volume... meticulously researched... an absorbing read" (Margate Civic Society)

"amazing ... a page turner ... highly recommended for anyone who has either had fond memories of Margate or would be interested in the history" (Jeanette, goodreads.com)

ISBN: 978-0-9559219-5-7

A Victorian Cyclist
Rambling through Kent in 1886
Stephen & Shirley Channing

Bicycles are so much a part of everyday life nowadays, it can be surprising to realize that for the late Victorians these "velocipedes" were a novelty disparaged as being unhealthy and unsafe – and that indeed tricycles were for a time seen as the format more likely to succeed.

Some people however adopted the new-fangled devices with alacrity, embarking on adventurous tours throughout the countryside. One of them documented his 'rambles' around East Kent in such detail that it is still possible to follow his routes on modern cycles, and compare the fauna and flora (and pubs!) with those he vividly described.

In addition to providing today's cyclists with new historical routes to explore, and both naturalists and social historians with plenty of material for research, this fascinating book contains a special chapter on Lady Cyclists in the era before female emancipation, and an unintentionally humorous section instructing young gentlemen how to make their cycle and then ride it.

A Victorian Cyclist features over 200 illustrations, and is complemented by a fully updated website.

"Lovely… wonderfully written… terrific" (Everything Bicycles)

"Rare and insightful" (Kent on Sunday)

"Interesting… informative… detailed historical insights" (BikeBiz)

"Unique and fascinating book… quality is very good… of considerable interest" (Veteran-Cycle Club)

"Superb… illuminating… well detailed… The easy flowing prose, which has a cadence like cycling itself, carries the reader along as if freewheeling with a hind wind" (Forty Plus Cycling Club)

"a fascinating book with both vivid descriptions and a number of hitherto-unseen photos of the area" ('Pedalling Pensioner', amazon.co.uk)

ISBN: 978-0-9559219-7-1

Travels in Taiwan
Exploring Ilha Formosa
Gary Heath

For many Westerners, Taiwan is either a source of cheap electronics or an ongoing political problem. It is seldom highlighted as a tourist destination, and even those that do visit rarely venture far beyond the well-trod paths of the major cities and resorts.

Yet true to its 16th century Portuguese name, the 'beautiful island' has some of the highest mountains in East Asia, many unique species of flora and fauna, and several distinct indigenous peoples (fourteen at the last count).

On six separate and arduous trips, Gary Heath deliberately headed for the areas neglected by other travel journalists, armed with several notebooks... and a copy of War and Peace for the days when typhoons confined him to his tent. The fascinating land he discovered is revealed here.

"offers a great deal of insight into Taiwanese society, history, culture, as well as its island's scenic geography... disturbing and revealing... a true, peripatetic, descriptive Odyssey undertaken by an adventurous and inquisitive Westerner on a very Oriental and remote island" (Charles Phillips, goodreads.com)

ISBN: 978-0-9559219-8-8

West of Arabia
A Journey Home
Gary Heath

Faced with the need to travel from Saudi Arabia to the UK, Gary Heath made the unusual decision to take the overland route. His three principles were to stay on the ground, avoid back-tracking, and do minimal sightseeing.

The ever-changing situation in the Middle East meant that the rules had to be bent on occasion, yet as he travelled across Eritrea, Sudan, Egypt, Libya, Tunisia and Morocco, he succeeded in beating his own path around the tourist traps, gaining unique insights into Arabic culture as he went.

Written just a few months before the Arab Spring of 2011, this book reveals many of the underlying tensions that were to explode onto the world stage just shortly afterwards, and has been updated to reflect the recent changes.

"just the right blend of historical background [and] personal experiences... this book is a must read" ('Denise', goodreads.com)

ISBN: 978-0-9559219-6-4

www.ingramcontent.com/pod-product-compliance
Lightning Source LLC
Chambersburg PA
CBHW040255100426
42811CB00011B/1267